JIM LABARBARA

THE MUSIC PROFESSOR

Jim LaBarbara
"the Prof"

JIM LaBARBARA

THE MUSIC PROFESSOR

A LIFE AMPLIFIED THROUGH RADIO & ROCK 'N' ROLL

by

Jim LaBarbara

LITTLE MIAMI PUBLISHING CO.
Milford, Ohio
2011

Little Miami Publishing Co.
P.O. Box 588
Milford, Ohio 45150-0588
www.littlemiamibooks.com

Cover design by Mike Stretch, BrandGarden, Mason, Ohio.
Cover photography by Joel Quimby, Cincinnati, Ohio
Photos from the author's collection unless otherwise indicated.

Printed in the United States of America on acid-free paper.

ISBN-13: 978-1-932250-92-3
ISBN-10: 1-932250-92-1

Library of Congress Control Number: 2011937115

Contents

Acknowledgments

The love of my life, my foundation, my wife, Sally: Many have said she should receive "sainthood" for putting up with me all these years. Thank you for your endless patience the last couple of years and for affording me the space and time to go through this creative process. You're a great "sounding board."

My proudest achievement my children: Jimmy and Shelby and their families for their love and faithful support—Jimmy, his wife, Amy, and my grandson, James; Shelby, her husband, Dan Tepe, and my granddaughter, Colleen. Shelby thanks for answering my infinite computer questions.

I am thankful for my parents Jim and Eva LaBarbara: Two of the most generous and loving people the world will ever know. They shaped my values and, by example, showed me a strong work ethic. They let me dream and sacrificed so that I could achieve those dreams. I miss them dearly.

My brother, Sam: He has always been there for me. I am so blessed to have Sam and his family in my life. Thank you for your unselfish commitment to look after our mom and dad.

My listeners: I am privileged that you allowed me to be a part of your life; whether I was in the dashboard of your car, in the transistor under your pillow, sitting on a shelf in the kitchen, or with you at work—wherever. Thank you for your support on the air and at appearances, because without you this wouldn't have been possible.

A special thanks to the hundreds of entertainers who took the time to share their stories with me so that I could share them with you.

Randy McNutt, author: What can I say to a guy who answered my endless questions about the book business and gave me the best advice. Thank you for setting the wheels in motion so that this book could become a reality. I am most grateful that you recommended me to Barbara Gargiulo at Little Miami Publishing.

Jim Blommel my radio friend: Your belief in me as a writer has never wavered.

Arnold Barnett: For your friendship and for giving me the push and guidance to reinvent myself as a talk show host many years ago and, therefore, extend my career.

Louis Mazzaro, Tony Ficarri, and Anthony Crivelli—my Stowe High classmates: Thank you for your enthusiasm, the laughs, and the constant reminder—"When is the book coming out?"

Tony Rosiello, my close friend and confidant: Thank you for your loyalty and daily reminder that it is all about family—people getting together breaking bread and sharing friendship, because without it we have nothing.

Jack Heffron, the talented writer: You were the first to read both of my early manuscripts. Thank you for your early confidence in me as a "storyteller" writer. Your input was invaluable.

Joe Seta president of the Italian men's club, the "Fratelli Uniti": For being an early booster. You booked me as the featured speaker to talk about my "memoir" at the groups "20th Annual Christmas Eve Morning Breakfast"—ten months before it was published!

* * *

Barbara Gargiulo owner of Little Miami Publishing Company: Thank you for being my biggest believer. You agreed to publish my story during our first conversation. I called Randy McNutt that day and told him, "She's the one, I want to work with her." I appreciate your tireless work as we went over the manuscript; I lost count is this round six or seven. I respect your guidance—"let's think about that one," "do you really want to say that," "maybe you should use that for another book." I am grateful to you for turning me into a writer.

This is the microphone I use in my home recording studio.
PHOTO BY JOEL QUIMBY

Introduction

My friend, the late disc jockey and scholar, Dr. Bill Randle asked me time after time,

"When are you going to write the book?"

"I'm not a writer. I'm a disc jockey."

"Just write it."

Well this is it, a memoir of my life in and out of radio and how I remember it. My biggest surprise was the discovery that I was several different people on the radio over the years. They shared many of the same characteristics, but each had his own persona. Jimmy Holiday was more subdued than J. Bentley Starr, and I redefined Jimmy LaBarbara's image a number of times. Saying my own name on the radio was very difficult for me. It was so much easier to be somebody else, a Holiday or a Starr. I've had a couple of guardian angels in my life and a Hell's Angel saved my life. I've tried to paint a picture of the ladies in my life, including one that was a dog. There are things I've done over the years that I'm not proud of, and I hope I don't embarrass my family too much with these stories.

I especially wanted to share my conversations with Bill Randle when he was the head of the Broadcasting Department at the University of Cincinnati, and I was his student working on a master's degree and teaching. Bill introduced Elvis Presley to a network television audience. Johnny Bench was the best man at my wedding and my best friend for a number of years. Those happened to be the glory years of the Big Red Machine, and I was right there.

I had the pleasure of interviewing and partying with some of the biggest stars in the history of rock 'n' roll, and you'll learn about some of them in their own words. When I got into radio, this new, exciting music was starting to take off, and I was a professional musician who was single and close to the same age as the performers, so it was easy for me to relate with them on a number of levels. This helped my interviews. I enjoyed their music, and I was truly interested in their story, and here's my story.

CHAPTER 1

My First Record Hop

The high school dance in the school gym was a huge event in the fifties and sixties. The aroma of popcorn filled the air. The guys were on one side of the gym, the girls on the other, and the couples going steady were dancing or just walking around holding hands. The gym lights were dimmed, but there was one light that stood out. There was a gooseneck lamp on a card table over a 45 rpm record player in the far, right-hand corner of the gym. Oh yeah, the skinny guy with the glasses standing there—yep, that was me, and I was on crutches. During my sophomore year, I injured my leg lifting weights trying to get bigger for baseball. I was playing the records because I was in love with Pinky Lorenz, the pretty majorette who lived down the street. When I found out she didn't have a date but was on the dance committee, I volunteered to play the music so I could hang out with her. The stage crew was glad they didn't have to do it, and they even gave me a microphone. I made some dedications, and I felt very comfortable introducing records. I discovered I could create a mood with the great ballads of the Platters, the Penguins, and the Five Satins. If I saw a guy slow dancing with a girl I liked, I could break that up quickly—

just play a fast Chuck Berry record. It was an empowering position to be in, and I enjoyed my newfound celebrity. The kids loved the music and asked me to play at the next dance. I agreed. I was on crutches, and I couldn't dance anyway. My buddy Chieffo, the big football tackle, asked me to make a list of the records I needed. He'd get me the records, and they always had somebody's name on them: "Joan M." or "Mary S." I didn't question where he got them, but I was grateful I had a fresh supply every dance.

Rock 'n' roll music was always about the guy trying to get a girl, and it worked for me. Pinky was my date for the Junior Prom. At the end of the night, in her doorway, I asked if I could kiss her. She kissed me. I turned around and walked right into their screen door. Years later when I passed her house, I could see the indentation of my face in that door.

It's funny how things work out. If Pinky had a date that night, I wouldn't have played the music and never would have gotten into radio.

Rock 'n' Roll—the new music

My introduction to this new music happened a few years earlier. My buddy Ronnie Miller was two grades older, and his record collection consisted of Joni James, the Four Aces, and the Four Coins. I was just getting into this music when a change occurred. I saw the movie *Blackboard Jungle*. In it, Glenn Ford was the good guy teacher. The school kid punks were Vic Morrow, Sidney Poitier, and Jamie Farr. They called him a square "daddy-o" and smashed his 78 rpm big band records. Those records symbolized conservatism at a time when we were on the cusp of a rock 'n' roll revolt. The movie's soundtrack featured this wild record with a sound we had never heard before, "Rock Around the Clock" by Bill Haley.

When we found out Bill Haley was coming to the Syria Mosque in Pittsburgh with a show billed as the "Biggest Rock and Roll Show," we had to make the scene. I sat in the first balcony with Ronnie and his brother Gary. In the row behind us were five guys fashioned out in shiny sharkskin suits—yellow, red, blue, orange, and purple. They accessorized with sunglasses and canes. They were easily the coolest guys in the whole place. I remember it like it was yesterday. Twelve acts, eleven black and one white, but the audience was predominately white. LaVern Baker wiggled out in a dress that was so tight she must have been sewn into it. Somehow when she sang the seemingly innocent "Tweedlee Dee," she became a sexual tease. Bo Diddley beat up his guitar singing "Bo Diddley." Clyde McPhatter, wearing his army uniform, joined the Drifters, and when he sang the nasty "Honey Love," the audience went crazy. Thirteen-year-old Frankie Lymon and the Teenagers, featuring their incredible bass singer Sherman Garnes, did the split when they danced, and the Platters, with the lovely Zola Taylor, sang "The Great Pretender."

Zola Taylor would one day marry the much younger Frankie Lymon and was one of his three wives who sued for the copyright of his hit "Why do Fools Fall in Love?" after his death. She was his second wife and in court claimed she had been sexually active with Frankie as early as this tour in 1956. She claimed they married in Mexico around 1965 but couldn't produce a marriage license and lost. No wonder he was so happy on stage. The male black entertainers during this era always wore suits on stage, and the ladies looked respectable in evening dresses. A big black guy, six foot two and 250 pounds, was introduced as the "King of the Blues," Joe Turner. The sweat was pouring off him as he performed "Flip, Flop and Fly," and he sang a song I knew, "Shake, Rattle, and Roll," except the lyrics were changed. He was singing about a lady in the bedroom with the light shining through her dress, and they were gonna shake, rattle, and roll in the bedroom. I was thirteen, playing trumpet in big bands and jazz groups, but I was knocked out by this newfound music. The loudest applause of the evening came when the emcee introduced the only white act on the show, Bill Haley and the Comets. Everybody was yelling and screaming except the guys behind us wearing the sunglasses and fancy suits. They got up in unison and gave Bill Haley the finger and the Italian sign as they walked out. I asked one guy what was wrong, because Haley had the number-one record in the country.

He said, "Man, he ripped off Joe Turner's original 'Shake, Rattle, and Roll.'"

"Wait, I don't understand."

He told me to listen to Porky on WAMO.

Porky—"The Daddio of the Raddio"

Bill Haley was terrific. He sang "Crazy Man Crazy," "Rock Around the Clock," and he sang "Shake, Rattle, and Roll," but it wasn't in the bedroom, it was in the kitchen, and they were innocently shaking pots and pans. Porky Chedwick was a deejay who did a show on a little suburban radio station in Homestead that was tough to pick up where I lived; however, the next day I started listening to Porky, and I soon understood what those guys in the fancy suits meant. The "Daddio of the Raddio," the "Platter Pushin Papa," "Pork the Tork," the "Boss Man" played only the original hits by the original artists. Porky was a white man who didn't care about the pigmentation of a man's skin. He'd play The Moonglows' "Sincerely," not the cover by the McGuire Sisters; LaVern Baker's "Tweedlee Dee," not Georgia Gibbs's; and Little Richard's hits, not Pat Boone's covers. He played these race records to a racially diverse audience four years before Alan Freed, but he was never on a powerful mainstream station. He butchered the English language, but no one cared because he was a great communicator. He was a guest on one of the local Pittsburgh television dance party shows, and a white group—the Four Coins of "Shangri-La" fame—performed their newest record. The television host asked Porky if he liked the record, and he said yes it sounded good.

"That's great, then we can expect to hear this on your show."

Porky responded, "Oh no man, the cats would hang me."

I saw that and thought he was so honest—no bull. On several occasions, I remember him saying something like: "Porky dedicates this to Butch Jankowsky who was killed in a car crash the other day. Butch was a regular at Porky's hops, and this is also for his girlfriend Marilyn and his cousins who are listening on their porch." He'd play Donald Woods's "Death of an Angel." The record's background vocals were overshadowed with crying, and when he sang the line, "There was a death of an angel," a sobbing scream would wail through the speaker. You could feel Porky's pain in 1958 when he told us about the fire in Chicago at a Catholic elementary school that took the lives of ninety-two children. He proceeded to dedicate the Platters' new record "Smoke Gets in Your Eyes" to them. Most radio executives would say he crossed the line of good taste and on-air responsibility. Was the station's switchboard jammed with calls about his insensitivity? I'm sure no one called to complain about his misjudgment. Porky was the most believable and sincere deejay I ever heard. I didn't realize at the time, but he had a huge influence on me. He was so honest and passionate about the music he played. I thanked him on a couple of occasions, and I sat next to Porky at our fiftieth Stowe High School reunion. He was ninety-one years old at the time and looked as young as most of my classmates. He'd called me on the telephone: "Jim the Barbara, you have been porkified!" That's all he said, and to the uninformed, it sounds like nothing, but to be "porkified" from Porky was an honor; it was the ultimate.

Bill Haley

Going back to my first rock 'n' roll show, there was no doubt that the stars were Bill Haley and the Comets. Years later, Bill described how the Saddlemen, a country group, were transformed into international rock 'n' roll stars with "Rock Around the Clock." He told me: "We were playing country music, and I got the idea to mix rhythm and blues with the western sound. So we employed a saxophone, a drum, a slap fiddle, and a rhythm guitar. At that time, we had an accordion, and we experimented and did a few things like 'Mulberry Bush' and 'Ten Little Indians' and things like that. It was a completely different sound. About 1954 there was a fellow around town who started a record company, Essex, back in Chester, Pennsylvania. They came up with this tune 'Rock Around the Clock' that I didn't like too much, but we added the saxophone and then we brought in a lead guitar player. We did away with the accordion and switched him over to piano, and we did the thing, and I didn't think anything would happen. About a year later, it was submitted to Columbia Pictures to be in a movie called *Blackboard Jungle*. They wanted some background music. They called it youth music instead of the big band music a lot of movies had, and that was the rise of Bill Haley and the Comets."

Bill explained to me that "Rock Around the Clock" was released a year before the movie came out, but it didn't do anything because "the jocks didn't grasp it." I don't think his record company had a clue what this sound was because on my 78 rpm record, Decca called it a fox trot.

Six months after the movie was released, it was sandwiched in between Perez Prado's "Cherry Pink and Apple Blossom White" and Mitch Miller's "Yellow Rose of Texas," and it was on its way to number one. Bill and I were talking about that moment when he knew he had a smash. I guess money talks. They were playing Wildwood, New Jersey, making about $250 a week for four men playing seven days and two matinees. All at once his agent, Jolly Joyce, was shouting and waving telegrams. "You made it!"

Bill said, "Jolly are you cracking up or what?"

"No, no. Look at all the offers."

It was astronomical. From $250, the offers were up to $5,000 a week.

"We just couldn't believe it was all happening."

CHAPTER 2

My Defining Moment

Bill Haley knew the exact moment he made it. We all have those special moments that stand out. Mine happened in May of 1966 when I was in my early twenties. I was getting ready to go on the air for the first time on one of the most powerful Top 40 stations in the country; it was my dream station, NBC–owned, 50,000-watt WKYC in Cleveland. General Manager Bob Martin hired me out of Erie and was with me in the studio. Moments before I went on, I pushed my headphones back so I could tell him, "What a great opportunity this is for J. Bentley Starr." Bob said, "I didn't hire J. Bentley Starr, I hired Jim LaBarbara. Use your real name; you don't have to put anybody on." I panicked for a second and then recovered. He heard my tape; I'm J. Bentley Starr the "Intrepid Leader." I was Jimmy Holiday—every day is a holiday with Holiday. I could easily be him. I was Holiday in Titusville, in DuBois, and I used that name on the college radio station. I knew those guys, but Jim LaBarbara—I didn't know if I could be him. When I decided I would make radio my career, I gave myself a timeline and a goal. I was in my early twenties, and I made it. I never pictured myself getting old; anything after this would be a bonus. I spent years honing my craft, and I reached my goal. The only catch was, I didn't know Jim LaBarbara.

Young man with a horn

I was always setting goals for myself to reach. The first goal I remember setting happened when I was eleven, and I saw the movie *Young Man with a Horn*. The story was based loosely on the life of Bix Beiderbecke, a jazz trumpeter played by Kirk Douglas. Doris Day was the singer, and the soundtrack featured Harry James. I fell in love with the trumpet. I got a newspaper route delivering the morning *Pittsburgh Post Gazette* newspaper, saved my money, and bought a brand new ninety-seven-dollar trumpet. I played it two to five hours every day. I later discovered that Frankie Avalon, Hugh Masekela, and Chuck Mangione were inspired to play the trumpet because of that movie. I was only in elementary school when I saw the movie, but I set a goal: I was going to be first chair, first trumpet in the high school band. By the time I hit the ninth grade, I was first chair, first trumpet in the senior high school band, an honor that normally went to a senior. I was good enough that for two summers I had a scholarship to study music at Carnegie Tech's School of Fine Arts (currently Carnegie Mellon University), and my senior year, I was named the first student band director in our school's history.

I was a dreamer like most kids, and I set goals to reach. I really believed you could do anything and be anything you wanted to be. I wasn't alone in these thoughts. Neil Sedaka is a songwriter performer who has sold millions of records going back to the late fifties. Neil was another dreamer, and he was surprised that I knew he introduced himself at a party and signed autographs as Danny from Danny and the Juniors of "At the Hop" fame: "How did you hear that? I did. I was a ballsy kid. I said, 'I wonder how it feels to be famous,' and I had a three-piece combo in the Catskill Mountains. I said, 'Let's spread a rumor that I'm Danny, and we're all Danny and the Juniors.' I wanted to see how it felt getting recognition, and I liked it."

Williamsport, Pennsylvania

The second goal I remember happened when I was just about twelve. A sports magazine had a picture of the Little League World Series Champions of 1953 at the original field in Williamsport, Pennsylvania. I looked at that picture every day. I told my buddy Rudy Rudison, our star pitcher, that we were going to play there next August. Pretty strong stuff from a kid nobody knew could play. Yes, that year my Red Sox team beat everybody, and I made the Sto-Ken-Rox All-Star team. I hit a three-run home run against North Pittsburgh, and we won three to nothing. Carl Stotz, the founder of Little League Baseball, came to watch us win our next game, and we were off on a great train ride to Williamsport. I reached my goal, well not exactly. We didn't win the championship. I never talked about winning it—I just assumed we would once we got there.

In my mind, I had achieved my ultimate goal. I was officially a WKYC disc jockey, a WKYC VIP. I was going to be the sub filling in for vacationing personalities, and I would do the *Sound Eleven Survey* countdown show on Sunday nights that was heard over half of the United States. I'd count down the top hits and tell little stories about the records. All of their jocks took a lot of vacation so I'd be working all summer. The only catch was I had to be Jim LaBarbara, and I was never him on the radio.

Jimmy Holiday in Titusville

I wouldn't mind being Jimmy Holiday; I thought it was a good show business name that I created. "Every day's a holiday with Holiday." My first paid personality radio show happened in the summer of '62 before my senior year at Allegheny College. I was hired by WTIV in Titusville, Pennsylvania, to do the midday show, but after a couple of days, they moved me to afternoon drive. It was a day-timer, and the first night I got to town, I waited until the station went off the air around nine and practiced with the equipment until 2:00 a.m. Those were the days of cueing records on turntables and playing commercials from tape machines. I was dead tired when I headed back to my room at the YMCA only to discover the Y was closed. I had a room, so I thought it was okay to pull down the fire escape and climb to one of the floors. I was climbing the fire escape when I was blinded by police lights. I explained what happened and that I desperately needed to sleep. They invited me to stay in one of their rooms at the police station's "crow bar hotel." I surprised them and took the offer. I didn't sleep much, the bed was too hard—not great accommodations. Jimmy Holiday became instantly known in that little town playing pop and rock 'n' roll on the afternoon drive show. I moved from the YMCA to the Shadyhall Retirement Home on Main Street: one room, common bath, and two meals a day. It sounded like a great deal, but at every meal without fail, whoever I was sitting next to would break wind and just smile. I actually lost weight that summer. My boss owned a good rock station in nearby Franklin. His two star jocks were crazy guys, and they would get me the typed headlines to read on Sunday afternoons because they had access to the newswire service. Bob Sauber, the owner, often monitored our station from his summer home in New York State. I was naïve and read what they sent me. Once there was a nuclear test set to go off near his summer home; another time it was a story about a nearby Indian tribe. I said "horse s——t" in their language several times. Franklin was like us, a day-timer, so the morning guy had to turn on the transmitter every day. One night they removed its whole control panel and replaced it with a fish aquarium. The morning guy, half asleep, went nuts trying to get the station on the air.

Bob Sauber hired me with the understanding that I would work full time even after school started. I agreed that I would commute from Allegheny College in Meadville to Titusville, a pretty bad drive in the winter. A week before classes began, he fired me. I missed a day because I was sick, but one of the jocks convinced him that I wasn't sick but partying at my apartment. If I was, it was with the eighty-year-old ladies in the retirement home. I think it was Bob's way of letting me out of my commitment to commute. Years later we talked at length, but he didn't remember firing me. I still have a copy of a letter signed by hundreds of people asking Bob to bring Holiday back to WTIV.

Graduation decision—Boston or DuBois?

During my senior year at Allegheny we got a radio station and they asked me to do the first personality show. One night a week I'd play disc jockey Jimmy Holiday, but I wasn't going to make radio a career. However, my girlfriend who attended another school broke up with me because she didn't approve of radio and despite my denial thought I was headed to a radio career.

While home on a break my senior year, I got together with Joann, singer Lou Christie's cousin. She worked at KDKA radio in Pittsburgh. We met a couple of years earlier when I was selling magazines over the telephone. Randy Hall, KDKA's all-night man, was leaving for the Cleveland station WERE. She introduced me to Randy and, after listening to my tape, he said I was good enough but thought they would shy away because they hired him right out of Penn State. However, if I didn't get the KDKA job, he could get me a job in his hometown DuBois, Pennsylvania. KDKA hired an older guy from their sister station in Chicago, but thanks to Randy I got the DuBois job, a split shift early afternoon, and evening from six to midnight, plus sales. I took the job expecting to stay a few months before heading to Boston University and a graduate scholarship in religion. I'll never forget at graduation, a couple of my female classmates asked, "Jim, when are you leaving for Boston?" I said, "I think I'm going to spend a few months in DuBois as a disc jockey." They looked at me, and one said, "What a waste," and walked away. On a day when everyone was wishing each other the best, this was a put-down—a big rejection. Rock 'n' roll music wasn't pop culture in 1963. Many in the academic world had a great disdain for this so-called music. Although Elvis had put James Dean's act to music, to them he was just a greasy hillbilly. These girls weren't buying the pop music some thought was loaded with sexual innuendo. To them, the disc jockeys who pandered this music were held in low regard. I wanted them to like me, but I was confused by the dichotomy of being a disc jockey. On the one hand, the disc jockey was the pied piper who people loved; on the other, he was disliked by some academicians. I would make a big decision that summer. If I went to Boston, it was about helping people, dedicating myself to the Lord. The other choice was radio, all about fun and money. I felt badly about my decision, and I didn't walk into a church for years. Even in the army, I stood outside. I can't tell you the number of times I doubted my decision.

The day after graduation, I drove my little Morris Minor convertible to DuBois, and Jimmy Holiday was off and running. I quickly discovered I wasn't a salesman. The station gave me a list of possible advertisers to call on that included the local florist, the Dairy Queen, and others that never were on radio. They had no intention of ever buying radio time. I concentrated on my show, playing rock 'n' roll and talking about the local high school kids, and I got plugged into the community. I was the first rock jock the station ever had. I played a piece of the Four Seasons' song "Candy Girl" and saluted a "candy girl" every night. I'd give her name and a quick bio, about a ninety-second bit. I told stories about the records, did comic bits, and worked on creating my persona.

Randy stopped by the station to see me one night. I did a quick interview with him, and then I said, "Everybody in town knows you as Scotty; Scotty it's all yours." I gave him my headset, and I left a surprised Randy Hall alone to do a show. I went to the local diner where they always had us on and listened. About an hour later, his pretty wife found me and begged me to get back to the station because they had a previous commitment.

I did experience a life lesson when I answered an ad for a radio/television job in Richmond, Virginia. I took a day off to interview at the 50,000-watt powerhouse WRVA radio and television. It was for a night radio show and a backup TV weather announcer position, but I didn't get the job. I had a long drive back to DuBois and while I was going through the state border town of Frederick, Maryland, I noticed a car following me. It was late at night when the car pulled in front of me. I had a crow bar in the back of my seat and I picked it up as I got out of the car. I held it along the side of my leg as a man with a flashlight approached me, when I realized he was a police officer I told him I'd put it back in the car. He said I was speeding and that I went through a stop sign and a red light. I asked where, but he told me to follow him. I explained to the judge at the police station that my old Morris Minor convertible couldn't possibly go that fast and once again asked where the signs and lights were located. I had to downshift to second gear to get up hills in that old car. The judge asked me to put my wallet and money on the table. They took all the bills and told me to leave. It wasn't much but I said, you might as well lock me up because I need some money for gas to get back to DuBois to do a radio show. I wasn't allowed to make a phone call but he let me keep a few dollars for gas. The police followed me out of town. When I got to Pennsylvania I told the police my story but they just smiled and advised me not to go through that town again. I had been caught in an old fashioned speed trap.

The wildest show on the station was the *Sunday Morning Polka Party* hosted by Ben Fingerowski. Ben Fingers was our sales guy, and he'd get together with a couple of Polish gentlemen to party for a few hours. One of their sponsors was Modern Dairy Milk. The first time I stopped to visit, they got me: "Jim, you've got to drink with us. Please tell the folks what you think of Modern Dairy Milk." Well, they poured the milk out, and the containers were filled with whiskey. They were hammered every Sunday morning. Ben was trying to read the news, but somebody had set fire to it while he was reading, somebody else was mooning him, the record was playing at the wrong speed, and nobody noticed. The show was just unbelievable and sold out every week.

President Kennedy is dead

I'll never forget November 22, 1963. While I was doing my day shift, Teresa, our receptionist, came into the studio crying and said that President Kennedy had been shot. I ran to the wire machine. The Associated Press wire service had started the story three times. I had to wait for it to come over the wire. By the time I had it, our general manager, George Williams, who lived in an apartment over the station's studio, took it and broke in on the air. Since we were a CBS affiliate, we went to the network news. For the next several weeks, the music was like a dirge—instrumentals, very somber music, and no more playing disc jockey. Radio didn't know what to do. We gradually went back to playing the regular music. The music charts reflected that somber attitude—Bobby Vinton records, the Village Stompers' "Washington Square," and "Dominique" by the Singing Nun got a lot of air time on our station. Speaking of the Singing Nun, Jeanne Deckers really was a Belgian nun, and Debbie Reynolds starred in a movie about her. Although she inspired millions with her music at a time when we really needed it, she met a senseless, tragic death. Four years after "Dominique," she left the convent and opened a school for autistic children but had heavy financial problems because the Belgian government wanted money from her record royalties, which she claimed was given to the convent. In 1985, because of financial difficulties, she and her female companion of ten years both committed suicide by an overdose of barbiturates and alcohol.

Beatlemania

Less than three months after the assassination of our thirty-fifth president, the time was right, the country needed a pick-me-up, and we got it from four long-haired lads from England who sang old American rock 'n' roll. I loved the early Beatles, and I played the heck out of them on my night show. Teenage girls were suddenly hanging out by the radio station to see me because I was their connection to the Fab Four. Beatlemania had hit! Girls would give me Beatles' dolls, magazines—everything Beatles.

Bobby Goldsboro was in Roy Orbison's band when the Beatles did their last British tour before coming to America. Bobby said Roy was just about as big as Elvis in England, and it was his first English tour.

Roy Orbison told me that during the tour he was reporting for a

British musical paper and that he predicted their success. He had the clippings where he wrote this article in late '63 and, of course, it came to be in 1964. He said, "What I told them was that if they kept their hair like it was and let it be known that they were English and came to America and did a show like the *Ed Sullivan Show*, then they would be as big here as they were in England."

When Roy sang songs like "Only the Lonely" and "Crying," he not only sang them, he lived them. In 1966, while riding their motorcycles, his wife, Claudette, was hit by a semitrailer truck and died instantly. Two years later, while he was in England on tour, two of his sons were killed in a fire at his Hendersonville, Tennessee, home. Everyone reacts to tragedy differently. Roy told me: "I went right back to work and emerged myself in my career. I did a film, and I did scoring for a film, plus an around-the-world tour that I kept doing."

My late brother-in-law James Rocco was a big fan of Roy Orbison and created the Sassoon Jeans commercial with Roy singing, "Oh, Pretty Woman" that brought him back in the spotlight in the late seventies.

What did he say?

Mr. Gray owned WCED radio, the local newspaper, and the main hotel. One night we went off the air because of technical difficulties. Truthfully, it probably was my fault. In the studio, we had this giant patch panel with patch chords all over the place. We carried CBS network, Pirates baseball, Steelers football, plus other events. I was always switching patches, and I plugged in the wrong one. To correct that, I switched another patch and then another, and no one knew how to fix it. They had to find the engineer who designed it. Luckily, he was retired but still living in the area. Mr. Gray called and asked, "What's wrong?" I told him we were off the air, and he was serious when he said, "Jim, make an announcement; break in and tell people the station is off the air." I looked at the phone and said, "Yes sir." I know that sounds like an old joke, because how could I possibly tell people we're off the air when we can't get on the air.

I found the sound

I used the name Jimmy Holiday for several reasons. I thought it sounded show biz, and if I did something wrong, I didn't want to embarrass my family with my real name. One day I bumped a lady's back bumper with my little Morris Minor car. There was no damage, but she was pregnant. I didn't want to take any chances, so we called the police to file a report. The next day in the DuBois paper the story read: "Jimmy Holiday a.k.a. Jim LaBarbara was in a car accident." Well, so much for protecting my real name.

Our program director said to me, "I heard the guy on WBZ in Boston use that same intro to a record the other night." I said something like: "Great minds think alike." I borrowed jokes and material from the big guys and adapted it to fit my style. There was no internet for show content, and years later I was flattered to hear from jocks that did the same while listening to me. I'd spend hours in front of a radio switching stations to hear what the jocks had to say. It was a time of learning and adventure for me. I was searching for a sound, and I wasn't hearing it listening to air checks of my program. One night a lady stopped by the station with her daughter, who happened to be in the Miss Pennsylvania Beauty Pageant and was a big fan of mine. She was one of the prettiest girls I had ever seen, and I found myself thinking about her. I'd pretend I was talking to her on my show. A short time later when I heard a tape of myself, I finally liked what I heard. This is the sound I was looking for; I wasn't a radio announcer, I was communicating one on one. I was positive I could make it in radio; I would never use the scholarship in Boston.

I got a nice ego boost one weekend when I stopped by to talk with Bob Conners, a disc jockey at WEEP in Pittsburgh. Bob went on to have a long career at WTVN in Columbus. The first thing he said was, "You sound good. That was a funny story you told." His family lived in St. Mary's, Pennsylvania, and he heard me on his way through DuBois. Bob introduced me to a disc jockey who had been sleeping on a station couch, Jimmy Rail. I don't know why he was using the name Rail, because he was already better known in other markets as Barney Pip. In the midsixties, Barney was a night star in

Chicago radio and did funny bits, including blasting his out-of-tune trumpet.

Bobby Vinton

Bobby Vinton and I had a close call. Bobby was the featured star at the big county fair near DuBois. He had a number-one hit with "Roses Are Red" and a million-seller with "Blue on Blue." He was becoming a big star, especially with the teenage girls. After the show, we were walking to our car parked in the middle of a field. I suddenly noticed about a hundred teenage girls who had spotted Bobby. Bobby was taking his time talking to someone, and I said, "We gotta go." He kept talking, and the girls were running over the hill. I yelled, "Bobby, we've got to get to the car!" We won the foot race and beat the girls, but there was no security, and we were trapped in a car surrounded by screaming teenagers. They started rocking the car. Our driver slowly drove away, but it was scary for a moment. Bobby joked with me years later that he couldn't believe how strong those little girls were. He added, "Hey, let's go back and see if they're still there."

Surprise, surprise

The DuBois National Guard asked me to do a record hop for them because they were trying to recruit people. It was peace time. The guard's commanding officer said, "Holiday set an example, sign up." I hurt my leg in high school and was told I'd be 4F, so I did. Whoa, what a surprise—I passed my physical. I had Air Force ROTC in college for two years, and I could have entered as a second lieutenant, but I dropped it knowing I couldn't get in. I was off to Fort Knox, Kentucky, and basic training. When I did my last radio show, I was greeted by a bunch of teenage girls who gave me gifts. It was a different era in radio when disc jockeys were stars with loyal followers even in little DuBois. That was the last anyone ever heard Jimmy Holiday on the radio.

CHAPTER 3

J. Bentley Starr

I would have been terrific as Jimmy Holiday on WKYC in Cleveland that day. I was totally comfortable being Holiday on the radio, but NBC radio didn't want him; they wanted Jim LaBarbara. I was never him on the radio, and I was getting nervous as my engineer gave me the signal that my microphone was open. I was about to go on the air. The general manager, Bob Martin, hired me from a tape of a J. Bentley Starr radio show. I had been Bentley for the last three years. I had his act down to perfection. I could tell you all about him.

J. Bentley Starr was born in Fort Knox, Kentucky. That place was a real treat. The sergeant yelled, "Any college grads?" I didn't raise my hand. "Good. We need some smart recruits to 'police' the area." They had to pick up all the cigarette butts, candy wrappers, and garbage. I tried to stay low key and under the radar, but that didn't last long. The sergeants acted like I was some tough guy. I found out why when one asked me about Jimmy Holiday. I had listed it as an alias, and most guys with an alias were criminals. "You're a what? A disc jockey?" They made me a platoon leader, an acting sergeant, and gave me the worst, the trouble makers, and if a guy went AWOL he was added to my platoon. This was peacetime before the Vietnam War, and I will tell you I was not the best soldier. The night before graduation from basic training, our first sergeant and drill sergeants got together for a little beer drinking with all the platoon leaders to wish us well. A Sergeant Smith did a special toast to me. He announced that after thirty-five years in the army, he was retiring, and in all his years, he had never had a recruit like me. I stood up and thanked him for the compliment. He yelled out, "LaBarbara, you is the biggest 'f——k up' I've ever seen!" Everybody laughed hysterically.

We got our next assignment. Somebody liked me because I was going back to Fort Knox to be a clerk typist for a colonel. I had the easiest job, and the colonel had a blonde civilian typist. He explained my job: clear the window ledges—no dead bugs or flies—and just make sure the coffee pot is always full. That was it. I had plenty of time to daydream about radio. I came up with a new name: J. Bentley Starr. "J." for Jim, "Bentley," a fine British car, and "Starr" because that's what I wanted to be. I thought my next move would be to a bigger market. I targeted Erie, Pennsylvania, and the number-two rock station. WJET was by far number one, but WWGO was making noise. During my last couple of months at Fort Knox, I sent a postcard a day to WWGO in Erie. I'd write about me being the next "Starr of Erie radio," an idea for a contest, or a song they could play. I gave them a date when I'd be getting out and how they could contact me. I never got a response, but I'd write back as if I did—"I agree with you," "Thank you for the kind words," "Oh, that's funny." It kept me sane. I graduated from basic training and went to the station and dramatically announced my arrival, "Here I am."

Rejection

Well, not exactly. I went back to DuBois; by law they had to give me my job back. However, I was given strict orders—no more Jimmy Holiday, and they would pick the music. They didn't want a high-profile disc jockey on the air. I was going to start the next week. An old girlfriend said, "What are you doing here? Everybody expected you to move on to a bigger city."

I had time to think about this because I had been here before. I knew very well what failure and rejection felt like. I mentioned that when I was twelve we lost in Williamsport in the Little League series, but I didn't tell you how we lost. In the bottom of the final inning, there was a play at the plate with the bases loaded and the score tied. Instead of keeping the ball in my catcher's glove, I tagged the runner with the ball. He knocked it out of my hand with his knee as he scored the winning run. The next morning one of my teammates threw a copy of the *Williamsport Gazette Bulletin* on my bed. My picture was on the front page with the caption "LaBarbara Loses Ball." The *Grit* newspaper picture caption was similar, "LaBarbara Lost Ball." There were pictures of me dropping the ball from three different angles. The *Pittsburgh Post Gazette* had a picture of us getting off the train with the caption, "They're Still Heroes to Their Followers." I didn't leave the house for more than a week except to play in baseball games and deliver papers. I blamed myself for the loss, and I wasn't alone. I was walking with my teammate Rudy when a friend of his stopped us to talk about the game. He said, "LaBarbara lost it for you. If I ever see him, I'll kick his ass." Rudy looked at me and said, "Meet LaBarbara." He walked away. I read back over the newspapers, and on the day we lost, one paper had the line, "It's Friday the 13th; You better have your lucky rabbit's foot." I've been superstitious about Friday the 13th ever since; I really thought we'd be the champions. A few of us in our uniforms later appeared on Marty Wolfson's DuMont television show, *Musical Sketch Pad*. He was a cartoonist who drew pictures. On the program, I was the caricature "Little Johnny Strikeout." How appropriate was that? Here I was in DuBois, once again feeling not wanted.

Go Radio—Erie, Pennsylvania

The day before I was to start, I got a phone call from WWGO Erie: "Are you as good as you say? We need a night man. Our guy just quit to go across the street to WJET." The radio station's general manager sounded familiar. He turned out to be Larry Perrotto, the guy who engineered my first show in 1959 on WMGW in Meadville, Pennsylvania.

I turned down a couple of scholarships and could have played baseball at one college, but I decided on a great premed school, Allegheny College in Meadville. My senior year in high school I watched my grandfather die a slow death from cancer, and I was convinced I had to be a medical doctor. After my college interview, I stopped by the local radio station WMGW, and I told the station boss I'd be attending Allegheny in September, and I wanted to do a radio show. My background? I had the lead in the senior class play, and I did record hops, emceed shows, and played in bands. He looked at me like I was crazy. Six months later, I stopped back and said, "Remember me?" One of their jocks, Eric Johnson, convinced them to give me a one hour a week show aimed at the college crowd. I'd interview college VIPs and play pop music. Larry Perrotto was my engineer that first show and said "You're a natural; you're gonna' make it. I wanna' be with you." The college show didn't last very long; I was fired after my third program for playing a suggestive record by the heavy breathing April Stevens called "Teach Me Tiger." Seven years later while working in Cleveland, I told her the story, and she said, "Honey, I'm so sorry." That same record was good enough for one of the Apollo crewmembers to take into space. She never had a hit with it but did have a number one with her brother Nino Tempo, "Deep Purple." It took five years, but Larry and I were once again working together.

Bentley hijacked the station

I drove my new, old light blue 1959 Jaguar XK150 with red leather, spoke-wheel sports car 150 miles to Erie on a few hours sleep. The receptionist laughed when she saw me. She still had all the postcards I sent. I was so tired, but I wanted to go on seven to midnight. I felt terrific; my adrenalin was pumping, and about eleven o'clock that night, I got an idea. I was going to hijack the station. WWGO had the transmitter controls in the same area as my on-air studio. I had control of the station. They couldn't take me off. When the all-night man came in, I locked him out after putting the news microphone in the hall. He was a college student and didn't care; he studied. I put a huge desk in front of the door and stacked cabinets on top and barricaded myself in the studio. I was replacing a guy who left to go across the street to "Jet," the number one station. It was shameless self promotion: "Hey everybody, look at me! Here I am." It worked. The next morning by 9:00 a.m., the whole city knew I was in town, but my boss wasn't happy because I missed playing some commercials. He fired me a couple of times, but I had to tell him to watch his language because I had the news microphone in the hall turned on. Everybody heard him talking to me. A local high school football team came to break the door down. During most of that time, I played one record—"C'mon and Swim" by Bobby Freeman—and introduced it differently every time. It was my number one hit, my number five hit—whatever I wanted it to be. It drove me crazy; I can just imagine what listeners thought. My boss would get on the microphone again telling me I was gone. Finally, he said I could keep my job, and he'd give me a day off to get rest. "Did you hear that I'm not fired? How about a raise?" He wouldn't agree on a raise, but I still had my job. The *Erie Morning News* on August 21, 1964, ran a picture of me behind a turntable: "J. Bentley Starr, roving disc jockey who drove into Erie radio 'Gangbuster' style the other day set a new record in Erie radio by keeping himself locked in the WWGO radio studio and doing more than thirty consecutive broadcast hours without a break or anything to eat. Today Mr. Starr is enjoying some peaceful tranquility at management's request." I've been asked a number of times if this was a planned station bit. No, I just did it spontaneously when I saw the transmitter in the same area. Most radio stations have their tower on a tall hill away from the studio. Our studio happened to be in the tallest building in town, and our antenna was on top of the building. A number of jocks copied this over the years, but it was a planned station stunt. All the engineer had to do was shut off the studio from the transmitter and go to a backup studio. That was impossible in my case because I controlled the transmitter. Oh, I forgot about my Jag sitting outside collecting parking tickets. My little stunt proved to be costly.

I was J. Bentley Starr, "Your Intrepid Leader." This incidentally predated my friend Jack Armstrong, who would call himself "Your Leader" in Cleveland. I did both a British and American countdown show every night. I was probably one of the first to do a nightly British countdown show. Hey, my name was Bentley, and I drove a British Jaguar. The Beatles opened the door for all the English acts.

Peter Noone, the leader of Herman's Hermits, told me the first time he saw the Beatles was before they made records. The boys were singing in a field in Manchester like our county fair, but because they had been playing in Germany for five hours a night, for them to do a one-hour show was like a day off. Rock 'n' roll was always about the guy trying to get a girl, and this was true in Peter's case. He recalled seeing a girl he knew at that show, Angela Denna: "We never had a chance with her after that. There was no way we ever could be cool. Now she wanted a Beatle, or a guy like that. We all grew our hair, and we got the same boots. I became the singer because the singer obviously gets the best chicks."

Peter Noone, of Herman's Hermits (center), my son, Jimmy, and me.

The Beatles and me

One of the first things I gave away on my show were tickets to see the Beatles in Pittsburgh on September 14, 1964. It was their first real concert tour of America—thirty-two shows in thirty-four days. I had two special tickets to give away to see the Beatles' concert and attend their press conference with me. I got a real tearjerker of a letter from a girl with a physically disabled cousin who just had to see the Beatles. I picked her as my winner. I needed pictures taken of me with the guys, and she promised she would take them. My car was filled with stuffed animals and gifts for the Beatles from their Erie fans. I'm sure it all went to charity or the dumpster. When I got to the press conference, my guests were already there, and because one was handicapped, they sat in the front.

I had our cheap station tape recorder on the Beatles' table along with the fifty or so microphones. There were a lot of jocks besides the host station KQV jocks. Keep in mind, rock 'n' roll was still in its early years, and many of the disc jockeys were announcers with deep voices from the big band era who had to play this music. A few did a good job of faking it, but others had a real dislike for the music. Some of the jocks were really obnoxious and pompous. I asked a question or two and I talked with them at their table. I wanted to know, "The 'Yeah, Yeah, Yeah' in the song 'She Loves You,' was that inspired by your Liverpool friends Gerry and the Pacemakers' song 'I Like It?' Where did you get it?" They all stood up and mocked me singing, "Yeah, Yeah, Yeah." Everybody got a good laugh. I've seen that example of the Beatles' humor played back many times over the years, a piece of Beatlemania.

The Civic Arena show was a sellout of 12,603 mostly hysterical young girls, who paid $5.90 for a ticket, and the Beatles walked away with $37,000.00. A big Pittsburgh promoter at that time in 1964, Tim Tormey said the highest he ever paid one headliner touring across the country was $3,500.00. The Beatles' fee for that show was $35,000.00, but Tormey negotiated it down to $25,000.00 plus 60 percent of the gross sales, whichever was higher, and they ended up getting the higher fee.

The KQV guys did a good job, but nobody cared. Clarence "Frog Man" Henry, the Exciters, the Bill Black Combo, and Jackie DeShannon came out before the Fab Four and were all greeted by shouts of "We want the Beatles!" I felt sorry for Jackie. The Beatles sang twelve songs, but you couldn't hear anything because of the screams. It was an exciting night for this young disc jockey, but honestly, none of us had any idea how big they would become.

I got a thank you note from the girl who took her handicapped cousin and a reminder that they were expecting to go with me again next year when they came back. She sent me the pictures. Oh, you can see my hand shaking Ringo's and John's, George's and Paul's, but not one of me with the guys. The pictures upset me because the station needed them. However, what really bugged me was that she expected me to take her again. She had used her cousin. The sights of that backstage get-together stayed with me—a group of disc jockeys being obnoxious and dozens of people in wheel chairs.

Peter Brown was with the Beatles' management company and closely associated with the group from the beginning on and was John's best man when he married Yoko. I interviewed Peter when he wrote *The Love You Make: An Insider's Story of the Beatles*. Peter told me how frustrated the Beatles were on that tour and why they didn't care to tour. At some concerts they didn't even bother to sing because no one could hear them; they wanted to get the hell off stage and out of the hail of flashbulbs and jellybeans. Peter wrote something that bothered people: "As the tour progressed, the Beatles became aware of a ghoulish phenomenon. The deformed goblins and cripples of John's schoolboy drawings had come to life to haunt them. Everywhere the Beatles turned, they seemed to be surrounded by the unfortunate; children crippled by various diseases, blind children, the retarded, the terminally ill. It was the crippled children who sat in the first five rows of every concert, so the Beatles looked out over a sea of wheelchairs. And it was inevitably the afflicted who got backstage passes. Desperate parents would present these children to the boys, and one of John's primary memories of touring was the twisted hands reaching out for him."

* * *

When I first got to Erie I started hanging out at a popular bar, and every night after my show I had a prime seat waiting for me at the bar. After a couple of weeks, I thanked the bartender for saving me a seat, but he had no idea who I was. So much for thinking everyone knew me because I was on the radio. It turned out no one ever sat in that chair because it had a direct line to the door, and a guy was shot in that seat a few weeks before I got to town.

I later became involved with the hottest band in Erie, The People. Tom Hanks did a movie in 1996 called *That Thing You Do* about a fictional Erie group. The People was the only group making records at that time in 1964. Every night when I would enter the Brown Jug Club, they would sing to the tune of the Elegants' "Little Star": "Where are you, J. Bentley Starr?"

The Supremes, Lou Christie, Dee Dee Sharp

In November 1964, WWGO presented the Caravan of Stars Show for two appearances. It was extra special because I had so much time to spend with everybody. The Supremes would become the number one female singing group of all time, but they weren't the headliners. They were way down in the billing. The headliner, Johnny Tillotson, who had hits like "Poetry in Motion," was walking around the hall holding hands with his pregnant wife talking about how beautiful it was. Bobby Freeman thanked me for playing his record "C'mon and Swim" over and over when I locked myself in the studio. I know he thought I was crazy. Dee Dee Sharp, the "Mashed Potato" girl, looked like a princess in her white gown, and she got excited telling me about a young man who kept calling her. She didn't know what to think of him, but she was sure her religious grandmother would not approve of this brash boxer named Cassius Clay. Dee Dee said, "Bentley please don't tell anybody about this." And I didn't. Brian Hyland of "Sealed with a Kiss" fame seemed very quiet. He told me he had been mobbed by a bunch of female fans earlier on the tour. Lou Christie didn't believe him. I started calling him "Bashful Brian Hyland" on the air, and it caught on. I have a picture of Lou, Brian, and me backstage, and forty years later when we were together, we reposed for the picture. The Supremes were so elegant and classy. When the tour started, they were jokingly referred to in Motown as the "no-hit Supremes," but by the time they hit Erie, they had two number one hits: "Where Did Our Love Go" and "Baby Love," and they were just about to hit the top again with "Come See about Me." Lou Christie had a thing for Diana Ross and didn't hide it. Mary Wilson looked like a little girl, and Florence Ballard was the sexiest with her beautiful skin color and great figure. I tried to spend time around her. I was surprised years later when she was kicked out of the Supremes for being overweight.

Those tours were fun but didn't pay much. The headliner got between fifteen hundred and twelve hundred dollars a week for fourteen shows, but most acts got between four hundred and six hundred dollars. The Supremes got six hundred—two hundred dollars for each girl. Out of that money, the artist probably had to divide the money: 10 percent manager, 10 percent agent, pay taxes, and, of course, they had to pay their own room and board. Oh, they had to get their own transportation to the bus at the start and the end of the tour. At the end of the tour, some singers were lucky if they ended up with twenty-five dollars a week.

The Crystals had a higher billing than the Supremes, and while we were sitting in the dressing room, I asked, "Girls, what's the difference between the Motown sound and the Philles's sound?" None of the girls could give me a good answer except, "We record for Philles Records, and we record for Motown—it's a Detroit sound." Years later, musicologists would spend hours analyzing the differences. Philles Records was formed by record producer Phil Spector, whose trademark was his "wall of sound" production where he layered one thing on top of another.

Phil Spector produced those early hits for The Righteous Brothers and is often referred to as a genius in the recording studio but very eccentric. Bobby Hatfield of the duo laughed when I mentioned Phil's quirky personality: "Oh yeah, and just about all the stories you hear

The Righteous Brothers, Bill Medley and Bobby Hatfield.
The term "Blue-eyed Soul" was first widely used to describe their music.

about Phil are true. He's a different kind of person."

I heard Phil started screaming hysterically on an airplane as it was taxing down the runway. Bobby explained, "He got on the plane, and he looked around, and he didn't like the looks of the people sitting around him, and he started thinking ah, ooh, I'm on a plane with a whole bunch of losers. So he started yelling. The FBI were waiting for him when they got back to the runway—but that's a true story."

He wasn't Bill Black

There was one Erie night club that brought in national entertainment, not the giant names, but second tier. The sign promoted the Bill Black Combo, an instrumental group that had a number of chart hits including "White Silver Sands." I had just seen them when I was with the Beatles; they were good friends of Elvis, and Bill had played with him. After their show, I went backstage to say hi, and I talked with the group's leader privately to refresh his memory. He was livid, and he told me the whole story: no, they weren't the Bill Black Combo. The owner promoted them that way. They had nothing to do with it. They were actually a very good group and didn't need this. I kept my eye on the club and to my knowledge that never happened again.

Johnny Maestro

Johnny Maestro, the great lead singer of the Crests' "Sixteen Candles" and "Step by Step," and, later, the Brooklyn Bridge was in town for a week, and we worked together. Three years earlier, he was one of the hottest singers in the country. The record company bought him a fancy car and gave his mom a fur coat. But after the hits stopped coming, he had to pay everything back, including the car and the coat. These weren't gifts, they had been charged in his name. I guess he signed a record contract that said he could make records, but it didn't say anything about getting paid. He once said, "The Crests never made money on any record. I got one check that was for seventeen dollars." Yes, he was another victim and got cheated out of his money. As I recall, he needed money to get back to New York because his wife was having a baby.

The Four Seasons

The Four Seasons were in town, and although another station was promoting their appearance, they wanted to get together with this "Italian guy." We sat around in their room. Nick Massi was the old guy; Tommy DeVito managed to get into most of the pictures and acted like he was the boss; of course the big tall guy was Bob Gaudio; and Frankie Valli was the great lead singer. The station didn't have a recorder for me to use so we went outside to a pay phone. I have a picture of me talking on the phone with Frankie and Bob. It's actually pretty funny; here I am interviewing the number one American group, and we're in a phone booth. My Cincinnati friend Rick Steiner's Broadway hit *Jersey Boys* really tells their story. After seeing it, I understood: Tommy was the leader; he was also the one who got them in debt to the mob for over a million. Frankie and Bob paid off all those mob debts. In the nineties, I was sitting in Frankie's trailer backstage while he was eating a steak, and he put ketchup on it. When I mentioned I saw in a tabloid that Tommy was an actor working with Joe Pesci in the movies, Frankie snapped: "Did you ever see him in the movies? No. You know that guy carrying the clothes bag into the Vegas hotel behind Pesci? That's Tommy DeVito." After watching *Jersey Boys* I understand why he said that.

Johnny Bizzarro Day

One of the perks of being a disc jockey was you got to meet celebrities—national and local. At that time, no one was more famous in Erie than Johnny Bizzarro. I decided to have a Johnny Bizzarro Day party at my house. Bizzarro, an acquaintance of mine, was a top-ranked lightweight boxer; he won fifty-six and lost eleven. He fought Carlos Ortiz for the world lightweight crown two years later. I lived in a rented house on the Erie Peninsula with a few friends. It was an incredible party with plenty of food and pretty girls. Everything went smoothly until we got evicted the next day. Apparently some biker guys insisted the ladies who lived next to us attend the party. The ladies happened to be nuns who resided there and taught economics to the young ladies at the local girls' Catholic college.

Bikers want to fight me

I boxed a little at the Boys' Club when I was a kid, but I was no fighter. However, that was about to change. I played the Shangri Las' "Leader of the Pack" and told an old dumb joke: "Do you know how you can tell a happy motorcyclist? By the bugs on his teeth." I guess one biker didn't think it was funny. I got sick when I saw my beautiful Jag. Someone had taken eggs and smashed them over my hood; the egg shells were embedded in my paint. I decided to go home before hitting the bar scene. One of my roommates, a fellow disc jockey, was hiding in the closet crying. This guy was six foot three, a lot bigger than me, and shaking like a baby because the menacing motorcycle guys stopped by looking for me. I was furious! They messed up my car, and they came into my house. I was a crazy guy in my early twenties and not much of a street fighter, but this was personal. I went out looking for them. I found Jesus, at the drive-in diner—a huge, bearded, tough fat guy who weighed about three hundred pounds. I sat next to him and put my arm around him: "I understand you're looking for me." I had my right arm free; I'd get the first punch. He was surrounded by his biker buddies, and he said he didn't do it, but he knew who did. I surprised him. He was the biggest, and the others apologized. My next stop was the bar I hung in, the Brown Jug, and Spech, a big, quiet weight lifter who was probably the toughest guy in Erie. He could have killed me.

"You're looking for me—let's go outside. But before we knock each other all over the parking lot, tell me why we're fighting? Why did you do it?"

He didn't. O'Brien, a biker from Buffalo, was hanging and heard me say it on the radio. I told Spech exactly what I said; it was a dumb joke.

"You know me I wouldn't disrespect you guys."

No, we never fought, but that night every biker in Erie was looking for O'Brien. A couple of days later our receptionist came into the studio and said, "You have a bunch of motorcycle guys in the lobby, and they won't leave until you see them." I came out, and they hugged me and called me righteous. They asked for some dedications, and I had some new friends. They told me O'Brien wouldn't bother me again, that he was back in Buffalo. They took care of him.

I didn't see the knife

I rented a house in a residential neighborhood near downtown with a couple of friends. One of our housemates invited Whitey, a guy who had some trouble with the law but was trying to get his life together, to stay with us. I gave the okay after he promised no underage girls— nothing crazy. I soon discovered he was stealing money from me. He owed me around a hundred dollars—that's a lot of money when you're making eighty a week. We kicked him out, and he promised to get me the money. A couple of months later, I saw him in a bar. I sat next to him, put my arm around his shoulder and punched him in the stomach a few times to convince him to pay me. I was very discrete; no one noticed. Well, almost no one. He said, "Watch it, the Indian has a knife on you." The Indian was a local who was always juiced. Gary Montgomery, a friend, saw this and said, "Bentley let him alone. I'll get your money." Sure enough, the Indian was about to stick me under the table with his knife. Gary saved my life. A few weeks later, Gary got my money back. He was a good guy who would reenter my life later, shortly before his life took an unbelievable turn, but that story is for another chapter.

Oh, I had another memorable brush with death. I was popular in the black community. It might have been because of my name, J. Bentley Starr. I did spend time in an all-black bar with black friends. Some white guys told me about a black house of ill repute. They really talked this place up. Late one Saturday night, after I had too much to drink, I decided to check it out. It was in the worst part of town, but I parked my car under a light. I knocked on the door, and an attractive lady answered. I told her, just like the guys told me, "Johnny sent me." She closed the door; I didn't think I was going to do anything. I was just going to look at the girls. All of a sudden, I felt cold metal pressing against my head. Standing in front of me was a big black woman holding a gun against the side of my head telling me in a rather uncivil manner to get out of there, and she started counting. I instinctively jumped over the porch railing into some bushes, and I dashed to my new car. I floored the gas and smashed the back end of my new Mustang into a wall. Hey, I forgot—the Jag was a stick, and the Mustang was an automatic. A few days earlier, I had traded my Jag for a '65 Mustang 2+2 Fastback V8, poppy red, the first one in Erie. I got out of there alive and never went back.

I know I'm J. Bentley Starr the "Intrepid Leader," but what happened to Jimmy LaBarbara? I was this good, clean-cut Italian kid. I was so innocent that the first time I kissed a girl I didn't, but I told everybody I did. It happened in Chucky Galba's basement during his birthday party. We were in the seventh grade playing spin the bottle, and I had to kiss a cute little girl with lots of freckles named Mary. We went behind a closed door, and as I recall, I gave her a quarter to tell everybody we kissed. At graduation I looked at her and thought how stupid I was because she was one of the prettiest girls in our class. My life was spinning out of control, and things were about to get worse.

Encouragement from Joey Reynolds

A disc jockey friend of mine on the easy listening Erie station, Rodger Miller, was a friend of Joey Reynolds, who was a star on WKBW in Buffalo, a station you could hear all over the East Coast. Joey did crazy bits with special sound effects, and the Four Seasons sang a special radio intro for his show. He is acknowledged as radio's first "shock jock" before the term was coined. He made comments that made adults cringe and gave a lot of program directors headaches. Joey invited us to visit with him at the station. His little gold mine was a huge trunk in his studio filled with horns, toys, tapes, and junk that he used on his show. He listened to my air check, and he gave me encouragement: "You're good enough to work here, but I'm not leaving. You sound like Bobby Mitchell from KFRC San Francisco. Are you Bobby?" I was thinking about getting out of radio, but now, with his positive comments, I was going to give this business a few more months. He really motivated me, but I didn't know how long I could hang on.

I was a walking chimney

My friend from the radio station in Meadville who encouraged me to get into radio was now working at an Erie television station. Eric Johnson was married, and from time to time, I was invited for a home-cooked meal. I was a smoker; I'd sometimes go through five packs a day. Cigarettes were a lot cheaper in 1964, and I thought I looked cool holding one. No one smoked in his house, and I guess I stunk the place up. On more than one occasion, my ashes would hit the rugs or sofa, and I know I made a little hole in the sofa from a hot ash. One day I got a call from Eric, "Congratulations, my wife just told me you quit smoking." Well, not exactly. I did a bit on the air and pretended I was quitting; I had no intention. I had actually gone more than three hours without one when he called. I felt so bad I tried to give it a day. I did, but the next day, I went to the hospital because my whole system was a mess. It was a big deal for me to quit because I was constantly smoking. Sometimes little fires would break out in the ash tray when I was on the air. I burned my pillow smoking in bed. That was it. I gave up smoking cold turkey. For the next six months, I kept finding packs of cigarettes everywhere—in coats, dresser drawers, shirt pockets, and the car glove compartment. I never had another cigarette. My wife, Sally, was a smoker, but she quit after our daughter, Shelby, told her what she wanted for her fifth birthday. The only thing Shelby asked for was that her mommy stop smoking, because she didn't want her to die.

My last year in Erie, I lived in a sleazy boarding house. We shared a common bathroom, but it was cheap. I came home late one night and found a wino neighbor of mine blocking the door. I started to push him aside when I saw his face. Somebody did a number on him; he was a bloody mess.

"Who did this?"

He said, "He went that way."

I ran down the street, but I couldn't find anyone. I was so frustrated about everything, and it really hit me. I was a college graduate, and this is how I was living. It was embarrassing.

Don't tell anyone I'm on WIXY

I was just about to get out of radio and begin a teaching career in Pittsburgh when things suddenly changed for me. I gave an air check to an engineer friend who was working at WDOK in Cleveland. The station featured a mixture of specialty shows—Italian, Polish, a lot of ethnic shows. WDOK was now under new ownership and switched

formats to Top 40, WIXY 1260. I got a call from their program director, Gerry Spinn. Joey Reynolds, yes the same guy, had left the station for Detroit. Somehow Gerry found my tape, but he couldn't
promise me anything. However, he wanted to hear me on WIXY.
They moved the all-night guy up and asked me to do his shift until
they found a permanent host. Gerry said, "Don't quit your job until
we see what develops." I was to start the next night, but I was going to
continue to do my shows in Erie. I was so excited, I told my boss, the
general manager, and at first he was happy for me, but then told me if
I took the job I'd be fired. I couldn't believe it; he was my friend.
What a dilemma. I was just filling in. I didn't tell anyone, but after
doing two shifts, midday ten to one and afternoon drive two to seven,
and doing production and recording commercials from 7:00 to 8:00
p.m., I drove to Cleveland to do the all-night show. I had already
accepted the part-time job. I'd been doing the midday show for
months while they were looking for a jock for no extra money.

WIXY was broadcasting from its transmitter. I entered the studio
and major market radio. Bobby Magic had a waste basket over his
head screaming into it as he introduced a record. He was preoccupied
talking to a girl on the phone. He quickly showed me the equipment
and left, leaving me on my own to figure things out. I did bring tape
to make an air check of J. Bentley Starr. I did a lot of the same talk
bits and record intros that I used earlier in the day in Erie. Overall
things went smoothly, and I liked hearing the stations reverb in my
headsets. At six o'clock, the morning man, Ray Otis, came in; he had
a great deep voice and had worked at WHK in town and KXOK in St.
Louis. We had a good conversation, but the next morning, he was in a
bad mood so I didn't bug him. I called Gerry Spinn after my second
show; he still hadn't taken the time to hear me. The third morning,
Ray didn't show, but left the general manager one hell of a note. He
quit. Howie Lund, a local radio vet who rhymed everything, was now
doing mornings. Howie was a reformed alcoholic who, years later,
would kill himself by drinking a bottle of Lestoil, a product used to
clean toilets. You really have to hate yourself to do that. I had
wrecked my car, nothing serious, but I was sleep deprived. I left the

program director a note saying I couldn't come in the next day, but I'd be in the day after for the weekend. I called Gerry later that day, and he screamed at me, calling me every name. He wanted to fight me. He was crazy. I said, "You'll get your chance someday." He still hadn't heard me on the radio. That was the end of my WIXY career, but I had a few air checks as a memory. Of course I couldn't tell anyone.

Thank you Steve Popovich and Bob Martin

I was the music director at WWGO and the next week Steve Popovich, a record promoter from Cleveland, came in, but he didn't hear me on WIXY. However, he told me Jim Gallant, the all-night guy at WKYC, wasn't happy and that I should give General Manager Bob Martin a call because they were between program directors. I took Steve's advice, and to my surprise, Bob Martin wanted to see me. I took a day off and visited 50,000-watt WKYC, one of my dream stations, owned by NBC. Mr. Martin seemed to like my WIXY air check, and I told him the whole Gerry Spinn story.

He asked, "Do you have any more of this material?"

"Oh yes, this is what I do on the air."

He asked me about money, and I told him I had received a raise to ninety a week, but I was going to get bumped to a hundred dollars in six months. I drove back to Erie, but since he didn't hire me, I didn't think he was interested. A couple of days later when I finished my show, I got a call. "Jim we'd like you to work with us at WKYC." I thought it was another jock in the market who took pride in bugging me, and I hung up. Then I got another call. "Jim this is Bob Martin. You visited with me the other day. If you hang up again, I'm not calling back." I was offered the summer fill-in job. I'm glad I didn't hang up. Earlier in my career I had a guy call me and say, "This is Rick Sklar with WABC in New York. We're interested in you." I was sure this was a put on, and I hung up on him twice. Everybody in the business knew Rick Sklar was the program director of the number one rock station in America, WABC. Years later when Rick was promoting a book, I asked him if he called me. He didn't remember, but Erie was a market he listened to for young talent, and if someone hung up twice, he told me he wouldn't call back.

CHAPTER 4

Cleveland Wants Me !
Not Holiday or Starr?

J. Bentley Starr was a little crazy, but he would have been a nice fit playing rock 'n' roll on WKYC. Of course I knew everything about him, but Mr. Martin didn't want him any more than Jimmy Holiday. He was sold on Jim LaBarbara, and it was time for him to talk for the first time on WKYC. I did a pretty straight show that night. I wrote Jim LaBarbara on a piece of paper and kept it in front of me so I wouldn't forget my own name. I didn't use the "Intrepid Leader" lines, and I couldn't say things like, "You're listening to a Starr by the name of J. Bentley." This was one of the most difficult things I ever did, and I didn't know where to begin. Who am I, Jim LaBarbara? The next night I filled in for Jim Gallant on the all-night show and at 6:00 a.m. Harry Martin and Specs Howard entered the studio. I visited with them three years earlier when I was working on the air in Titusville. Specs Howard was an Allegheny College graduate so I thought I had an in. His critique: I had some talent, but I needed to work hard if I wanted to make it. Harry Martin, his partner, heard a bit of it and said I needed to project more. He began singing the scales very loudly and explained that he was a professional singer who once performed with the Harry Simeone Chorale. His advice was to take singing lessons. I took his advice, and during my senior year, I did take vocal lessons, walking to the other end of campus every day to practice my scales. I was happy to tell Harry that I took his advice just as he suggested. He laughed, "You dummy. I was putting you on. Specs, look, they hired the dummy." He proceeded to walk the halls telling everyone, "They hired the dummy."

I reached my goal working on this great station in a major market, and I had nothing else planned. Anything else would be a plus. I never thought I would get old, and I never pictured myself getting married and having a family. I don't know exactly why, but I knew I'd die young.

Maybe it was the movie *Rebel without a Cause* with James Dean. Dean was this troubled teenager we all identified with to some degree. He crystallized the image of youthful rebellion as no one ever had. He showed us that it was okay to be a teenager, especially a vulnerable, alienated one. I had a red jacket like he wore. I wasn't cool enough, but we all wanted to be James Dean. He died in a Porsche Spyder at age twenty-four. Awhile back, I rode my Harley to visit James in Fairmount, Indiana. His tombstone is one of the smallest in the cemetery. Somebody left him a pack of cigarettes, matches, sunglasses, a lighter, and several pictures. It was a Sunday afternoon, and I stood by myself for a good half hour before anyone stopped by.

Maybe it was something else that had me thinking I would be a young corpse. My dad was a truck driver for a florist. During the holidays I would help him with deliveries, and we visited a lot of funeral parlors. One of my best friends was Anthony Musmanno, and he lived above a funeral home. If his dad didn't have a customer, we'd hang out in his basement. Patsy Aluise, Vince Valicenti, Henry Tumpa, Dave Oliver, and I would shoot pool, play ping pong, or practice singing as a group we called the "Cashmiers." In all fairness, I couldn't sing. I had chorus one semester, and when it came time for the big concert, our director took me aside and asked me not to sing: "Just pretend you're singing." I did and got a B for the semester with the notation, "Follows directions well." One day at school, Anthony totally ignored me until I finally caught up to him: "Why won't you talk to me?" He started to cry and told me he saw me in a dream. He went downstairs in his house, the funeral home, and saw me in a coffin. I gave him a hug and told him, "I'm okay"; he said his mom said it was good luck.

The day the music died

There was something else that made me think I'd die young. I had a *Pittsburgh Post Gazette* morning newspaper route from the sixth grade until I left home for college. I'll never forget the front page story on February 3, 1959. It was the first death of a rock 'n' roll star—not one, but three. Buddy Holly, Ritchie Valens, and the Big Bopper, were killed in a plane crash. Buddy was a favorite of mine because I could sing along with his records, and he looked like an average guy. His self-contained group of two guitars, bass, and drums would become the prototype for countless groups in the coming years. He was also one of the first to write, produce, and perform his own songs. That plane crash was later immortalized in a song about the day the music died, in "American Pie" by Don McLean in 1971.

Years later as a disc jockey I talked with Don, and we joked about the fact that we both wore those cool, black horn-rimmed glasses like Buddy, and we were newspaper boys. He told me, "I tell people that's the only job I ever had. I started making music when I was fifteen, and when I was sixteen, I was able to make enough money just giving guitar lessons to make more money than most of the kids who had jobs, and I gave these little shows and stuff. Buddy Holly's death and the memory of his music stayed with me."

The *Buddy Holly Story* movie in 1978 with Gary Busey came out as a direct result of "American Pie." According to my conversations with Don, the song and the movie had one thing in between them and that was a book written by a guy named John Goldrosen called *The Buddy Holly Story*. Don told me about a letter John wrote: "He said, 'Before your song came out, I was trying to shop this book around and nobody wanted it. They said, what the hell are you writing about some dead rock 'n' roll star,' nobody cared about these guys when they were around, let alone when they are dead. That was the way it was back then. Rock 'n' roll was a side issue, not mainstream. If one of these guys happened to die in a plane crash, bring on the next guy. But that's not how it was to the people who heard the music or to Goldrosen who wrote the book. He said after "American Pie" came out, he immediately got a publisher, and then they auctioned the book and made the movie. Maria Elena, Buddy's widow, said he got more publicity after "American Pie" than he got in his whole career."

Dion

Dion and the Belmonts were on that Winter Dance Party tour. Dion told me why he wasn't on the plane: "At the time, it was a financial issue decision on my part. They were solo performers, and I guess they didn't have the overhead I had traveling with a group. It was just a matter of dollars and cents, and I thank God I wasn't on it. That's baffling at that age; I was in my teens, and suddenly the floor slips out from underneath you. Three friends and fine performers just don't show up in Fargo, North Dakota, at the next job, and you heard that their plane crashed. It's just baffling even at my age today. We just finished the tour and made the best of it, but it's hard to measure what that does to your inside."

Dion explained to me that they were having bus problems, and that's why they took the plane: "It was an old bus. It was breaking down. It was in the heart of winter in the Midwest, temperatures were way below zero. We had a few frightening calls on the bus. In fact Buddy Holly's drummer, Carl Bunch, got frostbite on his feet. I know the Big Bopper had brought a sleeping bag just to stay warm on the bus. We were having quite a bit of trouble. I don't know if that was the motivation. It could have been one of the motivations to take that plane. They wanted to get laundry and haircuts. Once in a while, performers would do that, especially on a tour where you were being bused around the country. They'd want to fly into one job and have that free day." The ticket cost thirty-six dollars to ride the plane.

Bobby Vee

Fifteen-year-old Bobby Vee remembers the radio station asking if local talent would donate their services to the show. They had the remaining acts: Dion and the Belmonts, the new Crickets, and Frankie Sardo. Bobby told me, "It really should have been cancelled. We called the station. We were a little garage band—we didn't even have a name for the band. I stood on stage, and Charlie Boone, the disc jockey that hosted the show that evening, turned around and looked at me and said, 'What's the name of the group?' I looked at the floor. I didn't know what to say, and I said, 'The Shadows,' and he said, 'Ladies and gentlemen, the Shadows.' That was a launching pad for me." There was a booking agent in the audience who was impressed with Bobby Vee, and two weeks later, he was sending them out on appearances.

I asked Bobby if Tommy Allsup and Waylon Jennings of the Crickets performed that night. He recalled, "It was a very emotional evening. I remember my brother Bill had forgotten his guitar strap, and he borrowed a strap from Dion, and we talked to Tommy Allsup. I didn't know who he was. I was expecting to see Jerry Allison and Joe B. Mauldin of the original Crickets. I hadn't heard Holly had a new group of Crickets. Tommy was the guitar player. He had played on 'Heartbeat' and some of the later Holly records. I just remember looking at his eyes and thinking, boy he was there physically, but he was miles away; he wasn't there at all. Waylon Jennings went on and did a Ritchie Valens tribute. He sang 'Donna.' There were people who arrived at the show that night, (the media not being what it is today) that didn't find out about it until late in the afternoon, or for some of them until they arrived at the venue. It was an emotional night."

Jerry Allison

Jerry Allison was the Crickets' original drummer and one of Buddy's closest friends. They met in the seventh grade and learned to play rock 'n' roll together in high school. He was the one who married the "Peggy Sue" they sang about. On their first hit record "That'll Be the Day," Norman Petty is given credit as one of the songwriters. I questioned that, and Jerry confirmed my thoughts: "No, we already recorded it before he ever heard it, but that's one of those old rock 'n' roll whiz deals."

Jerry told me the part about the group getting back together was pretty true in the movie *The Buddy Holly Story*, but they were disappointed in other parts. "They called me 'Jessie,' and they called Joe B. 'Ray Bob.' Actually when Buddy moved to New York, and we started going our separate ways, we made a deal that we would get another lead singer, and Buddy would work just as Buddy Holly. If it didn't work out, we'd get back together. We already missed playing with each other, and we were trying to get a hold of Buddy at the Surf Ballroom in Clear Lake, Iowa, the night of the last show. We called, and he had already gone. Later on, Waylon Jennings said that Buddy had mentioned to him a couple of days before the plane crash that he was going to do a tour of England. He wanted to get back together with Joe B. and I and have the original Crickets. Waylon said, 'What about me?' and Buddy said, 'We're going to take you as a singer not as a bass player.' So I think Buddy had the same thoughts as we did of all getting back together."

Something that has always bothered me was why Buddy needed the money so badly that he did that tour. Jerry surprised me when he said, "I think he probably did because Norman Petty was holding a bunch of Buddy's money on like some threat of a lawsuit or something because I think Norman Petty really hated the thought of losing Buddy, the management of Buddy. I think there was some kind of hassle. Joe B. and I weren't in on that deal. We didn't really know what was going on, but I think Buddy actually did need money, and he couldn't get his own money from Petty. That's the way it always struck me."

Petty was the Crickets' manager and producer and recorded them in his Clovis, New Mexico, studio. Norman had a way of manipulating numbers and probably took an enormous slice of the group's income for himself. His books were in such a mess that those involved took whatever he gave them. There was no money coming from Petty. Buddy's wife, Maria Elena, was pregnant, and Buddy decided to make some quick money and do the tour. She later had a miscarriage.

Buddy's guitar player, Tommy Allsup flipped Ritchie Valens for the seat. On the toss of that coin, Ritchie lost his life, and Tommy Allsup would one day open a club called the Heads Up Saloon, a tribute to the coin toss that saved his life. Ironically, Ritchie was very excited and said, "That's the first time I've won anything in my life."

Waylon Jennings, Buddy's bass player, gave up his seat to the Big Bopper, who was sick with a fever. When Holly heard that Waylon wasn't going to fly, he said, "Well, I hope your old bus freezes up." Waylon joked back, "Well I hope your old plane crashes." That friendly kidding would haunt Jennings for the rest of his life.

Young James Dean dies in a car crash, my friend Anthony sees me in a casket in his dad's funeral home, and I read the story of the plane crash over and over as I folded my newspapers. I was convinced I'd be a young corpse.

*Sam the Sham ruined my first WKYC commercial recording session,
but I had to laugh. I've never seen him without his turban. He traveled
in a 1952 Packard hearse with maroon velvet curtains.*

CHAPTER 5

Creating Jim LaBarbara

WKYC was my dream station, and in my mind, I had made it. My only problem was me, Jim LaBarbara. J. Bentley wore a sophisticated ascot and drove a '59 Jaguar. LaBarbara wasn't even allowed to drive the station's VIP car because the first time I was behind the wheel, I backed out of the parking space in the garage and promptly smashed into a pole.

After I got my own shift, my first PR bio page read: "WKYC's Jim LaBarbara is unique. . . . He wears the wrong clothes, drives the wrong car, and has been known to drive the wrong way through a one-way street. But he is loveable. (He has endeared himself to his audience because of sheer innocence.)" It went on to describe my education and radio background. It ended with, "The only thing Jim says is, 'What did I do?' If he ever finds out, we'll all be in trouble." This wasn't exactly the image I had in my mind.

The beard

I needed to create a persona, an image for LaBarbara. Alan Douglas, our late evening talk host, had a terrific beard, and he suggested I'd look good in one. At that time, not many guys had beards. I thought it was a great idea; I could hide behind my beard. I was always self conscious about my appearance; my nose was too big, and my complexion wasn't good. A kid in school told me he knew I liked his cousin Judy, but she thought I was ugly. I believed him and never asked her out. My sophomore year, I got a big hit in a baseball game. I had a crush on a senior cheerleader, and that night at the school dance, I was feeling pretty confident, so I made my move: "Gloria, you wanna dance?" This beautiful goddess looked at me and whispered, "Get lost." The guys saw me and asked, "What did she say?" I told them, "She said, 'ask me later.'" LaBarbara wasn't Dean Martin, he was Jerry Lewis. In the James Dean movie, he wasn't James—he was the kid on the motor scooter, Sal Mineo. I grew a beard, and I took Alan's advice and used Dippity-do, a gel, holding product, on the beard to make it look neat. One hot afternoon, dressed in my elegant sharkskin, blue VIP suit, I felt a little strange on stage introducing a rock band. The sun caused the Dippity-do from my beard to drip all over my shirt and suit. I was a mess. I've kept the beard over the years. However, because of military regulations, I was clean shaven except for my moustache when I was in the army reserves. I have no desire to shave my beard. I would feel naked without it.

How much money?

When I got my first WKYC paycheck, I knew something was wrong. I took it to Bob Martin, our general manager, and he apologized for the mistake. I asked if I could be paid by the week instead of the month. He responded, "This is your weekly check, but we didn't include your talent fee, an extra one hundred per week plus whatever commercials you read." I actually started to tear up and cry. Bob asked me, "Didn't we discuss salary?" No, we never talked money except that I told him I was making ninety dollars a week in Erie. I made almost thirty-eight thousand dollars a year during the time I was with WKYC, NBC. That was a lot of money in 1966, '67, and '68.

To put that in perspective, in early 1968, I was sitting in a Euclid Avenue bar with Duke Sims, the Indians' starting catcher, who was holding out for more money. Kenny Suarez, the backup catcher, had just signed for eighty-five hundred dollars, but Duke told me he wasn't going to spring training until he got a fifteen-thousand-dollar contract.

The first commercial I did in Cleveland was for the Dave Clark Five show. I must have done five takes, and I apologized to the engineer and producer. I said, "I guess I'm no Jim Stagg." Jim Runyon on his show often praised Stagg for his impeccable grammar when they were on WKYC a couple of years earlier. They burst out laughing because that was Runyon's way of making fun of Stagg. Apparently Stagg would take forever to do a commercial. Just as I was wrapping up the spot, a strange bearded man wearing a turban entered the studio laughing and ruined my commercial. He yelled, "Hey man, what's going on?" It was Sam the Sham of the "Wooly Bully" fame. I couldn't be mad, because he just wanted to say hi. I kidded him about a radio report I heard while I was visiting my parents in Pittsburgh a few weeks earlier. He drove his hearse through the Squirrel Hill Tunnel the wrong way, and traffic was backed up for hours. Sam and I laughed about it, and he explained, "The way that spaghetti bowl is, you know, coming in you're on one ramp, and you think you're headed right for the city, and the next thing you know, you're headed in another direction. Yeah, it was crazy."

The Dave Clark Five was a huge British group that came over on the heel of the Beatles. Years later, their lead singer, Mike Smith, told me his first impression of America was arriving at Kennedy Airport and hearing fifteen thousand kids screaming his name. He didn't understand how people three thousand miles from his home knew his name. He added, "I could not believe how big the buildings were, and I thought everybody was talking with a fake accent." That Sunday night, they played in front of seventeen million people on the *Ed Sullivan Show*.

WKYC was a strong union station, and the disc jockey never touched a record. When you wanted a record or a commercial, you pointed at the engineer. I had a problem because I'm Italian—I talk a lot with my hands. I could be in the middle of a sentence, and the record would start. The engineers were trained to let the record go when you moved your hand. They set up a button for me to push that would set off a tone to signal the engineer to release the record. An engineer could make or break your show. One night I went into my intro about the group, but the engineer played a different song. I asked him why, and he said because he wanted to hear it. Of course he made me sound bad on the air. I know they were testing me. I never said anything, and it never happened again. Depending on the day or the shift, I could have as many as three different engineers working my show. We sat in a huge studio with nothing but a microphone, a cough switch, a table, a podium, and two chairs, one high and one low. Jerry G. and I liked the higher chair with the podium.

Jerry G. and Jay Lawrence

I was officially a WKYC VIP, a Very Important Personality, and with that came a lot of perks, including our own secretary to answer fan mail. It was a little overwhelming that every day there would be a stack of fan mail on my desk. I got a lot, but Jerry G. got the most. Personal appearances were crazy, and disc jockeys at WKYC were held in the same esteem as some of the artists we played. I remember an appearance at an Akron shoe store where they had to get me in the back door because a couple hundred kids were blocking the front door. I autographed pictures and answered music questions for a few hours. That summer was unbelievable. I filled in on all the day shifts. Jerry G. was the star afternoon guy. He had his own engineer, Phil Music, and they worked well together using a lot of audio drops. Those audio bits could be anything from laughter to a line from a movie that Jerry would respond to. If he had an appearance, I'd tag along with him just to see how it was done. I was the one he wanted to do his show when he toured with the Beatles in 1966. Every hour Jerry would be on the "Beatle Beat," and he would have an interview with one of the guys. He'd say, "Jimmy, say hi to Paul or Ringo." It was incredible. Jay Lawrence, our midday guy, had a great sense of humor and an infectious laugh. I learned a lot watching him do his show. Jay lived in a huge house on the lake, but because it was so big, he had doors boarded up because they never used those rooms. Jay, the "Jaybird," always wore a wool sport coat to work. It could be ninety degrees. He told me, "Jimmy, I live in an air-conditioned house, I drive to work in an air-conditioned car, I park in the garage next to the station, and our station has air conditioning. I'm never outside."

I'd been at WKYC a few months when I got a call to emcee a show at a theatre about forty-five minutes outside of Cleveland. I took one of the high school kids who helped with the phones, Bud Stalker. I introduced a couple of national acts, but after the show, the surly guy who hired me told me to get lost. He had his big bodyguard with him, and he wasn't about to pay me. I was upset, but I was new at the station, and I didn't want to cause problems. On the way back to Cleveland, a guy driving the wrong way almost hit us on the interstate. It wasn't a good night. A few months later, Jerry G. was having a fit in the office because the same guy gave him a bad check, but he called the cops on him. I told Jerry about my experience with this jerk. Jerry gave me a lecture about speaking up. That never happened to me again.

Years later, the program director of KMPC Los Angeles introduced me to Gary Owens, and a voice yelled over the intercom. It was my Cleveland friend who took phone requests, Bud Stalker, now Gary's producer. Gary Owens always liked my radio work and nominated me for *Billboard Magazine*'s Radio Personality of the Year in 1973.

One of my close Stowe High friends was passing through Cleveland. Sonny Dudzinski was an officer in the military, and he wanted to show me his classic red Porsche. He said something I thought was strange as he was leaving: "What are you going to do after radio?" I tried to explain this was my career, but he just looked at me like I was crazy. Now at that time, I was on top of the world. I never thought about my next goal. It's been more than fifty years, and I've gone through a lot of changes. I've often thought about his comment.

I was glad to see Sonny because it brought back memories from the old neighborhood. He and I conducted a most interesting research project that I have referenced a number of times over the years. It took place during summer vacation before the ninth grade at the North Park Swimming Pool, at the time one of the largest in the world. It came about from sheer boredom. We would lie on our stomachs to get a tan and watch the girls walk by. We discovered that if a girl had well-developed calf muscles, she would also have a full figure. If a girl walked by with nice calf muscles we'd look up to check, and we were seldom wrong. Although unscientific, this study was conducted on hundreds of girls that summer by two young boys.

Annette Funicello and Connie Francis

I grew up in a pretty innocent era. All the guys had a crush on Annette Funicello, the Mouseketeer on the *Mickey Mouse Club*. She told me their ears were specially made, and if they lost them, they cost fifty dollars to replace. Her hit record "Tall Paul" wasn't about Paul Anka; she recorded it before she met Paul. However, after they met on a Dick Clark tour, they dated for about two years, and she added, "'Puppy Love' and 'Put Your Head on My Shoulder' were both written for me." Ironically, she later married Paul's manager.

Now, the Connie Francis song "Frankie" was about Frankie Avalon. Connie Francis said she told Neil Sedaka and Howie Greenfield, "Every time somebody writes a song about a city or a boy, it's a hit. I'd like to sing a song about a boy," and they asked what boy. She said, "Frankie Avalon—he's so popular, and so many girls are in love with him." So, they wrote it.

Connie said, "There are so many cute stories about that era, Jim. Neil Sedaka was writing all these hits for me, and I said, 'You can sing; you don't have to have a great voice. Go in the studio and cut something yourself.' He said, 'I don't know what to write for myself.' That night I was writing in my diary, which I had kept for about sixteen years, and it had a key on it. He said, 'Let me look in it,' and I said, 'Nobody sees my diary.' So that night he went home. 'Oh, I'd like to look into that little book, the one that has the lock and key,' he wrote for the 'Diary,' which then became his first song."

Neil told me that he recorded "Oh Carol" for his girlfriend at the time, Carol King. Yes, the "Tapestry" lady. He said she idolized him and recorded "Oh Neil" for him.

No, Connie didn't date Frankie or Neil, but her first real love was Bobby Darin. Connie told me she met Bobby when he was a bus boy in the mountains, and he brought a song to her manager's office. She said, "I recorded 'My Teenage Love,' and Bobby did all four background voices. It was one of my early misses. It was by Connie Francis and the Blue Jays, and he was the Blue Jays."

Bobby Darin called Connie his "sweetheart" and wanted to marry her, but her father didn't want them together. One night when Connie was doing the *Ed Sullivan Show,* her dad came looking for Bobby with a gun. He escaped by climbing out a men's room window and down the fire escape. Well, so much for love.

In late December 1973, I was cleaning out my station mailbox, and I found a note that was a couple of weeks old: "Call Bobby Darin," and it had his phone number. I just stared at that note for the longest time, and I felt guilty that I didn't see it sooner. Bobby Darin had died a week earlier.

Shy guys meeting girls

I was so shy and innocent; I would blush if a girl looked at me. I was an insecure, self-conscious teenager when it came to girls. I discovered in later years that I wasn't alone. Neil Diamond, the great songwriter performer, told me that he was an awkward kid who didn't have too much grace with girls. Neil said, "I began to find I had physical needs as I became a teenager. If I wanted to go out with girls, the only way I could get up enough nerve to ask them to go out was, I used to write little poems to them, and that's really how it started, writing poetry to girls. When I was sixteen, I started to take guitar lessons. The first day that I learned a chord progression, I wrote a song, and I've been writing since then. It just seemed like a very natural thing, something that I fell into naturally."

Kenny Loggins, of "Footloose" and "I'm Alight" fame, became a songwriter performer to impress the girls. He had been in Catholic school—eight years of grammar school, and then four years of high school. Kenny told me, "By the time I was a junior in high school, I still had very few girl friends—meaning 'girl friends.' I didn't know how to talk to girls; they always seemed like creatures from a foreign planet or something to me. They all seemed so different. So in order to meet them and try to break the ice with them, I started singing and writing songs. That was a way to get to a party, meet people at a party. If you take your guitar, you're always invited. The problem is you spend most of the time at the party singing, and you end up meeting very few people anyway."

Music director or disc jockey?

Besides doing my radio shows, WKYC named me the station's music director. Years later I would realize what a powerful position that was. I met with the record label promotion people every week, checked local and national record sales, and compiled our Sound Eleven Survey. I did the music and air shift for several months until someone from NBC corporate said I couldn't do both. The decision was easy for me because I loved being on the air.

Ron Iafornaro, the local Liberty Records guy, and I became good friends. Because he was a bachelor, he and his fellow promoters would have weekend parties at his place. I must differentiate between these parties and the typical record company promotion party. Those parties were hosted by a label to promote an artist or a record and often featured professional ladies, alcohol, and food. Ron's parties were unique because nobody was pushing a record—just people in the industry getting together to socialize. Some of the local guys were Doc Remer, Louie Newman, Pat McCoy, and Rory Bourke. Rory became a Hall of Fame songwriter with songs like "The Most Beautiful Girl." The parties would start on a Friday night and go all weekend. I stopped by on a Sunday afternoon to watch the Browns' game when suddenly a guy came down from an upstairs bedroom. He had fallen out of bed and fell asleep under it. "Party Pat" Fitzgerald couldn't believe it was Sunday and that he missed his Saturday show on an Akron station. Jocks from all the stations would party. Later in my career, I worked for a couple of paranoid program directors who frowned on fraternizing with people from other stations. One of the soul deejays, Michael Payne, entered with the help of several young ladies wearing hot pants, boots, and mesh stockings, singing "Michael the Lover." At one party I met an attractive black lady and we decided to date. She stopped by the station to make arrangements, but after she left, a couple of my fellow jocks took me aside and suggested that maybe it wasn't such a good idea to date a black lady. I was the new guy, and it was 1966. I took their advice and ended it.

Terry Knight

One of the best self promoters I ever knew was Terry Knight. He stopped by while I was on the air and asked me to play his new record. It was "Lady Jane" and I told him "no," that I'd play the Stones' version. Terry was a former CKLW Windsor-Detroit jock who called himself the "sixth Rolling Stone" because of his early support of the group. There was a story that said the group told him if he came to England, they would make him part of the Stones. He quit his job, and when he went to England, they basically told him to get lost. That story has never been confirmed, but it is interesting. I played his record "Better Man Than I" earlier, and I told him to get me something like that, and I'd play it. There was a recording studio nearby, the Cleveland Recording Company, with the great engineer Ken Hamann, and before I went off the air that night, Terry came back with a song called "A Change On the Way." I liked this song about the generation gap and and played it immediately. That was the beginning of our friendship. As an entertainer, he went through a lot of changes. He'd invite me to La Cave, a coffeehouse, and there he was in a robe like a flower child singing folk songs. He went through another phase where he was a lounge singer a la Bobby Darin. He wasn't a good singer, but he knew how to entertain on stage. Terry invited me to be the co-host on a national afternoon television show he was putting together. The set was going to be in the round, and musical guests like the Mamas and Papas, Neil Diamond, and the Loving Spoonful would perform acoustically. He saw a large gap in the market because the big daytime shows at the time were Mike Douglas and Pat Boone. I was told they shot the opening of the show in his New York apartment where he had this huge armored knight. I thought it was a great idea, and there was definitely a market for it, but when I took a radio job in Cincinnati, that ended my involvement. WKYC jocks alternated with the CKLW jocks at Cedar Point Amusement Park in Sandusky, and every other week we had the stage. I introduced Terry Knight and the Pack, and afterward Terry asked me what I thought of the group. I told him, "Terry you're terrific, but get rid of the kids. You don't need them." He didn't take my advice, and the next time I saw him, he was wearing a suit carrying an attaché case walking into Crosley Field in Cincinnati on June 13, 1970, to star in a television show we were taping called *Midsummer Rock*. Oh, he wasn't going to sing and perform, but the Pack's Mark Farner and Don Brewer were. They were now known as Grand Funk Railroad, and Terry was their manager/Svengali. That was the last time I saw Terry. He made it big with Grand Funk, but they ended up suing him, and he sued them. They sold more than twenty-five million records, but they fired him because they were concerned with his fiscal responsibility, and he sued for breach of contract. It wasn't a smart move for the group because he only had three months left on his contract. At one point, he repossessed the band's gear before a show at Madison Square Garden. Terry came out the supposed winner when he procured a multimillion-dollar settlement from the band.

Grand Funk's Mark Farner told me, "Terry did some things that weren't honest." On the VH1 special, Terry said, "The guys said that Terry Knight wears a black hat, but I don't mind wearing the black hat because I wear it to the bank." It was years later, and the band didn't like hearing that.

What happened to Terry? Mark said, "Terry turned state's evidence on the big dog that he was involved with. When we split, he had enough money that he bought some Lear jets and was chartering these jets, and part of what he got into was he was running drugs, cocaine. They busted him, and he dropped a dime on a big boy that he was getting the stuff from or somebody higher up in the chain and turned state's evidence. He was put in a protection program."

My old friend came out on top with the Grand Funk lawsuit, but he lost his three best friends, and his life spiraled out of control while he lost those millions because of bad investments and drugs. Terry eventually beat his cocaine problem, and he got clean. He ended up a lonely man with few friends. He was living in a Temple, Texas, apartment with his daughter when her boyfriend attacked her. Terry, in a final unselfish act, defended her but was stabbed eleven times before he died in November of 2004.

Alan Douglas

Terry Knight and I actually did a show together. The *Alan Douglas Talk Show* preceded my late show on WKYC radio. This particular show featured disc jockeys. One was "Murray the K," the famous New York deejay and his wife, Jackie; our own afternoon star Jerry G.; a young deejay turned singer from Detroit, Terry Knight; and the youngster—me. I was in good company. In 1974 while visiting New York, I talked with Alan. He was at WNBC, but he had just been fired and was leaving the Big Apple to work at WXYZ, ABC radio, in his hometown of Detroit. He was excited to be going home and was very upbeat. I was shocked to read that he had committed suicide November 26, 1974, following his first show on WXYZ. His body was found in a leased automobile parked alongside Detroit's Westside Parkway. The news report said he had a slashed artery below the elbow of his left arm and bled to death. I never believed he killed himself. I was told one of the last guests on his show was teamster boss Jimmy Hoffa, who months later would disappear.

My Corvette

I was getting more comfortable with being Jim LaBarbara, but I needed something that would enhance my image. I was wearing a t-shirt and Levis when I visited Luby Chevrolet on Euclid Avenue. I decided I would buy a Corvette. The salesman gave me that up-and-down, who-are-you look and said they didn't have any, but just at that moment, a lot boy heard us and said, "Yes, we have two on the second floor." I looked at them, a bright blue and a British green one with a tan interior. The salesman said, "The best deal I can give you on the green one is $4,600." I proceeded to give him $4,600 cash, and I said, "I'll take it!" The salesman said, "No, we can't sell it. It has to be prepped." I told him: "I'm going to get a beer. I'll pick it up when I get back."

Bill Winters, our early-night guy, was the only other single guy at WKYC, and he took me under his wing. His advice was, "You make good money; when record promoters buy you a drink, you buy them one." When I filled in on the day shifts, we'd hit the clubs after he got off the air. One night he handed me an envelope.

"What's this?" I opened it. It was his letter of resignation. "You can't quit." He told me I should be doing his shift.

I said, "No, let's get the letter back."

"I can't. I put it under the GM's door."

Bill left, and I moved into his shift. Bill had a drinking problem, but you'd never know it. He actually hid little scotch bottles behind records in the studio. He was more of a Drake-type jock—time and temperature—and not so much a personality, but he didn't have any trouble getting another job at CKLW Detroit and then WCBS FM New York. Years later I visited him in New York, and he wanted me to join him on CBS, but I wasn't interested in leaving Cincinnati. That station, WCBS FM, became a powerhouse in New York. Bill passed away at a young age. Once, at WKYC, when he got back from vacation, he proudly told me, "I didn't get the job." His family was from the Carolinas, and he stopped at a small station in an even smaller market and auditioned for a job. The program director said he needed more work; he wasn't ready. Bill had a great voice and of course was a big-time talent. When I became a voiceover performer, I heard a similar story about Don LaFontaine, the most recognized voiceover talent of his day. He auditioned for a Don LaFontaine sound alike but didn't get the job.

I know it sounds crazy, but I didn't want the early shift. I wanted all night where I had the freedom to try more bits and be more creative.

Appearances and the Choir

Jim Gallant did the all-night program, and his act was talking with listeners on the air, but you only heard him talking. He would repeat what the person was saying. He had a loyal following, and many of his regulars had unusual nicknames. Jim's wife, Mary Ann, was a former Miss Ohio and the fashion coordinator at a department store, but she also ran a booking agency. She could have given her husband most of the gigs, and no one would have blamed her, but she spread the appearances around. I had the big Saturday night teen dance at the Painesville Armory. Carl Reese, from WJW, was one of the guys who ran it, and he wanted a teen jock to host it. We plugged the heck out of the jock appearances on the "VIP promos," complete with background music from the Routers' "Let's Go." I was on the air until 10:00 p.m., so the party was in full swing when I arrived in my Corvette. I'd jump on the stage in time to introduce one of the stars, who would lip sync their latest hit, and I had a lot of station giveaways to pass out to the kids. The guy who booked the national *Upbeat* television show made sure their guests appeared with me. Sometimes they went on before I got there so I'd ask: "How did you like Bobby Goldsboro? Okay, I'd like you to welcome the group that has the number five hit on our Sound Eleven Survey: the New Colony Six." I adopted the band, the Choir, as my band. In the summer of 1967, I broke their record on my show. "It's Cold Outside" by the Choir, the kids in the robes, became a number one hit for five consecutive weeks in Cleveland. Years later at a WIXY reunion weekend, my fellow

jocks Armstrong, Kirby—everyone—took credit until Jimmy Bonfanti, the Choir's drummer, called and said, "No, Jimmy was the first
to play it." You know I soaked it all in. After I left Cleveland, the
nucleus of the Choir—Jimmy Bonfanti; Wally Bryson; and Dave
Smalley; along with Eric Carmen from the Cleveland group, Cyrus
Erie—became the Raspberries. The Raspberries had some big hits,
including "Go All The Way" and "I Wanna Be with You."

I think I got a nice compliment at a Cleveland radio reunion
weekend. A very attractive lady and her husband told me they were
faithful listeners to my show when they were in high school. After
graduation they separated when he went to Vietnam. They married,
but not each other, but eventually got together. They wanted me to
know how important a role I played in their lives. She said the first
time they made love was in a car, and I was on the radio playing The
Association's record "Cherish." They thanked me; I smiled and
thanked them for sharing that information.

I've been involved in a lot of crazy radio promotions over the
years, and one got me on the cover of a national magazine in October
1966. It was billed as the "World's Most Unusual Race." It featured
Harry Martin from our morning show and me in a floating bed race
in Lake Erie off the Ninth Street Pier. The beds were complete with
pontoons and two Mercury twenty-horsepower engines. The picture
shows me waving, looking happy. In reality I was screaming for help
because I'm not a good swimmer, and I was drifting way out and sink-
ing. Boats would get close to say hi, and of course, they created more
waves, and that made it worse. There were hundreds in attendance,
but our station people were partying and not paying attention to me.
They finally got me to shore. To my knowledge, there was never
another floating bed race.

I was in an ostrich race that seemed harmless until an ostrich
turned around, bit our night guy Bill Winters on his upper thigh, and
almost cost him his manhood.

Every station was trying to outpromote the others, and disc jockeys were all vying for attention trying to find that certain gimmick.
However, I would describe the overwhelming majority of on-air peo-

ple I've worked with as shy, and some are real introverts. One disc jockey would hide behind the station van because he didn't want to talk with listeners. He was afraid of people. There is a lot of insecurity that the industry itself creates.

When is he getting a real job?

My parents were always very supportive of me, but I don't think they were too crazy about me being in radio. I believe they thought I was going through a phase, and I would eventually get a real job and move back to Pittsburgh. Here was their National Honor Society son who one day was going to be a doctor, or maybe a minister, playing disc jockey. Once I started working full time in radio, I was seldom home because I worked a six-day week, and I never took a vacation. I used those two weeks for army reserve camp. They tried to surprise me once, when I was in Erie. They drove around trying to hear me on the radio but couldn't find me because I neglected to tell them I wasn't Jimmy Holiday anymore, and I wasn't Jimmy LaBarbara. I was J. Bentley Starr the "Intrepid Leader."

I know they got a kick seeing me and listening to my stories. I was at WKYC, and I wanted to show them my new Corvette because to me this was a symbol that I had made it. They had never seen me with a beard, and when one of the neighbor kids was admiring my car, I jokingly gave him a flower and said, "Peace, wear a flower in your hair." Mom wasn't too happy with me. She thought I was acting like some hippie. I spent a lot of time trying to convince her I wasn't.

I got an emergency call in Cleveland to come home. My father was very sick and in the intensive care unit at a hospital. When he saw me, he got a big smile, but he rang the buzzer for a nurse. I was really worried. The nurse leaned over him, and he said as he pointed to me, "This is my son the disc jockey; he's on the air in Cleveland." I thought I was going to cry, because for the first time in my radio career, I realized my father was proud of me. WKYC was a powerful station that you could pick up in certain places in Pittsburgh, and Dad listened to me often.

Childhood memories

I missed being home. My family is Italian on both sides. So you can imagine that most of my family memories revolve around huge, extended family gatherings with lots of food. Those times were really something special, especially Christmas Eve. Our custom was to all gather at Grandma's house in Stowe Township, outside Pittsburgh, early in the day and sing and play Christmas songs. It was the day that every time you shook hands with Grandpa, you'd find a coin in your hand. It could be a penny. It could be a silver dollar. I must have shaken hands with him twenty or thirty times throughout the day.

Christmas dinner was always a typical Italian feast that lasted forever. I'll mention here that I once complimented Grandma on her delicious soup. I loudly proclaimed: "Grandma, this soup tastes like *piscia*." I was quickly given a slap to the back of my head, and my mother apologized to my poor shocked grandma. You see, I had just insulted my Grandma's soup in front of everyone, and in a vulgar way. It was an Italian word I heard a lot but didn't know what it meant.

On this particular Christmas Eve I'm remembering, I was the youngest grandchild so I got to be Santa's helper—the gift runner. Grandpa would act as Santa, give me a gift, and I would deliver it to Mom or to Aunt Dora—to all the family gathered there. It was always so special to get gifts from my aunts and cousins, because the presents were always surprises, like some toy I hadn't asked for. I had so much fun I didn't want to go home. They were having a hard time getting me to move this night. Grandpa had a brilliant idea. He went upstairs and shouted for me to come up. On the way up the stairs, I knew the window was open because I could feel the wind blowing in. It was already dark outside, and it was freezing. "Hurry, hurry!" Grandpa shouted. "Come here Jimmy, or you'll miss him!" As I ran breathlessly into the bedroom, Grandpa was standing in front of the open window pointing to the sky: "Look! There he goes. It's Santa, and he's on his way to your house. You'd better get there, or he won't leave any toys for you!" I ran to the window, and I swear, I will never forget that moment as long as I live. I looked up, and I don't know what it was I saw—maybe a shadow, maybe just something in my imagination—but at that moment, I really believed I saw Santa Claus and his reindeer streaking across the sky. We had to leave Grandma's right then because I had to get home for Santa. Ah, that Grandpa, such a wise man.

How wonderful it would be if we could have Mom, Dad, Grandma, Grandpa—the whole family together again. Those times with the family were special. If only we could go back for just one day like that!

I lived in a poor ethnic neighborhood, only we didn't know we were poor. Our family never took a family vacation, but our refrigerator was always packed with food, and friends were always stopping by for something to eat. We never had a family car, but my dad worked for Harris Brothers Florists in Pittsburgh as a delivery man, and we rode in the store's truck if we were going anywhere—Mom and Dad in the front, and my brother, Sammy, and I sat on crates in the back. My dad had to quit school in the eighth grade to help support the family, and he was making deliveries for this florist almost his entire life. He worked seven days a week and every holiday, but he never complained. I did acquire my father's work ethic. When I was little, I wanted to be Roy Rogers, and I had a gold Roy Rogers cap gun, so I was always Roy when we played cowboys. My uncle loved bubble gum, and he gave me all his baseball cards. I had a beautiful Schwinn bike with chrome fenders that I was sure impressed the girls. Okay, maybe I didn't really believe that. I had a paper route and made payments on a new Bach Stradivarius trumpet. My life was pretty good compared to some.

Ray Charles's tragic childhood

Ray Charles was acknowledged as the "Genius of Soul," but his childhood was tragic. He told me that he wasn't born blind, and before he lost his sight, he stood by helplessly as his younger brother George accidentally drowned in a wash tub. He choked up and said, "As young as I was, I've never forgotten that scene, and for a long time, I kind of felt responsible. I was about a year older than George, and it just looked like somehow or another I should have been able to save him. Obviously, I couldn't because I was as small as he was. You see something like that, and you think everything: Why didn't I do this, or why couldn't I have done that? For a long time I had a terrible time trying to rationalize myself with that. One does not get over that very quickly."

Ray Charles's blindness was a slow process, and he knew he was losing his vision. He said, "Yes, I knew it; my mom told me. She always gave me the facts. She'd sit down with me and try to show me a way to deal with whatever the situation was. I was only about five when I started to lose my sight, and you really don't comprehend nearly as much as when you've been seeing for twelve or fourteen years. When you're five, a lot of things you hear, but it doesn't have the same effect. I was afraid, but as long as I was around my mama, I didn't care what happened. That was my solution."

Ray Charles was ten years old when he lost his father, and by the time he was fifteen, his mother passed away. Ray described his feelings: "After my mother passed, I was lost. It was just me. I was always taught not to beg. The next three, four years were extremely tough for me. As bad as it was, I learned a lot from it." Ray Charles had given me his life story years before the move *Ray* was made.

CHAPTER 6

Backstage

Early in my career, I enjoyed being backstage during a concert. You could hear the concert through the stage monitors. That all changed over the years as more performers used only earpiece monitors and, under those conditions, it's the worst place to hear a show. Sometimes a performer's behavior can disappoint you.

We promoted the Rolling Stones' show at Cleveland Arena on June 25, 1966, and I was one of the VIPs on stage. It was a tour to support their LP *Aftermath*, and I played "Paint it Black" and "Under My Thumb" in heavy rotation. One of the guys in the opening act, The McCoys, told me, "We heard you on the radio last night. We're not from Dayton, Ohio, we're from Union City, Indiana." They were upset, but that's what their record company told me. Their hit "Hang on Sloopy" was a giant, and I played it a lot. Yes, it bothered me a little that these high school kids, instead of saying, *Thanks for playing our records. By the way, we are not from Dayton, but we were discovered in Dayton by the Strangeloves ("I Want Candy") when we did a concert with them,* chose to be abrasive.

A teenage listener of WKYC won a contest and was invited backstage to meet the Rolling Stones in their dressing room. She made a cake and was excited to give this to her favorite band. The Rolling Stones took the cake from this little, bubbly thirteen-year-old, laughed about the cake, and proceeded to throw it into a nearby toilet and flush it. She started to cry while they continued to giggle. We all thought they were jerks. I made a comment to one of my fellow jocks that I'd never play another one of their records. Of course that was difficult to do, but I sure didn't go out of my way to play them. They were despicable in every sense of the word.

On June 16, 1972, I was doing a morning show on KTLK in Denver, and a girl invited me to see the Stones. I really didn't want to go because when I last saw them I didn't like them personally, and professionally, they just stood around on stage and had no act. It was the Stones Touring Party, and they had their hit "Brown Sugar." Stevie Wonder opened the show and almost fell off the stage several times. His backup singers didn't notice, and neither did most of the audience. The crowd went wild when Mick Jagger and the guys came on. They were a lot more professional than six years earlier. Mick worked the audience like Wayne Newton playing to the blue-haired angels in Las Vegas. I became a Rolling Stones fan and, on September 14, 1989, was totally knocked out by their *Steel Wheels'* tour at Riverfront Stadium when they did "Start Me Up."

We hosted the Righteous Brothers' big show at Public Hall, and I got there early to hang around backstage when there was a commotion. Bill and Bobby came in wearing trench coats and were at the piano on stage checking things out when a security guard tried to chase them away. I explained to a red-faced guy that they were the Righteous Brothers.

Most recording stars were very nice, but in August 1966, at the Cavalcade of Stars Show at Euclid Beach, I was one of the emcees, and Bobby Miranda of the Happenings gave me a hard time because their song "See You in September" wasn't number one on our Sound Eleven Survey. He was really upset. I thought, wait a second, I play your record every night, sometimes twice a show, and you're yelling at me? My friend from Pittsburgh, Lou Christie, sang his controversial hit "Rhapsody in the Rain." He wrote it and told me there were only nine thousand copies released with the dirty lyrics, and they are collector's items. We introduced an eighteen-year-old singing hopeful Tony Thomas, Danny Thomas's son. He was a really nice kid, but he never had a hit. If it's not in the grooves, it's not going to happen. I got shocked for the first time on stage at that concert. I was standing in a little puddle of sweat when I grabbed the microphone to take off a soaking wet Mitch Ryder. It hurt, but I kept it to myself.

I was beginning to wonder if acting stupid was part of the job description if you were a rock star. A teenage girl was backstage to meet the Loving Spoonful. One of the guys in the group got her camera and threw it around to other guys in the group. She was in tears running back and forth, and of course, the camera hit the floor and broke. I don't remember who it was, but I do remember John Sebastian wasn't involved.

Entertainers were always stopping by the station. One thing that separated me from a lot of the jocks was that I really was interested in the singers, and I wanted to know the story behind the song. I was single and about the same age as most of the artists we played, and I had a musical background, so we'd often hang together and party.

One night at dinner, I asked Del Shannon (he had numerous hits, including "Runaway"), "What's your real name?" He showed me his driver's license—Charles Weedon Westover the third. He said, "That's it, but don't tell anyone."

The great comedian Jerry Lewis's son had just scored with a couple of top five hits. Jerry and I were talking in the station hallway. I asked him, "What advice did you give Gary?" He said, "Just make sure you can look at yourself the next day in the mirror." A simple sentence but more complex than you might think.

The Shangri-Las

When I did early evenings on WKYC, the Shangri-Las were my studio guests, and afterward, we went out for a late dinner. We were going to have dinner, drinks, and then party. The girls were every young man's fantasy on stage—tight tops and pants, motorcycle boots, and bouffant hair. They were the first female punk group complete with a tough girl's persona. I understand they ended up getting screwed out of royalties despite selling millions of records, but that's another story. Mary Weiss, the lead singer, had sexy, long blonde hair. However, I got turned off immediately at dinner when one of the girls used a vulgarity to say, "Mary, pass the . . . butter." They were rough girls from the Queens, and any romantic thoughts I had quickly disappeared as I listened to them and watched them eat. After dinner I suddenly remembered I had another commitment.

I've wondered if their crudeness was a self-defense mechanism to purposely chase guys away. I never had success with the so-called "easy ladies." Some girls undeservedly had that reputation. A high school friend I hadn't seen in twenty years married one of our classmates. The first thing he said to me was not hello but, "She was a virgin when I married her."

Lots of misinformation

I was a very naïve kid. I know this is going to sound trite and corny, but it was the fifties. I learned about the birds and the bees on the playground during recess, and we got a lot of misinformation. The first time I saw a naked girl was when one of the neighbor kids took several of us to his house to watch his older sister get out of the bathtub. She was yelling, we were running, and he was laughing. I don't think I saw much. What I do remember was that I couldn't sleep for a week in the third grade because I thought I got one of the girls pregnant. I hardly knew her, but I bumped up against her in the aisle in class. Okay, I'll say it, I was a virgin until I graduated from college.

Jim LaBarbara was a pretty innocent guy. However, Jimmy Holiday and J. Bentley Starr were just the opposite. LaBarbara's persona was beginning to take shape at WKYC, and I got some help from our afternoon star.

CHAPTER 7

Cleveland's Most Eligible Bachelor

Jerry G. helped define my image when he labeled me, "Cleveland's Most Eligible Bachelor" on his show. He pounded away at that, the rest of the station picked up on it, and the *Plain Dealer*'s Jane Scott began referring to me as "Cleveland's Most Eligible Bachelor" in the paper. It sounded exciting, but because of my shyness, I didn't date much.

I laughed about being called Cleveland's most eligible bachelor, but it did give me a little confidence. It was my first time in this bar on Euclid Avenue, but I felt comfortable, especially when I got surrounded by several attractive ladies who recognized me. The place was filled with a lot of tough-looking Italian guys, and it reminded me of my old hometown. A couple of the girls were hanging all over me. One in particular was excited to be with me and introduced me to an older gentleman in a black suit. He moved in close to me and whispered my name as he gave my cheek a little tweak and a pat. I wanted to tell him, hey I'm Italian, but I got the message these ladies were with him and his friends, and I wasn't welcome. It didn't matter that they weren't paying any attention to the girls. I went from this great euphoric high to quietly making an exit. I wasn't rejected by the girls; I was just doing the prudent thing.

Faye

Rock 'n' roll and pretty ladies go together, and I wanted that lady. I was doing very well financially in Cleveland and living my dream, but I didn't have her. I decided to contact my old college girlfriend, Faye. I met Faye when I was a disc jockey in Titusville the summer before my senior year. I only had a half hour before my air shift, but I had to meet her. She was wearing an orange blouse and white shorts. She was the pretty lifeguard from the swimming pool, but I didn't know it. I drove my little green Morris Minor convertible alongside her as she was walking home. I tried to talk with her, but she totally ignored me so I beeped my horn but got no response. In an act of desperation, I drove my car on the sidewalk behind her and gently hit the horn. She asked me to please go away, I was embarrassing her.

I told her, "Just let me drive you home, and you'll never see me again."

Promise?"

"Yes." I introduced myself as we were riding, "I'm just a crazy disc jockey, Jimmy Holiday."

She said, "Are you the one who sneezed on the air yesterday?"

"Yes, that's me."

She said, "You are crazy."

She wasn't very friendly. It was a short ride, and I had to act fast. As she was leaving the car, I told her I wanted to ask her out, but I didn't give her a chance to answer. I knew she'd say no. I told her that I was going to call her in a couple of days for a date. I said, "I want you to think about it." I started to really fall in love with Faye. She went to nearby Grove City College, and we dated through most of my senior year, visiting each other on the weekends. We broke up when I started doing a show on our new college radio station because I told her I was finished with radio. I believed I was, but she thought I was more committed to radio than her. A couple of years later we almost got back together. I was working in Erie and she agreed to visit me for a weekend. I decided to send her my first disc jockey publicity picture that was taken when I was in DuBois. It's a picture of me holding records. What was I thinking? After she got the picture, she sent a telegram to me—she wasn't coming, our relationship was over.

Throughout the years I've blamed it on that dumb picture and I never used it again. I didn't know it at the time, but that picture became the object of a practical joke between my wife and daughter. If Sally went on a trip, that picture would end up somewhere in her suitcase and wherever Shelby went, it was in hers. I hadn't seen it in years until a giant three-foot-tall blowup was auctioned at a WGRR charity event. Sally gave it to the station, not knowing what it meant to me. I was furious, but got over it when it raised a lot of money for a good cause.

I did talk with Faye, however, we would never see each other again. She was teaching in Rochester, but followed my career and heard me often on WKYC. She was engaged, but happy for me and remarked, "You did what you said you were going to do."

Deception and betrayal

Some classmates from Allegheny College threw a party for me. They talked about how Glen Beckert, the Cubs' second baseman, and I were their most famous classmates. It was funny to me because a few of these people wouldn't give me the time of day in school.

I thought back to the remark a classmate made to me on graduation day when she heard I accepted a radio job: "What a waste!" I wondered if she shared their feelings.

Three years after college graduation I was one of their most famous graduates because I was, what, a famous disc jockey? Somehow they confused me with that other Jim LaBarbara. The guy who's friends were trying to get him an invitation to the Fiji House during rush week our sophomore year. My freshman roommate and his buddy who slept under my bed that first year told me they were working on it. At that time, it was a social must to be in a fraternity on a small campus. One of my close friends that year was a transfer from West Point. Randy was older and the coolest guy on campus; all the fraternities wanted him. The third night of rush week, I still hadn't received an invitation to visit the house even though those two kept telling me they were trying to convince their brothers. I told Randy that somebody must be blackballing me, so when he went to their rush he mentioned me and was told that my name was never brought up for consideration. The next day, I confronted my ex-roommates separately, and both said "Jim, we're working on it." When I told them what Randy said, one told me: "You just wouldn't fit in at the house." The other guy was embarrassed and walked away. Ouch, that hurt! I wasn't cool enough to be in their fraternity. The last night of rush week, Randy stopped by to show me the invitations he had, and man was he rubbing it in; should he pledge here or there? I didn't say much. Suddenly he said, "You know what? They don't think you're good enough? I'm not pledging anywhere. Let's go get a drink." I'll never forget what Randy did. He was in that enviable power position where he could say, *"You can't treat my friend this way; this fraternity stuff is bull."* However, that hurt feeling of deception and betrayal from my friends still hurts. I learned a lot about people and friends that week.

I thought about those feelings of rejection when I was talking with Tony Orlando in 1971. Tony had hits with "Halfway to Paradise" and "Bless You" in 1961, but then didn't have a hit for a decade until he hit with "Candida" and "Knock Three Times."

Tony told me that during that time when he didn't have hit records, he was in an elevator with a couple of songwriters, and the one said to the other guy: "Hey you know what I've got—the next Tony Orlando record." Tony recalled, "I'm standing there, so I knew they knew I was the guy they were talking about, and they were putting me on. The other guy said, 'Oh, Tony Orlando, he's the youngest oldie-but-goodie that ever lived.' You know I remember just crumbling and saying oh wow this is terrible. In fact it was that comment in the elevator that day that I decided to quit singing at the time, and I headed a music publishing firm for three years. It still hurt. People call me now and say, 'Hey baby, how are you sweetheart?' It's a whole different—it's the old story you know."

I said that was very sad, and Tony added, "It really is, because you know what happens? You lose perspective about people. You don't know who your friends are—you know. That's why you always hear the music business is a very cutthroat business. Well of course it is because you really don't know who your friends are, and you don't even know who your enemies are, and that's even worse."

Susan

I was feeling more confident about being Jim LaBarbara. I had a date with a belly dancer and took advantage of the station's free movie passes for the movie *Blue Max*. One of our sales guys was with a beautiful girl, and we all exchanged pleasantries. The next day, I asked him about her. "She's Susan. She works for Wyse Advertising, a big client, and stay away from her." "Stay away from her"—that's all I had to hear. I called her, and to my surprise, she wanted to go out for a drink. She was a New Jersey girl who graduated from a Cleveland college and stayed. We were together during most of my time in Cleveland. Dating one of the prettiest girls in town did a lot for my self esteem. Susan, without my knowing it, helped to create my image. She gradually changed my wardrobe. She was used to some of the finer things in life, and that rubbed off on me. I never felt this way before. We would go for walks or just look at each other. I think I was truly in love for the first time. She went on appearances with me, and the young girls would hang around her asking questions about her clothes. Years later at station reunion parties, my fellow jocks would tell me how they tried to take her out, but she was loyal to me. One reminded me: "We couldn't believe how you treated her; you'd tell her, 'Susan, get me a beer.' You yelled at her when you lost at cards, and it was for pennies." I was afraid to tell her how much I loved her and never did because I was afraid of being hurt. That hurt would come later.

I lived in Lakewood on the Gold Coast in a big high-rise overlooking Lake Erie, where I could see little fires break out nightly in the water. My girlfriend, Susan, lived on the East Side. She told me before we dated that she had gone out a few times with a guy who was a little strange. One night after leaving her apartment, I noticed a car following me on the shoreway as I headed to the West Side. I'd slow down, he'd slow down. When I pulled into my garage, he was right behind me. As I entered the elevator, he got in. He was wearing army fatigues and said, "I'm a friend of Susan; she talks a lot about you." "Yeah," I said, "She talks about you. We've got to get together." We had a short conversation like we were at a party, but here we were in an elevator at 3:00 a.m. in the morning. I got off on the first floor, and he left. Shortly after that, he was arrested for chasing his new girlfriend down the street with a butcher knife. At the time, they found an arsenal of guns and knives in his car. I couldn't help but wonder if I had said the wrong thing a few days earlier, if he would have killed me. Susan and I were in my car a week later when we saw him drive by. We were shocked that he was out. He was jailed, but his father was a wealthy Clevelander. Shortly after that, he took his own life by driving into several parked cars.

* * *

I did refer to myself on the air as "Cleveland's Most Eligible Bachelor," but I said it a little tongue in cheek. Jim LaBarbara's image was developing rather quickly. I would say LaBarbara was more cerebral than Holiday or Bentley. A large part of my show prep was sharing artist and song information with my listener. This was a major part of the image I was creating. I guess I was doing something right, because in the January 21, 1967, edition of *Billboard Magazine*, they featured the Radio Response Rating for Cleveland. The top disc jockeys were Jerry G., for pop singles, at 30 percent (he was our afternoon guy and host of his own bandstand show); I was second, tied with WHK's Ken Scott with 20 percent; and in fourth was WIXY's Jack Armstrong. I was flattered to be in that company.

I took a lot of kidding from record promoters. Somebody asked me, "How do you know so much about the music?" The record promoter broke in and said, "His sister dates Paul Revere?" Everybody started asking me about my sister and Paul. I don't think they believed me when I told them I didn't have a sister. The promoters were my connection to the artist, and they gave me a lot of my material. I also got my show content from the performers and songwriters.

Billy Joe Royal recorded Joe South's song, "I've Got to Be Somebody." That song's title became my mantra in 1965; I had to make it. I was ready to quit radio. I was really down, and I wondered if the man who wrote it was going through a similar experience. Joe was listening to me in Atlanta and sent me a letter. He was having similar feelings when he was inspired to write the song. Of course, I shared this with my listeners.

Sonny and Cher

Sonny and Cher were riding high, and they packed the hall. The audience was made up of mostly teens and preteens. Parents liked them— they were married, and at the time, they presented a nonthreatening image of American counterculture. They were the hippest couple of the day with bobcat vests and bell-bottom trousers. Cher had long, straight hair and a bad complexion, and she didn't have much of a figure, but she could sing. Years later, thanks to plastic surgery, she would be one of the sexiest ladies on television. The strangest thing happened. The kids rushed the stage, and a couple of kids made it to Sonny and Cher. Sonny looked at them, put the microphone near their face, and said, "Okay, you're here now, what are you going to do?" They looked at him and jumped off the stage.

A decade later, Sonny and Cher had divorced, but I know he still had strong feelings for Cher. Sonny told me the song that was dearest to his heart was "I Got You Babe," and he explained, "The song represented how when two people pull together and are really going in the same direction, you're infallible. So it's a wonderful feeling. I don't think I'll ever have it again. You have no vulnerability. You feel like a giant, and that's the way I felt that day with Cher, and that's the way she felt. We felt so strong together. We felt like two karate fighters back to back you know. We didn't care about any of the outside elements. So, it was a wonderful feeling."

When I asked him what he enjoyed doing more, recording or television, Sonny Bono surprised me when he told me that he just wanted to be recognized. He raised his voice and continued, "Because, the one thing that really smashed me was that when we broke up, people said, 'gee poor guy, he should be selling pizza somewhere, and she's fantastic.' I thought, wow, after eleven years, this is the impression I left. I had built this whole thing. I had written all the songs—ten-million-selling songs. I had written the show I had created; I worked eleven years devoted to this act and, when everything was shaken down, I came out really holding a fig leaf. You know, I thought, I don't ever want to do that again. So, I want to do things and at least get recognized for what I do."

Sonny did exactly that when he changed his image and entered politics, becoming the mayor of Palm Springs, and eventually he was elected a member of the U.S. House of Representatives.

Charlie and Harrigan

Martin and Howard, our WKYC morning team left for Detroit, and we got the Dallas team of Charlie and Harrigan. Well, sort of. Harrigan (Ron Chapman) didn't want to leave Dallas, and Charlie Brown convinced NBC that the new Irving Harrigan could do the job. The new Harrigan was a guy in a radio class Charlie taught who could imitate them. He did a lot of the character voices in their bits and was a funny guy. Charlie's real name is Jack Woods, and he was one of the smartest radio guys I ever worked with. He was more of the straight guy, and he ran the show. They were good, but Irving had a habit of topping Charlie. Charlie would end the bit with a line, and then Irving would add another punch. Timing is so important in humor. They eventually worked it out and became big stars. It's funny how we remember people. Irving was a tremendous talent and the Lemon Pipers of "Green Tambourine" fame's first manager, but I'll never forget the time he got drunk at a station meeting. I can still picture his toupee floating in the toilet. He nonchalantly picked it up, ran some water on it, and put it back on his head.

We later had a fill-in guy working at WKYC who was once a teen idol in another market and would remind us. I think he was allergic to soap, and he had the habit of leaving his teeth in the studio in a coffee cup. I swear I saw that cup move on more than one occasion. I got tired of looking at his teeth during my show, and I moved the cup. He followed me on the air, and he was about twenty minutes into his show before he found his teeth, but that didn't deter him; he still left his choppers in that dirty old cup.

Me in Chicago?

Jerry G. left WKYC to join his old KYW boss Ken Draper at WCFL Chicago. Jerry was like a big brother to me. I decided in early 1967 that I was going to visit him while he was on the air in Chicago. After my night show, I got on a plane for my first trip to the Windy City and arrived in time to see Jerry do his last hour. The first thing he said to me was, "You've got great timing. Our all-night man is in Draper's office handing him his resignation." WCFL was 50,000 watts, and Ken Draper was a program director I admired and wanted to work with. Jerry introduced me to Ken; he knew about my work, we had a good conversation, and I left him my tape. Ken Draper may have been the most creative programmer in the country at that time, and he hired great talent. We talked a number of times during the next couple of weeks, and Jerry thought I had a good chance of getting the job. I believed I'd be moving until a former Chicago jock working in Los Angeles suddenly became available. Draper brought back the legendary Dick Biondi. It was a great move for WCFL.

Notebooks and security

Charlie Tuna would become a Los Angeles radio legend, but I first met him when he visited WKYC for a few days on his way to a Boston station. I liked that he carried a little spiral notebook and was constantly writing down show ideas. I started doing it and filled dozens of them with show prep material. Looking back over them is like a history lesson. We had a lot of radio guys hang out, but I never thought they were there to replace me. A Washington, D.C., deejay called me a few times, and I visited him at WEAM, a rock station in the D.C. radio market. I felt very uncomfortable because everybody seemed in a panic mode, like I was there to take their job. I didn't stay very long. I couldn't understand why everyone was so insecure. I discovered that was pretty normal in radio. Although I was crafting my new image as Jim LaBarbara, I felt secure in my talent. During my career, if I was on vacation, I always wanted someone as good or better to fill in. Hopefully they would say my name once an hour. I guess I was one of the exceptions. I filled in for a well-known Cincinnati morning man and got compliments from everyone, but later that day, I was told they made other arrangements for the next day's show. Apparently the guy went crazy when he heard me, because I had beaten him in the ratings years before when we were competitors. I filled in other shifts but never his. I was lucky that I was only there for a cup of coffee between stations.

No Buffalo

I was happy in Cleveland, but I interviewed for a better air shift at WGR Radio in Buffalo. It was chilly in Cleveland, and I was wearing a sports jacket as I headed out of town in my Corvette. Buffalo's weather made Cleveland look like Miami. A police officer pulled me over for going the wrong way on a one-way street. He didn't give me a ticket but gave me directions to WGR. The weather was miserable, even for a guy who grew up in Pittsburgh. I got out of my car and stepped into snow slush up to my knees. WGR was impressive with both radio and television. I met with the program director, and he was saying all the right things, but I was soaked. After listening to him for about fifteen minutes, I abruptly got up, thanked him for his time, but told him I was going to stay in Cleveland. I took him by surprise, because we hadn't discussed money. Maybe if it was a nice spring or summer day I'd still be in Buffalo.

Jack's hired—what about me?

In January 1968, Jack Armstrong from WIXY took over my early-night show, which I had inherited from Bill Winters. I was in my car when I heard the promos announcing his arrival that night. I called the station, and I kept asking, "Do I have a job, should I come in tonight?" No answers—everybody was in a meeting. The secretary didn't know. Finally late in the day, I got a call. I wouldn't be on the air tonight, but they wanted to see me. I went in expecting to be fired. Instead, I was named the new all-night man, and they let Jim Gallant go. That's the shift I wanted. While I was doing the early show, our general manager, Bob Martin had me listen to tapes of guys who auditioned for the evening show to get my opinion. I liked several, including a guy who was trying to get out of Boston named Larry Lujack. I was surprised they picked a guy in the market. WIXY's owner sent their lawyer to Columbus early that day and had the name "Jack Armstrong" copyrighted, so we had to call him "Big Jack." Jack was the fastest talking deejay I ever heard. He topped out at 386 words a minute and was in the *Guinness Book of World Records*. He was a few years younger than me, so I was no longer the kid. Jack liked my new green Corvette so much he bought a silver one with the big pipes. I had the number two parking space in the garage at night, but he took the first spot. One night, someone got past the security guard and stole his car, leaving mine alone. In my apartment, I had a three-speed vibrating leather chair. He bought two. WKYC had its own boat, but the sales guys usually got it. Jack couldn't get the boat one weekend, so he bought one like it. Jack wasn't on WKYC very long, and I'm not sure exactly why he got fired.

Max Richmond, the owner of WMEX in Boston offered me their early-evening show. I called Jerry G. who was in Chicago, but had worked for Max in Washington, D.C. Jerry's advice was, "Jimmy, sell shoes. You don't want to work for Max." I took Jerry's advice, and when Max called me the next day, I told him I decided to stay at WKYC but asked him if he would be interested in Jack. "He's coming over tonight, and he's looking." I put the two of them together. Jack later broke his contract with Max and fled Boston for CHUM in Toronto. I apologized to Jack several times over the years. Jack was tearing up the airwaves from WKBW in Buffalo when I called him to ask for his advice. He was in a down mood and said, "Everything I touch turns to s——t." He warned me not to leave WLW and work for Joe Finan in Denver because he had a bad experience at KTLK, but I didn't listen. I should have. He worked for a lot of great stations, but he seldom stayed long. Jack was very opinionated, but was right most of the time. He and I became better friends at the WIXY reunions and the Hall of Fame induction ceremony. At one reunion, my driver, an off-duty Cleveland police officer, hung with us. Jack was holding "court" in his room telling stories when he lit up a joint and passed it around. My driver left, and I apologized to him outside. I went back to the party, and I explained the situation to Jack. He took off with his stash, and I stopped him just before he flushed it. He was on top of the business. I once gave him my Arbitron rating numbers, and when he saw me the next day, he pulled out his computer and showed me they were even better than I said. We e-mailed back and forth, and I know he was really hurt when he lost his morning show in the Carolinas and then his voice-tracked oldies show in Buffalo in 2006. He died in March of 2008. Jack was the youngest of us in Cleveland. They said he died of a heart attack, but I truly believe he died from a broken heart. The radio business that he loved so much turned its back on him. At the time of his death, there were dozens of Armstrong imitators trying to do his act working in radio, but no one wanted the original. I can still hear him shouting out, "Yooooouuuuuuuuuurrrrr Llllleeeeedaaaaaa!" He was an incredible talent and the best at what he did.

CHAPTER 8

A Gift from the Hells Angels

On the way to the station, I was listening to the Alan Douglas talk show that preceded me, and I was intrigued by the lively discussion he was having with the notorious Hells Angels. When I got near the studio door, I was embraced by a large, bearded man wearing a Hells Angels' jacket, and suddenly I was in Alan's studio with all the guys and their "mamas" hugging me. Alan restored order, and I returned to the hallway. The Angels got into town the night before, and one of the guys recognized my voice. They were pounding on the NBC door as Alan was leaving the building: "Isn't that J. Bentley Starr from Erie?" Alan explained that "LaBarbara" was my real name, and if they came back the next night and appeared on his show, they would see me. Gary LeRoy Montgomery was my friend who just a couple of years earlier in Erie had saved my life when the Indian was about to stab me in a bar. The same guy who got my stolen money back for me just got his colors and was now a Hells Angel, better known as the "Monkey." He told the Angels how righteous I was, and they wanted to meet me. I talked with a couple of the group's leaders that night, but I'm not sure if Sonny Barger was with them. The Monkey and I renewed our friendship, reminisced about the Erie days, and promised to keep in touch. He was still the Gary I knew in Erie—one of the nicest guys ever. I didn't know he rode a bike. After he left, my engineer kept giving me strange looks, so after about twenty minutes, I started to say something, and he nodded toward a back corner in the studio. For the first time, I noticed a cute, little, long-haired hippie-looking girl sitting on the floor. I explained to her that everyone already left, but she said, "I know. I'm yours. Monkey won me in a card game, and he's given me to you." It was a nice gesture on the Monkey's part, but I wasn't interested. I had a girlfriend. She didn't want to go, but I called a cab for her and made sure she got down the elevator.

That should be the end of the story, except for something that happened in February of 1968. The front page of the *Cleveland Plain Dealer* told the story, but I didn't want to believe it. Two apparently innocent guys were gunned down, murdered in the early morning hours at Barto's Café, 3344 East Ninety-third Street in Cleveland. The gunman, who was wearing his colors, was Gary LeRoy Montgomery of the Hells Angels. He made the FBI's Ten Most Wanted Fugitives list, and they were going to gun him down. I thought I'd try to find him and get him to turn himself in because I knew he'd go back to Erie. I made the rounds and talked with members of other motorcycle groups, and the picture they painted wasn't pretty. He was one tough guy. A couple of months later, he was back on the front page, clean shaven and captured. The FBI later reported that there was a motorcycle gang war escalating, involving the newly established Cleveland chapter of Hells Angels and God's Children. God's Children had black and white members and didn't care for the Angels' whites-only policy. The police said James Tillet, a thirty-eight-year-old white man, was shot in the head when he went to the aid of thirty-eight-year-old Roosevelt Brown, a black man who was being beaten by the bikers. Brown was shot twice in the back. Ironically, Gary made a mistake—neither man was a biker. I heard from Gary a couple of years later when I was on WLW, and he was incarcerated in the Ohio State Penitentiary. He wrote a letter to me regarding something he heard me say on the air that some motorcycle gang might find offensive, and he explained that he wouldn't be able to help me. He gave me a much appreciated heads up. I have tried many times over the years to contact him but to no avail.

George Carlin and others

I was busy developing LaBarbara's on-air celebrity. The late-night show gave me more freedom to create and afforded me the opportunity to develop new bits, and with 50,000 watts, I heard from people all over the country. I did a schtick where I called myself the "Hippy Dippy Hang-up Man." I'd take calls to answer questions and solve problems. The bit always ended with me saying something dumb and hanging up. It was inspired by George Carlin's Al Sleet, the "Hippy Dippy Weather Man." One night I got a call from a guy who did the whole Al Sleet bit; he was terrific, and I told him. I then asked him, "What's your problem?" He proceeded to tell me how he had been a disc jockey in Texas but couldn't make it and that he was stuck being Al Sleet. It was the first of many conversations I would have over the years with George Carlin who, at the time, had just finished a college show and was on the road listening to me.

One night I got a call from a member of a very famous Capitol Records' singing group. I asked if the other guys were with him. He said no, he was in town to see his girlfriend but asked me not to say anything because he didn't want his wife to find out. I quickly said, "One, two, three, on the air with me is . . ." and proceeded to ask him about their new record. I didn't use a delay, and of course, the whole conversation was on the air.

I got burned when a guy from Mansfield, Ohio, called and thanked me for playing "A Little Bit of Soul." He said he was Jamie Lyons, the Music Explosion's lead singer. We had a short conversation. He was a pretty knowledgeable guy. Whew, then the calls started; this guy was an imposter. Apparently some people knew him, and the next night, I got a call from a guy who said, "He won't be bothering you again; we took care of him." This incident made me extra cautious, and I often gave entertainers who called the third degree. If a singer was traveling, he'd have to use a pay phone so you know he really appreciated me playing his record. I got a lot of those calls. A few who have reminded me they called were Troy Shondell, Jimmy Clanton, Paul Revere, Kenny Rogers, and Lou Christie.

Jay, Chuck, and I got fired

In early January 1968, WKYC's general manager, Bob Martin, was fired and replaced by WHK's general manager, Dino Ianni. Bob was the man who discovered me and gave me the biggest job of my career. When I said goodbye to him with tears in my eyes, he asked me "What are you going to do now?" I said, "I guess I'm going to stay here." I was naïve; he knew I would be fired. The new manager wanted to bring in his own people. Jack Armstrong had left the station before this. Among other things, Jack kept doing his gorilla character making throwing up sounds under Virgil Dominic's NBC newscasts. Jack thought it was funny, Virgil did not. Chuck Dunaway came in to work my overnight shift while I went back to early nights. I didn't know what to think, but radio can be a cruel business. I started getting calls from jocks asking me, "How does it feel to be a big shot one day and a nobody the next? Where will you be working tomorrow?" Of course, no one identified themselves. Those same guys today would be the ones making nasty, hurtful comments on the internet while hiding behind some alias. I was at the house of Charlie Brown, our morning man, and he introduced me to WHK's Russ "the Weird Beard" Knight. The Beard was the original from Texas, a huge man who looked like Satan. He asked Charlie if I was okay and then proceeded to tell me that the next day Hal "Hotdog" Moore, the WHK afternoon jock would be our new program director. A couple of days later, I was called into work early. I ran into Jay Lawrence, who told me he had just been fired. I met with Dino, our general manager, and I was fired. I went into the studio where Chuck Dann was doing his afternoon show, and I sat down, still in shock. A few minutes later, Chuck said, "They finally fired your sorry ass—it's about time." I looked at him, and he turned pale as a ghost and then said,

"No, I was only joking. They can't do that. I had no idea." He hadn't heard about Jay getting fired. He got called into Dino's office at the top of the hour when the news came on and was also fired. The last record he played was Sinatra's "That's Life." Although we were fired, we still had to work until the new guys came in. Hotdog interviewed both "Big Daddy" Johnson, the rhythm and blues jock from Baltimore, and Robbie Dee, from the soul station in Detroit, but NBC would not allow him to hire either one. It was very strange waiting around for them to hire our replacements and still do our shows. I stayed on the air for weeks. Hotdog called me in: "Did Dino tell you why we're letting you go?" I told him "Yeah, he said I had no talent." Hotdog said, "No, man. I'm getting a guy for half your price." I was the only one without a personal contract, but the union did get me a nice severance. That feeling of being on the air while seeing fan letters from my listeners coming in for the new jocks, who weren't there yet, has stayed with me. Record guys who were my friends suddenly were too busy to talk to me.

Human nature

I learned over the years that it's just human nature; people want to be with the winner. I should have picked up on that when I was twelve years old and played in the Little League series in Williamsport. People treated us like celebrities, pretty little girls hung around our team bus, and there were the adults who just wanted to be around us. After we lost, they totally abandoned us, and those pretty little girls didn't even say goodbye. Everybody wants to be with a winner.

That feeling of rejection happens at all levels. Sonny and Cher had famous Hollywood parties, but suddenly they were flat broke. Sonny knew why they were treated differently. He said, "I don't consider that a fault, because when you've got money you run in a circle of people who have money and can take care of themselves, and they expect you to take care of yourself. When you're not on their echelon—people run in certain echelons—they let you know it. You're treated different certainly."

They were down, but came back with a hit television show. Sonny smiled and said, "Then you get the same courtesies and the same everything. Yeah, it's nature. It's the way of life, and it's the way people will always be, that way."

Here I was twenty-six years old, and this was the biggest job of my career, and my army reserve unit was frozen, so I couldn't leave Cleveland. I was devastated. My last night was a Saturday show. When I got off at ten, one of the new guys who had been with us for a few weeks, Chuck Dunaway, took over. I was in the hallway leaving with my girlfriend, Susan, when he said to me, "Hey, you won't be doing anything for a while—listen to me. I'll show you how it's supposed to be done." That really hurt and embarrassed me in front of Susan. I knew my career could be over. Chuck had been with some great stations, including WABC New York. What he said was true, I could learn from him, but to say that to me was just being a jerk.

CHAPTER 9

I'm a WIXY Superman and Payola

It took me about two months to reappear on the air. By the first week in April 1968, I was a "WIXY Superman," the new WIXY 1260 all-night man. George Brewer, their program director, and I were acquainted because his wife and my girlfriend, Susan, both worked at Wyse Advertising. If I didn't have that connection, I don't know if I would have gotten the job. One of the owners was upset that I quit WIXY the first time. He didn't know the story. Norman Wain, one of the owners, was great to work for, but he didn't believe in paying anyone except the morning show. At a WIXY reunion, King Kirby, who did afternoons for years, told me he never got a raise and never asked for one because he made so much money outside the station.

WIXY broadcast from the station's transmitter, and we had a cast of characters. I was talking on the air when a strange looking man climbed through a window into the studio. It was Doc Nemo, who did an underground show on Sunday, and he had a bag full of drugs for me to sample. His often-stated goal was to turn all of Cleveland on. I wasn't interested, but he did leave me some samples. I later found a "Dr. Feelgood" who sold "diet pills" at a good price. It was during this time that my girlfriend got some marijuana cigarettes for us. I enjoyed smoking, but I never got high on the air. One of the people frequently sleeping around our studio was a guy with the hit group from San Diego, the Union Gap. We called him "Muther." He was in love with one of our secretaries. The "Wilde Childe" Dick Kemp did our early-night show. He was an older guy who had done his share of drugs but had once torn up Chicago radio. I came in early a couple of times to find him on the phone in tears talking with his ex-wife in Dallas. As the record ended, he'd be yelling, "This is the child from the wild," and the next moment, he'd be in tears again. I was always amazed at how he could turn it on and off. One night George Brewer, our program director, blamed me for getting the Childe drunk. Our transmitter and studio sat in a little valley, and after weekly meetings, a group of us would play trivia at a bar on the top of our hill. That day, the Childe, who didn't have a car but rode around on a bicycle, got drunk and wrecked his bike riding down the hill to the station. We all loved the Childe. He lived with a boa snake, Lady Jane, and a girl named Jet whose skin was almost orange colored. The most beloved of all the WIXY Supermen was Larry "the Duker" Morrow, our midday guy. He connected with our audience and stayed on Cleveland radio for more than forty years. I never heard anyone ever say a bad word about Larry. He was everyone's friend. King Kirby, our afternoon guy, rode around in a Cadillac limo with a lovely, long-haired, long-legged driver in a miniskirt. He wore his cape and crown and would often stop at Public Square so that he could wave to his fans. Whenever he called me, he'd say, "This is your king speaking." Someone was writing graffiti on our studio albums and no one knew who. It wasn't aimed at any individual—we all got it. They were very childish lines, but funny: "LaBarbara nudges his noodle, whacks his carrot, pulls his pud, and plays with his ding a ling." At a WIXY reunion weekend, the subject came up, and Kirby admitted he was the poet. Our news microphone was across from our deejay microphone in the main studio. Late one evening, Kirby came by to introduce me to a voluptuous miss somebody. A couple of hours later, King returned and gave me a detailed, titillating account of what they did.

It was only after he left that I discovered that he had tripped the news microphone, and although muffled in the background, our entire conversation went over the Cleveland airwaves.

Joe Finan

At six in the morning, Joe Finan took over. Joe had been a giant Cleveland personality until KYW fired him for payola in 1959, and he exiled himself to Denver. He did an excellent talk show. In 1968 we became good friends at WIXY, but he could be nasty. He'd get drunk and sleep on the lobby sofa, and I'd have to wake him. On more than one occasion, he'd take a swing at me, sometimes connecting. I'd swear and tell him: "You're on." While driving up the station driveway, I'd hear the record end and go thump, thump, thump; then he'd come on with his "Good morning Cleveland, this is Joe Finan." Sometimes he'd be twenty-five to thirty-five minutes late.

I liked to hang with him in the studio while he was on. He'd play a Neil Sedaka record and tell me, "I made 'x' amount of money playing that." He made thousands taking payola, and at the hearings in 1960, Joe Finan had the integrity to admit he was taking money. Joe said he blamed only himself. He was quoted as saying, "I allowed myself to be seduced. I was whoring." He could be one mean guy. He reportedly got a new driveway from one label and a swimming pool from another. The pool sprung a leak one weekend, and he called the record guy to get his ass over and fix it. The story goes that after he got busted for payola, the guy who gave him a driveway got a pick ax and slammed away, breaking it up. Once, after a few drinks, Joe broke down and told me how this was the lowest point of his life; he thought that everyone turned their back on him.

Dick Clark

The payola bust killed Alan Freed, but the most powerful disc jockey came out looking like a choir boy. In 1960 Dick Clark told the committee: "I have never taken payola. In brief, I have never agreed to

Dick Clark and I shared rock and roll stories on WLW in February 1979.

play a record or have an artist perform on a radio or television program in return for a payment in cash or any other consideration." They raised questions of payola and conflicts of interest. They listed thirty-three corporations of interest. I've done a number of interviews and appearances with Dick Clark. I've been the emcee for a number of his Caravan of Stars shows. He's a nice guy, but this was absurd. He had thirty-three companies, and he owned copyrights to 160 songs, 143 of them received as outright gifts. He quickly sold Sea Lark Music ("At the Hop"), January Music ("Sixteen Candles"), and Arch Music. He played the Crests' "Sixteen Candles" four times in ten weeks, but after his January Music became part owner, he played it twenty-seven times in less than ten weeks. Clark owned Mallard Pressing Corporation of Philadelphia, a record pressing plant. He did say he never leaned on anybody to use his place to press their records. He also owned one-third of Swan Records. He also owned Chips Distribution, a company that distributed records, according to John Jackson's *Big Beat Heat*.

So, because he didn't see any of this as a conflict of interest, Dick

Clark could acquire publishing rights to a song, have one of his people record for his own record label, have the record pressed at his plant, then have the record distributed by his company, play the record as often as he wanted on *American Bandstand*, and also have the artist appear on his show to plug the record, and then he was compensated for the singer's appearance. He didn't need to take payola for playing records because he owned everything. One investigator called it "Clarkola." Clark claimed he was a master music investor, but the payola people viewed it in a darker light. Dick had an interest in Duane Eddy's records. For instance, "Forty Miles of Bad Road" got thirty-three plays to twenty-four for Elvis. He paid $125 for 25 percent of Jamie Records, Duane's label, and later sold it for $12,025. Duane Eddy released eleven records between 1958 and 1960, and Clark played them a total of 240 times on his television show. If you look at some old 45s, you might see the name Anthony September as the writer or publisher of the song. He didn't write a note but got the money for himself or Clark. Anthony was Tony Mamarella, the producer of *American Bandstand*. In his book *Rock, Roll & Remember*, Clark said he didn't keep any money due artists who appeared on the *American Bandstand*. There wasn't enough money to pay all the artists, so Clark set up a system to pay as many of them as possible. The rest were paid by their record company—he gave the artist a check, the record company gave Dick a check, and the artist gave his check to the record company, resulting in a free appearance by the artist on the show. He said it was normal procedure in television at the time. I can understand the free appearances on the local bandstand shows, but his was a network show making a lot of money.

I asked Dick Clark what he did to get writer's credit for "At the Hop." He said, "Mac Davis had a song 'Stop and Smell the Roses' [1974]. It was a title suggested to him by Doc Severinsen and Doc is now the cowriter of the song. We were joking about it the other night. That song never would have happened if Doc hadn't given him that title and that's what I did for 'At the Hop.' They told me the song. I said it would never fly, its the wrong title—'At the Bop' [actually it was titled "Do the Bop"] I said change the title and it'll be a hit.

They changed the title and the lyrics and, as they say, the rest is history."

On a positive note, I did tell Dick I thought he was a great tranquilizer for the era. His sophisticated manner presenting rock 'n' roll made it a believable and viable thing, especially for doubting adults. Clark said, "That was part of the thing that made it fly. I was a reasonably respected looking fella. Although they didn't like the music, they figured well, maybe it wasn't all that bad. It was a very strange period of time as you know. The fifties were a very artificial period of time. We were all very innocent. We didn't often talk 100 percent truth. That's deep and philosophical."

Dick Clark did divest himself of all financial interests in recording, publishing, and other related fields. He got off with literally nothing, but that wasn't the case with Alan Freed.

Alan Freed

Alan Freed coined the term "rock 'n' roll," and he selected his own music, refusing to play covers of black artists by white performers. Clark was a clean-cut, low-keyed, a too-cool, made-for-television guy. I have tapes of both men interviewing Buddy Holly shortly before his death in a plane crash. Dick's interview was like vanilla ice cream. It was almost like he didn't know who was in the Crickets. Freed's interview is full of passion, talking about being with them on the road and the helicopter crash in Cincinnati that happened just as they were coming to town. He kidded Buddy about one of the Crickets always wanting someone to buy him a candy bar or something. Alan was a former musician who really knew music and its performers. Freed's arms would be waving, his tongue wagging as he howled, bellowed, and pounded the Manhattan telephone directory while he was on the air. His show props were a cow bell, a telephone book, and a stack of telegrams.

Alan Freed coined the term rock 'n' roll, but the phrase "rockin' and rollin" goes way back in the music industry. By the early twentieth century, the phrase was secular black slang for dancing or having sex; the 1922 Trixie Smith song "My Man Rocks Me (With One Steady Roll)" is often referred to as the first secular record to use the phrase rock and roll. In 1937, Ella Fitzgerald, with Chick Webb and his orchestra, had "Rock It for Me," a song full of double entendres. In 1947 Roy Brown wrote and recorded "Good Rockin' Tonight" that combined gospel with rhythm and blues.

However, Bill Haley told me Freed came up with the term from a record Haley did in 1955. He did the movies *Rock Around the Clock* and *Don't Knock the Rock* with Alan. I mentioned that Alan Freed coined the phrase "rock 'n' roll music," and Haley emphatically told me he got the term from his music. Bill said, "He used to call it the 'big beat' at one time. In those days, Alan was a high-pitched cat, and he could really get the kids going with him. He'd take his shoe off, or he would pound on the telephone book while he was doing his radio show just to emphasize the beat, and he called it the 'big beat.' Then I wrote a tune called, 'Rock a Beatin' Boogie.' He got that 'rock 'n' roll' from the music: 'Rock, rock, rock everybody, roll, roll, roll, everybody.' He took it from there, and he called it 'rock 'n' roll.' So actually he coined the phrase, but he took it from—in fact in those days he would admit it. I know for a fact that's where he got it."

In 1977, when I was working on my master's degree in broadcasting at the University of Cincinnati, I almost did my thesis on Alan Freed, and I was going to prove that, although his name was on the record, and he didn't write the song, he did contribute to its success. On Chuck Berry records, you can plainly hear the record's sound being augmented on the air by Alan pounding the phone book to the beat and his yelling in the background. I collected a number of Freed's air checks, and he was very consistent.

Alan Freed was a marked man after the payola bust. He was, although no one will admit it, blackballed from being on the air. Dick Clark didn't miss a beat, and he became a billionaire. I've documented Dick Clark's thirty-three corporations, but what about Freed? He had clearly been singled out.

Alan Freed pleaded guilty and was sentenced to a five-hundred-dollar fine, plus a six-month suspended jail term. The fine was reduced to three hundred dollars, after his attorneys pleaded lack of funds.

Yes, there were some very hungry disc jockeys who were putting the squeeze on record companies for money to play records, but Alan Freed wasn't in that category. Alan commented that while no one ever paid him to play a specific record, he regretted the way he had conducted some of his business activities.

Within five years, in January 1965, Freed would die broke and lonely. His best friend who he helped become a wealthy man, Leonard Chess of Chess Records, wouldn't even return a phone call. Leonard had promised him he would look after him, but, although he owned a Chicago radio station, he wouldn't hire him. Freed was only forty-three years old, and there are those who say that without any hope of being on the radio, he died of a broken heart.

I was subpoenaed

Did I ever take payola? I was the music director for three radio stations. I picked the music we played at Top 40 WWGO in Erie and for WKYC Top 40 in Cleveland until NBC said I couldn't be on the air and do both. I was the music director when I started at WLW in 1969, but the program directors eventually did the music. I was squeaky clean and never thought about it.

I've never talked about this, and the only person who knew at the time was my boss at WLW. In the early 1970s, they were gathering people for another big payola bust. It was huge—sex, drugs, and rock 'n' roll. I was subpoenaed to appear in Newark, New Jersey. I only had a couple of days notice, and they wouldn't tell me why they wanted to see me. I sat in a musty, dark room with a couple of FBI-looking guys who were firing questions at me, and I was never more nervous in my life. "Where were you? Who was with you? What did you do?" I was too scared not to tell the truth, but the event had happened at least two years earlier, and it was tough to remember. A Columbia Records promoter had a party sometime in 1970 to promote the novelty record "Rubber Duckie," a song sung by the Muppet character Ernie, voiced by Jim Henson. The song was named after

Ernie's toy, a rubber duck affectionately named "Rubber Duckie." They had a list of all the disc jockeys there, and I was the only one still in Cincinnati. However, I was the one they were after. Record promotion parties were common, and sometimes the artist would stop by. The food and booze was always plentiful, and it was a good chance to talk with other radio people in town. The highlight of this particular party was in the bathroom. Rubber ducks in the bathtub surrounded a beautiful woman. Yes, I was there. When I admitted this, they were pleased and about to hit me. "That's the reason you played 'Rubber Duckie.'" I don't even think I was doing music at the time, but I was doing afternoon drive. I tried to explain we only played X amount of records. WSAI was the teen station, and the station that "broke" records. He showed me a log they had of the airplays on WLW. I quickly pointed out that it only got played once or maybe twice in all that time on my show. It was a novelty record. However, it showed a bunch of plays between noon and one thirty. I was baffled; that was when the *Bob Braun Show* was simulcast on radio. I started to laugh, and they got upset. I explained, "They don't play records on Braun's show, but one of his singers, Rob Reider, sings a little part of that song as a bit." Apparently every time he said "rubber duckie," they logged it. I think they were embarrassed they brought me in, and that was the last I heard from them.

Mad Daddy

May 5, 1968, Norm N. Nite, who would one day write a series of *Rock On* books and become a disc jockey, put on a show at the Cleveland Arena called I Remember Rock and Roll. Norm once asked me why I didn't write *Rock On*: "You had all the information." I explained that I was busy doing a radio show. He was a fan of mine and got me to be one of the emcees, along with former Cleveland deejay, WNEW New York's Pete "Mad Daddy" Myers. The show featured Fats Domino, Chuck Berry, the Shirelles, and the Coasters. It was a great show, except Fats never showed up, and Chuck Berry took over, doing double duty. We stretched the show hoping Fats would make it, and he did make it in time for the food at the after party, but he couldn't understand why no one was talking to him. Pete Myers was better known in Cleveland as Mad Daddy, a rhyming, fast talking, wild man who said things like "mellow as jello" and "wavy gravy." He went to New York with big expectations, but his act didn't fly, and he became just plain Pete Myers. He became very successful as a mellow deejay and was working on the big, adult music station WNEW. He kept asking Joe Finan if he was happy being back in Cleveland. Joe was happy, and I thought Pete, who recently married a beautiful young New York model, was on top of the world. Six months later, on October 5, I read the story on the air: "Yesterday, former Cleveland deejay and WNEW radio personality, forty-year-old Pete Myers, died of an apparent suicide." He supposedly got dressed in his finest clothes, went into the bathroom with his prized collector's shotgun, listened to a tape of his old Mad Daddy show, and pulled the trigger. He left a note saying he was despondent that they were moving him from the one-to-four afternoon show, to the eight-to-midnight show. Years later when Chuck Daugherty joined our WLW staff, he told me he worked at WNEW, and he was the new guy in the afternoon who was to replace Pete. It wasn't Chuck's fault, but his career under the circumstances was short-lived at WNEW.

The Army Reserve Band

When I got to Cleveland I needed to transfer into a local army reserve unit. My girlfriend worked with a lady whose husband was in the 122nd Army Reserve Band. Barbara's husband, Harlan Miller, got an audition for me, and I became a trumpet player with the band. The Vietnam War was escalating, and the band wanted to stay under the radar. All hell broke loose when I played taps at a funeral, and someone took offense to my beard. My commanding officer, Chief Warrant Officer Irwin Walker, showed me the note—my beard had to go. I called the assistant adjutant general for the Ohio Army Reserve, Robert H. Canterbury, and explained my situation. I was on radio and that the beard was part of my image. We had a very cordial conversation, and he told me that the army reserve was designed for civilians like me to keep working, but that I needed to get everything in writing. I did, but a couple of days later I was told if I didn't shave my beard immediately, I would face a court-martial. The only exception to a clean shaven face is a neatly trimmed mustache. In May 1968, Jane Scott wrote in the *Plain Dealer*: "Unkindest Cut: Jim got word from the Army Reserve—off with the beard. So now he has a moustache that will really sink you." She picked me up, and I was feeling comfortable as Jim LaBarbara, beard or no beard.

A month later in the paper, Jane Scott kept the teens updated on why I wasn't on the air and that they could write Specialist Fourth-Class LaBarbara with the 122nd Army Reserve Band at Camp Grayling, Michigan, from June 14 to 28.

My first night at Camp Grayling a group of us went to town for a few drinks. I ran into Tom Kelly, a pitcher with the Cleveland Indians and his commanding officer. I ended up drinking and partying with them all night. I made it back just in time for formation, but I was drunk. As we were marching out to formation on this foggy morning, I kept thinking I forgot something. There were hundreds of soldiers lined up when the camp's commanding officer gave the call, "Bugler, sound your horn." Oh no, I suddenly realized what I forgot—my horn. The commanding officer got in my face and yelled, "Do you realize if this were Vietnam, that would be your weapon?" All I could picture was me trying to fight some Vietcong soldier with my trumpet, and I must have smiled. I was confined to quarters for the duration of camp, which was two weeks, and was given every detail available. Once again, I embarrassed the band, and even my closest friends wouldn't talk to me. It didn't take long for the word to get out about me, and the commanding officer from the other Cleveland unit—the same guy I was drinking with—asked for a "screw up" to send out on a detail. I spent a lot of days drinking with him and Tom Kelly. Another baseball player in that group was a former Indian who was with the White Sox, pitcher Tommy John. Thanks to them, I kept my sanity.

Glenville Riots

I was infatuated with black ladies since I was kid watching LaVern Baker wiggle out in a tight dress at my first rock show. I was in a bar on Euclid Avenue when I saw a shapely lady I had to meet. We hit it off and made arrangements for an early evening date before my show on July 23, 1968. There were a lot of people at her apartment, so we went to her bedroom to talk and listen to music. Several times, militant looking guys came in to interrupt us. She'd leave; then come back. She knew I was concerned. I was this white guy in this all-black neighborhood, but she kept assuring me everything was all right. At one point, there was a lot of commotion, and when she came back she told me to "leave—right now." A few hours later, I was getting ready for work when I saw the breaking news story on television. There was a riot in the Glenville section of Cleveland, the neighborhood I just left. What a mess. In the end, seven people were killed, three of them Cleveland police officers, and fifteen were wounded. That night two civilian tow truck drivers wearing uniforms similar to police uniforms were ambushed by armed snipers while checking an abandoned car. There was a six-mile area of looting and arson. The Glenville Riots were in full swing. While I was researching material for this book and reconstructing the events of that evening, I wondered if those were the militant members in that apartment and if I was to be a target. I never saw that lady again, and I never went back to that area.

Two nights later while I was on the radio, my unit was activated. One hour I was playing fun rock 'n' roll music, and the next, I was standing with a loaded M1 rifle on guard duty protecting the citizens of Cleveland during the Glenville Riots.

One of my favorite members of the Army Reserve Band was Ben Davis, a defensive back with the Cleveland Browns. We were on weekend duty at Camp Perry in Port Clinton qualifying with weapons. Ben and I had long talks about music and football. I mentioned how much I admired Dr. Martin Luther King; Ben said something like, "You can't be passive, you've got to be active, there is a cause." He was pointing out to me what was happening—the unrest, the riots.

We remained friends, but I didn't revisit that subject. I didn't understand Ben Davis, but I do now. He grew up in Birmingham, Alabama, in an area known as Dynamite Hill because of the large number of homes bombed by the Ku Klux Klan. He grew up in this environment, and Ben's sister Angela Davis was the well-known radical activist during the early seventies and a member of the Black Panther Party.

I really tried to get the guys in the band to like me. One night at Camp Perry, we had plenty of beer for everyone, and I hired a female entertainer to dance. We covered the barrack's windows, had a nice party, and I thought everyone enjoyed themselves. The next day, some empty beer cans were discovered, and I was thrown under the bus and disciplined by my commanding officer. I may have been looked on as a radio celebrity to some, but not these guys. I think everyone was relieved when I finally left the band and moved to Cincinnati.

The Donkey and me

Candy Forest was a young folk singer and our WIXY promotions director. She took all the jocks to the Cleveland Zoo to get promo pictures of us with animals. She wanted me to pose with a lion looking over me. I didn't object; a picture of me with the king of the jungle would be good for my image. I had to climb over the railing and stand on a narrow ledge above a moat wearing my handmade, slippery, leather moccasins while they threw rocks at the lion trying to position him behind me for the photographer. A zoo security guard got me away from the edge. He told me, "Do you know what would have happened if you would have slipped into the moat?" I said, "I'd just run to the door." He then explained it went straight to the lion's den. We got chased out of that section of the zoo, and I ended up having my picture taken with a donkey in the children's zoo.

WIXY was great about creating an identity for its jocks. One hundred thousand people turned out on Euclid Avenue for our first Christmas parade. The paper reported that Tim Conway was the grand marshal and Jim LaBarbara, the stations all-night man, appeared in a red flannel nightshirt and cap, holding a candle.

Paul Simon

We were the official station for Simon and Garfunkel, and we plugged the show big time. When I was music director in Erie and later at WKYC, I always made sure we played their records. Shortly before show time, Paul Simon came up to me and said, "Are you with that station?" and pointed to a big sign on stage that said "WIXY 1260." I said "Yes," as I extended my hand to shake, "and this is our night guy, the Wild Childe . . ." Paul cut me off: "Take it down, or we don't sing." We broke several of their records in Cleveland. I got Candy Forest, our promotions director, to deal with him. This egomaniac was ranting and raving over a sign. He was a brilliant songwriter but totally clueless about dealing with people. Over the years, I've had several opportunities to interview him and turned them down. He had a Broadway show, *Caveman*. I asked a Broadway producer friend of mine why it closed so quickly. He said, "Have you ever met Paul? You can't tell him anything." I guess he hasn't changed.

Stax Records, Sam Moore, and Wilson Pickett

A duo that really smoked on stage was Sam and Dave, the guys who gave us "Hold On, I'm Coming" and "Soul Man." They always looked like they were best friends. They looked like they were close, strutting around on stage, but something happened with Dave, and Sam told me, "I took it upon myself, and I said, 'I will sing with you, but I'll never talk to you again.' It was twelve years that Dave and I performed together that we never actually spoke to one another." Sam didn't go into details, but what upset Sam was that Dave shot his own girlfriend in the face after a heated argument. He eventually married her and that saved Dave from going to jail.

Stax Records had so many great acts, including Otis Redding and Wilson Pickett. They got an incredible sound out of Stax Records in

Memphis's Capitol Theater. It was a small theater, and Sam described it as, "A small studio, and the piano was out of tune, the curtains were dusty, the floors were rugged, and we were recording on an eight track at that time. We were recording live; sometimes we'd do three or four songs a day. That was pretty tough."

Sam Moore and his wife, Joyce, sat across from me one night at dinner, and next to them was Martha Reeves from Motown. Sam's wife's purse was on the table, and I watched it move on its own several times. I didn't say anything, but when Martha saw it she shouted, "Get that %$@#! purse off the table, I'm eating!" A little dog's head suddenly popped out of the purse. It was a funny scene.

Wilson Pickett had giant hits like "Mustang Sally" and "In the Midnight Hour." He recorded at Stax, but he was on Atlantic Records.

Wilson got the nickname "Wicked Pickett the Midnight Mover," not because of his gritty voice and stage movements, but his rendezvous with the Atlantic secretaries. He laughed and confessed, "Well, I did take a couple of them on the bus. The miniskirts were up a little higher than they were supposed to be. Noreen Woods, the secretary, said, 'My you are wicked,' so Jerry Wexler said, 'The name of his next album is the *Wicked Pickett*.'"

Wilson and I were talking about great session musicians when I mentioned the great sax player King Curtis. Wilson got excited and said, "You know, he gave the Coasters and all of them that style that they had. [He made a sound like a honking sax.] King Curtis could play in any session anywhere with anybody. He was versatile. The only thing I didn't like about King was, we'd go into a restaurant—he loved lemon pie—and he'd eat it with his whole face. Lemon pie would be on his nose; it would make my skin crawl. I said, 'King, why you got to put the pie all over your nose?' He said, 'Pickett, here, this is good luck, put some of this pie on your nose.' Lemon meringue pie, and you know he was very black; he was blacker than black with all that pie on his nose."

We had our second annual WIXY Appreciation Day at Geauga Lake Park on August 1, 1968, headlined by Gene Pitney, singing his hit "She's A Heartbreaker." We did a lot of shows, but the fan appreciation shows were the biggest. It was a thrill to be an emcee in front of an estimated 120,000 people.

In addition to my night show, I had a progressive rock show that aired Sunday night from 10:00 p.m. to 1:00 a.m. called *Red, White, and Blues*. I would play album cuts by acts like Hendrix, Cream, and Janis Joplin that wouldn't normally be heard on WIXY. It was one of the first shows of its kind on a mainstream Top 40 AM station. Although this was WMMS's music, and it would become one of the greatest rock stations in FM history, in 1968, they were no competition for us. I ended each show by playing Jose Feliciano's version of "The Star Spangled Banner," which at the time was very controversial.

It was a big day

It was a big day when we moved our studios from the transmitter to downtown Cleveland. Our studios were state of the art. Norman Wain had a use for our old studio equipment. He opened the WIXY School of Broadcast Technique. I was one of the school's first teachers. It was a nice way to make a little money. Our new location also afforded us a chance to be closer to our audience, and many pretty ladies took advantage of the situation to stop by the back door nightly to get a tour of the station.

A number of radio people frequented a restaurant on Euclid Avenue for lunch; it gave us a chance to socialize with other jocks. My eyes popped out when one of the soul jocks, who had just returned from a convention, started opening envelopes from record labels and artists. He'd smile and say, "So and so was extra good to me this year," or "This brother really got cheap on me." Here he was, nine years after the payola bust, showing us his financial take.

Mike Reineri replaced Joe Finan in morning drive on WIXY and possessed the driest sense of humor. He was a bachelor, and he'd play a little game in that restaurant with the help of newsman Bill Clark. They would carefully check out the ladies and put two twenty-dollar bills on their table in clear view. Bill or Mike would approach the lady and say something like, "Please excuse my rudeness. I'll understand if you don't want to answer this question because it's so personal. My friend and I have a twenty-dollar bet." He'd point to the table with the money.

"He says you are a thirty-five B, I say a thirty-six C—there's twenty dollars riding on this. I hope I didn't embarrass you."

"You won, I'm a thirty-six C," and then she'd join them at their table.

I was floored at the number of ladies they met with this sophomoric bit.

My craziest appearance

WIXY didn't have to answer to a corporate headquarters because it was owned by three former local radio salesmen. We reacted right now to whatever was going on, and our promotions were the best. A good example of this was also the wildest WIXY promotion that I was involved with. It happened on September 25, 1968. A girl named Francine Gottfried had captivated Wall Street traffic in New York with her forty–two-inch bust. Norman had me talk about it and say, "Anything New York can do, Cleveland can do better and bigger. Join me at East Ninth Street and Euclid Avenue at noon." It was unbelievable. More than ten thousand people, mostly men, showed up and stopped traffic. The girls stood on the top of a telephone company truck that a generous guy let us use. There were signs: "No Place for Twiggy's" and "Cleveland Is Better than NY." I was the station's bachelor, so I had to measure each girl. Guys in cars would beep their horns, then look over and see the girls, and get out of their cars. Yes, for a brief moment on this Wednesday afternoon, Clevelanders could forget the pressures of Vietnam, taxes, inflation, personal problems, and have a little fun. Mounted police came out to dispense the crowd. I couldn't decide between two girls with identical 43-24-37 measurements. Stomachs in, chests out, it was quite a sight, but suddenly the police were next to us. I helped the girls into Norman Wain's car, but when I tried to get in, he locked the doors and started to drive off. I chased them down the street until he finally let me in. He was the station owner, and he wanted me to get arrested so I could do my show from jail. The next day, the front page of the *Plain Dealer* read, "Disc jockey Jim LaBarbara, who did the measuring, could only respond, 'Ub, ub, ub, ub, ub, ub,' when asked about how he felt about his role." Yes, even for 1968, it was pretty chauvinistic. My girlfriend was not pleased with me.

The Cream

WIXY started getting the biggest concerts. When I was on WKYC, we had the shows and, if I was the emcee, I got a nice talent check. At WIXY there was no talent check, it was part of our job, but it was still a nice perk. I was involved with being an emcee for one of the Cream's final concerts. The Cream was a super group with Eric Clapton on guitar, vocalist Jack Bruce, and drummer Ginger Baker. We had a contest in the paper: just match the baby pictures of the WIXY Supermen and the Cream and win tickets with VIP treatment. Most people mixed mine with Clapton's. At that time, the top radio personalities were equated in popularity with the artists we played. It was a crazy sight backstage to watch Ginger Baker being led to his drums. I didn't think this stoned-freak druggy would make it through the day, but years later I was happy to read that he gave up drugs and became a Christian.

Party time

A couple of pretty ladies who worked at the "in" club, Otto's Grotto, had some great parties. I sat around with Sonny Geraci and the Outsiders, Tommy James and the Shondells, and the Young Rascals. It was an all-nighter. Sonny Geraci and I got into a heavy conversation about our Italian mothers' cooking. We decided if we could get the two of them together, we would have the perfect pizza. My mom always made the thin crust with everything on top, and Sonny's mom made the thick crust with not much on top. It would be his mom's crust and my mom's toppings. Wow—what a pizza! I don't know if we were high or just a little drunk. There was a lot of talent at that party. Tommy James was doing some drugs and smoking weed. He later had a problem with drugs that was well documented but got himself clean. I talked to him about how he kicked his drug problem, but he denied using drugs. When the microphone was off, I reminded him that we got high together. He said, "Yeah I know. I never like to talk about it." I didn't intend to embarrass him, and we talked on the air a number of times since, but I never mentioned it again.

Those pretty girls always had good parties. One of the ladies, a waitress at the club, was leaving to work at P.J.'s in Hollywood. I never dated her, but the night before she was to drive across country, we got together. She had been with John Lennon and Jimi Hendrix; we spent the night talking, but that's all. She would have been any guy's dream, and I liked her a lot, but in a twist, I didn't want to be just another number in her book. I didn't hit on her.

Vanilla Fudge

We waited and waited for the headliners to appear. I was the emcee for a show at Cleveland's Music Carnival in August of 1968. The Damnation of Adam Blessing, a local act, was opening for the Vanilla Fudge. I kept bringing them back onstage and stalling because the Fudge's plane was late. The group did four sets, and they played everything they knew, about fifty songs. They finally played "You Keep Me Hanging On," the Vanilla Fudge's big hit of the day. The kids loved the song, but while they were in the middle of an extremely long version of it, in came the Vanilla Fudge. Normally you'd never play another act's song, but the group was out of material, and we were all tired. Instead of being upset, the guys thanked the group over and over for keeping the crowd. The Vanilla Fudge was about three hours late when I introduced them.

WIXY is number 1, but I'm outta' here

Cleveland had three AM rock stations: WKYC, WHK, and WIXY, and CKLW in Windsor, Canada, boomed in like a local station. We battled it out with "world exclusive" records and incredible promotions. We were kicking butt, and everybody knew us by name, "Wicksy Twelve Sixty." I had been at WIXY about a year when the ratings showed we were the most listened to station in Cleveland. On January 31, 1969, at Cleveland Public Auditorium, we put on our WIXY Appreciation Day Show for our listeners. Neil Diamond, Tommy James, Canned Heat, Jay and the Americans, along with a couple of newcomers, Kenny Rogers and Bob Seger, were hanging with us in the wings. There was a strange vibe backstage; somebody was missing. We hired an announcer from another station to introduce the WIXY Supermen. When our name was called, we ran through a big paper banner that identified us, as our WIXY Pixie Girls cheered. We were all onstage except Johnny Michaels; they had just fired him. The announcer then introduced our newest WIXY Superman, Chuck Dunaway. Wait a minute, this was the same guy we just beat. The crowd gave him a cordial welcome. I was standing next to Joe Finan and the Wilde Childe. I told Finan: "I'm outta here. I quit." I told the Childe, "You've got your Texas buddy." He said, "Wait a minute, he's not my buddy." I was still upset about the comment Dunaway made to me on my last day at WKYC: "You won't be doing anything. I'll show you how it's done." I was to be an emcee, but I walked out followed by Finan and the Childe and missed a great show. We ended up at an old Irish bar in the Flats, a tough bar with an even tougher clientele. Finan talked me into not quitting until I found another gig but told me he was leaving. I got inebriated and never did my show. George Brewer, our program director never said a word to me about it.

I started looking for another job. WGAR in Cleveland was changing, and they wanted to talk with me. I was on time for my interview, but the program director kept me waiting in the lobby, and I couldn't help but think he did that on purpose. It was music day, and every record promoter in the city saw me sitting there. In those days, if you wanted to start a rumor, you just had to tell a record promoter; they were in touch with all the stations. I was embarrassed because I knew it would get back to WIXY.

The early-night show became available when the Wilde Childe left for our sister station in Pittsburgh. We had recording stars fill in. The ukulele-playing Tiny Tim had a shockingly high falsetto version of "Tiptoe Thru the Tulips" and did the show one night. My girl-friend, Susan, and I sat with him for a while, and we both agreed, he never broke character—his was no act. Suddenly he was this sad, pathetic person who thought he could sing, and he was no longer funny. He became really famous when he married Miss Vickie on the Johnny Carson Show.

Tiny Tim. I thought his act was a put on—it wasn't.

Tommy Boyce

Tommy Boyce and Bobby Hart, who wrote the Monkees' hits and had "I Wonder What She's Doing Tonight," did a terrific deejay show. We were going to dinner after the show, so I hung around in the studio waiting for them. A sexy sounding girl called in, and Tommy invited her to join us. Tommy was sure she was going to be a knock out. I learned early on that a phone voice can be deceiving. In DuBois, I invited a lady to stop by. She almost got stuck in the door trying to get into the studio. She wore this really cheap perfume that made me gag, and even today, I start coughing when I think about it. One lady who called me a number of times sounded terrific. She told me to check out her sister's picture that was in the paper. Her sister was attractive, so I was positive she would be too. Our conversation ended abruptly one night when someone took the phone away from her in the psychiatric ward of the local hospital.

We were sitting in the restaurant enjoying a drink when the mystery lady walked over to our table. To say this woman was unattractive would be an understatement. We all just looked at Tommy Boyce. What was he going to say, and how was he going to get rid of her? Instead, he pulled out a chair for her, introduced us to her, and proceeded to treat her like a princess during dinner. I think we all learned something from Tommy that night. Tommy remembered me and reentered my life later, but that's a story for another chapter.

It was clear I wasn't going to get a chance to move into the early show when we hired Chuck Knapp from Boston.

CHAPTER 10

WLW Cincinnati
"The Music Professor"

Jim Gallant, the man they fired at WKYC to make room for me, was the new program director at powerhouse WLW in Cincinnati. He wasn't home when I called, but his wife, Mary Ann, said, "I'm sure Jim wants to talk with you; he has an opening, and you'll love Cincinnati." Mary Ann was a former Miss Ohio who booked deejays when she was in Cleveland and took good care of me. Jim and I had dinner at the Sovereign Restaurant overlooking Cincinnati, and he made me an offer. I would do early nights 7:00 to 11:00 p.m. and be the music director. WLW was a tired sounding station playing the hit songs covered by groups like the Ray Conniff Singers. Jim wanted me to play the contemporary hits and oldies by the original artists, the pop music but not the real hard rock. It took a week for all the Avco Broadcasting paperwork to get done. My boss, Norman Wain, said, "If you were going to WABC [the number one rock station in America at that time], I couldn't be happier. WLW is a great station." He told me he listened to me every night and that he felt the station was safe with me and that's why he wasn't going to move my shift. I told him about WGAR. He knew they talked to me, but I was surprised when he said he wouldn't let me go to WGAR. I was getting tired of working on a teen station. I wasn't a kid anymore—I was twenty-seven, and it was time to move on to an adult station. I was on my way to WLW the first week in May, and my replacement at WIXY was Billy Bass, who had quit his early-evening show on WMMS FM to do all-nights. WIXY was hot, and everybody wanted to work there.

I was about seventy miles out of Cincinnati when my new 1969 yellow Corvette Stingray threw a rod. I took it to the closest Chevy dealership. It was off the main highway, but they couldn't fix it because they had to order parts. The day I went to pick it up, the owner looked at me and said, "It's not ready. You know, we are just country folks, and sometimes it takes us longer to work on fancy cars like this." He had heard me talk about my car experience on WLW. I learned an early lesson—to edit myself on this powerhouse.

The station put me up in the old Gibson Hotel. Bill Barrett wrote in the *Cleveland Plain Dealer* that he heard me talk on the radio about how nice it was to be able to walk around Fountain Square and that I could never do that at Public Square in Cleveland. Downtown Cleveland has had a rebirth in recent years, so that statement is no longer true.

On May 22, 1969, WLW ran an ad in the *Enquirer*. It was a caricature, a takeoff of *The Man of La Mancha*. I was in armor, carrying a spear on a horse. "Jim LaBarbara 'The Man of LaMusica' 7–11 p.m."

Jim Gallant gave me the title "The Music Professor." Gallant was carefully crafting my new image. Of course, I was no longer "Cleveland's Most Eligible Bachelor"—that wasn't going to work even if we changed the city name. This was a more sophisticated adult station. Jim liked the music information I used on my Cleveland show, and he wanted me to do more of it. "The Music Professor," I didn't care for it at first, but he thought I had the credentials. Gallant said, "You remember Kay Kyser the 'Ol' Professor,' the big band leader?" My dad had a bunch of his 78 rpm records, but I knew nothing about him. Kay had eleven number one hits and thirty-five Top 10 hits, was featured in seven movies, and had a top-rated radio show for eleven years on NBC. He was a popular band leader and radio personality of the thirties and forties, but in 1950, they totally walked away from the business. His big bit was *Kay Kyser's Kollege of Musical Knowledge*, where he featured a music-related quiz with songs and comedy. I respected Gallant's request, and I worked it into my show, but I thought it was hokey. I didn't feel comfortable calling myself the Music Professor.

My girlfriend, Susan, visited me on the weekends, but our relationship was changing. I never told her how much I loved her, and I never invited her to move to Cincinnati with me after being with her for three years. On a beautiful Sunday afternoon, we went looking for an apartment. I pulled into the driveway of the Forum Apartments in Clifton. A girl in a bikini stopped me. On one of the upper apartment balconies, somebody was pushing a refrigerator over the railing. There were a number of ladies in two-piece bathing suits by the swimming pool cheering this crazy guy on. The refrigerator made a huge crash as it hit the center of the driveway while its contents poured out. The girl in the bikini directed me around the refrigerator. I had the top down and almost got whiplash from turning to look at all the pretty ladies. My girlfriend said, "You are not moving here." The guy who threw the refrigerator over the balcony also had knocked down part of a wall in his apartment because he wanted to get evicted. It worked. Today, Jay Karp is a well-respected antique dealer and friend.

The Forum was a single person's paradise. I moved in the next week. Although we talked on the phone, Susan would never again visit me in Cincinnati. A lot of athletes lived in the apartments, and there was always a party going on somewhere. This is where the best looking single ladies lived. It was unbelievable. One of our single WLW sales guys lived on the floor below me. We had a couple of young ladies in his apartment for drinks, and after several, I decided to show one where I lived. After a few more drinks in my apartment, I got a brilliant idea. "Let's get naked and surprise them!" She agreed, and we took off to the next floor sans clothes. Here we were, "au natural," knocking on his door, and they wouldn't let us in. All of a sudden, people were in the hall, something must have just let out. We were standing with no towel—nothing. We made it back to my place, but of course, more people saw us. Lucky for me, I was new in town and nobody knew the crazy, naked guy. WLW would have had a fit. I guess I thought about it for a moment—excessive drinking, indecent exposure, my reputation.

The disparity of the disc jockey I had become and the college senior of six years earlier was alarming. Believe it or not, I was a lay preacher. I gave a number of sermons, but one that I still remember was based on a poem called "God Forgive Me When I Whine." I delivered it in November of 1961 at the Bethany Methodist Church in Meadville. I took a number of religion and philosophy courses. I was a member of the Thorburn Club, a group interested in the Christian ministry, and Dr. Hunter from Boston University offered me a graduate scholarship for religion. Boston is a Methodist school, and because I was a Lutheran, the church required another year of training in their liturgy to become ordained. I was recruited by several denominations and seminaries, but the one thing that turned me off was the talk of a big church in the proper suburb with the big car and big money, because I wanted to work in an inner city, integrated church. Money wasn't going to be a factor.

Charlie Murdock, our general manager, wanted to know all about WIXY. I explained the "WIXY spirit" that Norman Wain instilled in his staff. He was a near genius when it came to promotions. We reacted to things immediately. Of course, it helped that he owned the station. When the television stations promoted their fall lineup, we would run an ad on that same page with the WIXY fall lineup, complete with pictures and program description. On the other hand, when I was on WKYC in Cleveland, we ran a full-page newspaper ad, and the promotions department was all excited. It was a blank page except for the call letters in the bottom corner in small print. It might have been hip to some young ad executive on Wall Street, but those of us on the station thought it was dumb. WIXY's call letters were everywhere, and they were big and bold. Charlie asked me what I thought of WLW, and I was honest. It wasn't a radio station, because there wasn't a radio on anywhere, except sometimes in the sales department on the second floor and of course in Gallant's office.

There was nothing in the station lobby to indicate this was radio. The receptionist was clueless as to what or who was on the air because she was watching television. Charlie got a little red faced, and I backed off. To Charlie's credit, later that day, the television was replaced by a radio, and the lobby's transformation had begun.

I don't think Charlie was sold on me. I might have been on thin ice, but all that changed when the *Enquirer*'s Frank Weikel, the most widely read columnist in town, wrote on June 5, 1969: "While turning in early for the Reds' ball game the past couple of nights, I've had a chance to listen to the city's newest disc jockey . . . and the guy's got talent. The new addition to WLW is Jim LaBarbara." All of a sudden his seal of approval was a validation, and I was looked at differently. Apparently, Rich King was the only one at the station he ever mentioned. Frank would quote me often and use some of my one-liners. I thanked him several times and told him what his endorsement meant to me.

Nightly on my show I used a line about "fighting off the power of Morpheus." Morpheus in Greek mythology was the god of dreams. Another line I used was trite, but true in my case: "Music is my business and I hope my business is your pleasure." On one of my first shows, I did a sign off over Kai Winding's record "More." I said something like, "For you my lonesome lads, and especially for you my lonesome ladies. It's not good-bye, it's just good night, because I know that you and I will cross kilocycles again. And when we do—I'll teach you things you've never heard before, I'll sing you songs you've never sung. And if you stay by my side, this I promise—you and I will be forever young. I'm Jim LaBarbara, the Music Professor. Thank you for listening, and above and beyond all, love somebody tonight." I did variations of that for a few nights, and a girl I knew convinced me to use it as a sign off. In an early interview, I credited disc jockeys Jim Runyon and Randy Hall because I borrowed part of it from their sign offs. Over a period of time, I'd often be introduced at events with the band playing "More." I tried to drop my sign off at WLW, but listeners complained. At other stations I just said, "Love somebody tonight."

One of my first friends at the Forum Apartments was a guy I kept running into at the apartment bar. We had similar work schedules, and we both worked on WLW. Johnny Bench, the Reds' catcher, became my best friend, and for years we were like brothers. John lived in the apartment above mine, and we often used a broom to communicate. We would open the window and use a broom to bang across the other's window. He was pounding on my window with his broom and yelling, "You've got smoke coming out of your window!" I shouted back, "I know! I burnt a steak. I've got a grease fire!" Lucky for me, the West Virginia girls who lived down the hall saw the smoke and put the fire out with baking soda.

WLW carried the Reds' games, and my nightly schedule was easy. I'd come on at 7:00 p.m., work about fifteen minutes, and then work about twenty minutes after the game. I'd go to the game and leave in time to do my show, which was over at eleven when "Moon River" came on. Johnny Bench liked to stop by before we hit the clubs, and he'd intro some records and play disc jockey. He was good.

Johnny Bench and Pete Rose started calling me "professor," and suddenly everyone was referring to me as "prof" or "Hey professor!" Jim Gallant was right about "the Music Professor." I had a feeling it might work when our building's maintenance worker told me he listened everyday to my show because he liked my stories about the records. Every morning he listened to Stan Matlock on WKRC. I listened to Matlock the next day, and he proceeded to describe in great detail how many guppies a pregnant guppy could deliver. That was his bit; he gave out that kind of information several times an hour. I thought that made my job easier, because he trained the audience to be informed. I continually told stories about artists and records that no one else had. This was before the internet, and I was busy doing my research.

Andy Williams

I was proud to be a member of the WLW family. WLW was known as "the Nation's Station," and a lot of great stars worked here, including the Mills Brothers, Rod Serling, Rosemary Clooney, and Andy Williams to name a few. Andy told me he got his big break as a solo performer being a regular on the *Steve Allen Tonight Show*, getting national exposure and then recording with Archie Blyer on Cadence Records.

Thanks to my friend Denny McKeown, the gardening expert, on September 1, 1985, after a Reds game at Riverfront Stadium, I was the emcee for the Hope House Benefit Show. Denny was the show's producer and we had Andy Williams, Phyllis Diller, Marie Osmond, and Bob Hope. Andy and I had a chance to reminisce about why he and his brothers came to WLW. Andy explained, "We left WLS because AFTRA, the union, came in, and all the stations that had live entertainment had to close down because the union insisted that they pay for everything, [and that] was much higher than they were paying. They had to re-gear themselves. That was the beginning of the disc jockey. When they couldn't afford the live entertainment, they started playing records. So, we moved to Cincinnati. They had a show called *Time to Shine*. It was on in the morning. They hired us for two years. It was on eight fifteen to eight thirty. Grandpa Jones was on the show. We did a show every morning, and then we'd go to school. We lived in Cheviot or Price Hill."

When we talked about his Cincinnati memories, the first thing he said was that he started drinking beer here. "Everybody drank beer in Cincinnati. There were a lot of different beers at the time: Red Top Ale, Felsenbrau Supreme—a lot of those smaller companies have been bought up by larger companies. But before that, my parents were very strict. We never had any alcohol in the house. When we moved to Cincinnati, a grocery store near our house sent us over a care package. The first thing we did was to pour all the beer down the sink because we were really teetotalers. So I got corrupted in Cincinnati, and I've loved it ever since."

Andy Williams went to West High—Western Hills High School, and he was in the Triginta Optima (TO) fraternity. His recollection was, "We had I think the only fraternity house in high school. It was a little shack, but it was wonderful. I had a great time. I fell in love with my first girl in Cincinnati: Alain Evans. Alain Evans, I'll never forget her."

From Vivienne to my own TV show?

I was amazed by WLWT, our sister station's live shows. The day started with the *Paul Dixon Show*; followed by the *Bob Braun Show* from noon to 1:30 p.m., which was simulcast on WLW radio; and later in the afternoon the show *Vivienne!!*, hosted by Vivienne Della Chiesa. Johnny Walters, her announcer and sidekick, left for St. Louis just as I was coming in. Her show was being cancelled and was in its final weeks when Vivienne requested me to be her announcer. I did quite a few programs, and I loved it. Vivienne thought I was a nice Italian boy, and she would tell me: "Jimmy, the camera likes you; you can't fool the camera." I was her Ed McMahon; she would involve me in her conversations and tease me about my latest mod clothes. Apparently she wasn't the only one who thought the camera liked me.

I was called to the Avco Corporate office to meet with several vice presidents. I dressed very casual and was later reprimanded for my dress by Charlie Murdock. They talked to me about hosting a television show aimed at a younger audience. I was high on the idea of my own television show but not on the people they wanted me to work with. They were surprised I was passing on this opportunity. They showed me a pilot of a Sonny and Cher show. I had worked with them recently, and I had to think about it because it was nothing like the show you remember. We looked at a few awful pilots, and I was honest with them. They told me they were thinking of hiring former New York DJ Murray the K for our sister station in Washington, D.C., and then got mad at me when I said I wouldn't do that. I'd met Murray, and he was great in New York, but he needed a producer and a writer. I knew Avco wouldn't put up with his demands. Perry Samuels, our vice president of radio programming, stopped by during my show to tell me they hired him. I proved to be right, and they fired him after a short stay.

Avco Broadcasting took the money they were going to put into a weekly television show and came up with the idea to do a Midwest version of Woodstock. I wasn't consulted, but I was going to be on the show. It took place at Crosley Field on June 13, 1970, and was billed as the Cincinnati Summer Pop Festival, sixteen acts in fourteen hours. They called it a "gathering of the people." It was a great lineup of stars and future stars: Traffic with Stevie Winwood, Grand Funk Railroad, Ten Years After, Mountain, Alice Cooper, Iggy Pop, Brownsville Station, and a soon-to-be star, Bob Seger. My job was to do quick interviews with people in the audience. I got there early, before the gates opened at 10:00 a.m. It was a perfect atmosphere for a rock festival. It was raining, and the want-to-be hippies and flower children were playing in the mud. I got a camera man to shoot some people, but he couldn't because he said he wasn't on the clock. I tried to explain that this is your introduction for the show, but nobody would listen. They never used a video of a young mother breast-feeding her baby. In the end, all of my bits were cut out, at least with me on camera. Our program director, Cliff Hunter, had promoted me to the WLW afternoon show, and upper management didn't think it was proper for my image. It was a good show just because of all the talent, but Avco Broadcasting had former NBC *Today Show* host Jack Lescoulie under contract, and he anchored the broadcast. He was almost sixty years old and had no knowledge of pop music. To say he was totally out of place would be an understatement. WLWT condensed the fourteen-hour concert into a ninety-minute show that was later broadcast as *Midsummer Rock*.

The Inner Circle

A couple of Cleveland Indians' players told me: "When you get to Cincinnati, look up Pete and Billy at the Inner Circle Nightclub." I dropped their names at the door hoping to avoid the cover charge.

"What's your name?"

I introduced myself, and the guy said, "My wife listens to you every night." Pete Georgeton, the owner, gave me a hug, and said, "I want to advertise with you." The Inner Circle was in Corryville just up the street from my apartment, and it became my second home. I even took my phone calls there. It was a who's who for local sports celebrities. Sunday nights were different; the strippers and club owners from Newport would gather to relax. A number of Runyonesque characters could be seen standing around the bar. It wasn't uncommon to find notables like Frank "Screw" Andrews enjoying a beverage with his entourage, and nobody ever bothered them. In the pantheon of the old Newport gangsters, he was a trigger-happy example. He met a violent death when he "fell" out of a sixth-story window at Saint Luke Hospital. I later discovered he was an uncle to a couple of my Stowe High classmates. After Bengals' games, the team would be well represented, and the young ladies knew where to find them. Pete always had great entertainment, whether it was the white-haired soul singer Wayne Cochran riding his motorcycle down the steps, holding onto his bottle of Jack Daniels, the Orange Colored Sky, or the fabulous Mickey and Larry—it was the place to be. Pete treated me like a top-tier celebrity. I never paid a cover charge, somebody took care of drinks, the entertainers acknowledged me, and I always had a table up front. It all happened because I was Jim LaBarbara on the radio.

My WLW image was developing. I took possession of the Music Professor brand and became this high-profile bachelor who hung out with sports stars and beautiful women. I was plugged into the community, and I shared my daily adventures with my listeners. A well-known morning radio personality told me how he was jealous of the preferential treatment I received at the Inner Circle and other clubs. He said, "I used to think, who does he think he is to get all that attention?" I was married, doing a talk show on WCKY, and not into the club scene at the time he told me. It was like he was rubbing it in when he added, "Now I have the front row seats wherever I go."

Jackie Wilson

Jackie Wilson put on the best show I ever saw at the Inner Circle. My good friend Otis Williams, the King Records star, Jackie, and I hung out in his dressing room in between shows and had a lot of laughs. Jackie was on the Nick Clooney local television show earlier that day, and Nick asked if he was related to Nancy Wilson the singer. I told Jackie I was surprised to hear they were cousins. He explained they weren't related, but it was easier for him to say that because they were friends. During the course of the interview, I had to stop the recorder five or six times because we were interrupted by young ladies coming into the room crying and hugging Jackie. They all called him "Daddy," and he asked about their mothers and said to please tell them he was thinking about them. After the third or fourth time this happened, I looked at Otis, and we just started laughing. I asked Jackie if he knew these girls and their mothers. He said he had no idea who they were, but that this happened everywhere he went. I asked if they were his daughters, and he didn't know. Jackie was apparently very busy both on and off the stage.

Jackie did tell me he was influenced in the music business by "the late great Clyde McPhatter, who was originally with Billy Ward and the Dominoes, whose place I took when he left when I joined in 1953. It was my first venture away from home. I do a lot of knee bends on stage. I got those from a guy named Al Jolson."

Jackie Wilson sang in church as a youngster, but not in the choir. He had his own group, the Ever Ready Gospel Singers. Jackie said, "We sang throughout the Midwest. We had several programs with Sam Cooke when he had a group called the Highway Q.C.s, and then he sang with the Soul Stirrers, and we used to play with them too."

We discussed how that influence of gospel music had carried over into his act with the call-and-response sounds of the black church. I said, "You testify, and you talk about how lonely you've been: 'I'm okay now, and I'm looking for a woman, and do you have a woman?' Somebody yells out: 'Yeah, I have a woman,' or 'Hey, I need one.'" Jackie responded, "Definitely, it is a crossover from the gospel days."

He surprised me when he said his favorite song to sing was "Danny Boy": "I started singing that in the talent shows in Detroit when I was about eleven years old. I used to win all the time singing the falsetto notes. I always did love it since I heard it in a movie with Bobby Breen. It's a beautiful ballad."

Jackie told me, "Yes it is," when I asked him if it was true that he was a Golden Gloves boxing champion. He explained that he wasn't in high school: "No, believe it or not, I was a little too young. I was about sixteen years old, and my age went up naturally. I was eighteen to the people, and they scratched it out because I did win, but I didn't win legally. I had a mustache, and I was very good with my hands. I was a lightweight." I've seen other reports that list his Golden Gloves record as two wins and eight losses.

A signature song of Jackie Wilson is "Lonely Teardrops," and according to him, something did stand out at the recording session: "Yes definitely, Berry Gordy wrote it as a blues ballad, and when we got to the session, my manager, Nat Tarnopol, thought we should try a calypso beat because calypso was popular then. We changed the beat; it was supposed to be slow like 'Doggin' Around.'"

Jackie, the ladies are always grabbing you, trying to rip your clothes. Do you ever get nervous going into the audience?"

After being interrupted by another lady who had to see Jackie, we discussed the women at his shows. A lot of these ladies wanted a piece of him. I know it sounds like fun to step into that audience, but it could be dangerous. He admitted at times he got nervous: "I see how rough the crowd is that night. You can usually feel it and judge for yourself if you should go out or not. It's like a lion in a cage, and they tell you to walk in. You know better, and you take your chances."

In 1961 a girlfriend of his, Juanita Jones, shot and wounded Jackie when he returned to his apartment with another woman, Harlean Harris, an ex-girlfriend of Sam Cooke. Jackie was shot twice—one bullet resulted in the loss of a kidney, the other lodged too close to his spine to be operated on. No charges were ever brought against Juanita. Jackie told me a totally different story. He was Mr. Excitement, and he created hysteria onstage and off. The front page story said Jackie Wilson was shot by a frenzied fan. This was Jackie's version to me: "It was true, but it never happened the way people thought it did. I never took the time out to explain it to people. Actually, the gun was pointed in her direction, at her temple, her head. I was frightened to death for her; I grabbed it, and the gun went off, and I got it." He told me that kept him out of the business for about five months, and he added, "I stayed in the hospital about three of those months."

Jackie, Otis, and I had a lot of laughs together, and he confirmed that he wanted to continue singing, but he caught both of us off guard when he said, "I also want to act. I've always wanted to be a screen actor. I'm going to give it a try Jim." He told me he read for a play: "It's supposed to premier the first of next year off Broadway. I haven't gotten an answer yet, so maybe I'll start there and go into the screen business."

That dream of being a Hollywood actor never became a reality. Our conversation took place in May of 1974, and a tragedy would silence him in 1975.

In September of 1975, while Jackie was singing at the Latin Casino in Cherry Hill, New Jersey, he suffered a massive heart attack. Ironically, he collapsed while singing a line from his hit "Lonely Teardrops," the part where he sang, "My heart is crying." He was left comatose, and he never uttered another word. He died eight years later at the age of forty-nine. I remember feeling sick while reading a story about him being beaten while he was in the hospital. Somebody hated him so much they broke a chair over him.

His was a well-publicized funeral attended by more than fifteen hundred people, but there was one final indignity for Jackie. He was buried in an unmarked grave in his hometown of Detroit. In death he was a pauper. However, month's later, fans in Detroit raised money and bought a mausoleum and reinterred him and his mother.

The Forum Apartments

The two best things I did when I got to town was move into the Forum and visit the Inner Circle. The Forum was just one big party with a lot of interesting people. One of my favorites was Red Ryder. I told him I saw his car in Clifton. He was drinking and forgot where he left it. A few days later, I noticed its hubcaps were missing; a couple of days later, the wheels were off. This was actually a pretty nice car that was almost totally stripped by the time he finally picked it up. One of the girls living in the Forum got married, and a group of us went to the wedding. That's how the Forum was at that time; everybody hung out together. At the reception, in one of the apartments, Red Ryder and I were enjoying a little marijuana and intensely listening to a Jimi Hendrix record, making comments about musical parts we were just discovering. We were interrupted when one of the girls changed the turntable speed back to 33 rpm from 45. Red and I both agreed it sounded pretty good at 45 rpm.

How hard did people party in those buildings? It was a typical Saturday night, August 9, 1969. I was enjoying myself going from party to party, occasionally returning to my place to get another bottle. A couple of times I got crank calls telling me my National Guard unit had been activated. I got to bed around 3:30 a.m. when I received another call to report to the National Guard Armory on Reading Road. I humored the guy and told him I was on my way. The commanding officer of the Army National Guard called at 8:00 a.m. to inform me that I had been transferred; I was to report for duty immediately. A tornado had touched down at 7:15 p.m. in Reading and Madeira and Governor James Rhodes had activated our unit to assist in the damage clean up and to maintain order. The total count for the tornado: 4 deaths; about 250 injured, and 42 of them admitted to hospitals. The damage was estimated at fifteen million dollars. I was one of the seven hundred Ohio National Guardsmen activated to assist in the cleanup and maintain order. Our unit was withdrawn by Tuesday. I was in my Clifton apartment building partying, and we were totally oblivious to the tragedy that struck up the street. Although it appears I got off to a bad start on my new military assignment, I had a good stay with the unit. My six years were just about up, and whenever we had overnights, I made sure I brought a movie or two from our sister station WLWT to watch. In my six-year military career, this was the first time it was beneficial that I was on the radio.

Two of my favorite people at the Forum were Andy Luther and Dr. Marty Fritzhand. Andy worked at the hospital, and Marty was an emergency room doctor. They had a weekly card game in their apartment every Monday that went on for hours. I never played, but I'd stop by to watch a hand. A number of Bengals' players sat at that table, including Ernie Wright, Bob Kelly, Andy Rice, and Jess Phillips. One regular who watched every game was their pet boa constrictor, Julius Squeezer, who lived in a giant aquarium in the kitchen. All hell broke loose when he was missing for three or four months. Everyone thought he had passed away until Marty found him wrapped around the refrigerator coils.

The Forum was one big party, and it was the perfect place to be for my lifestyle. I had an easy, high-profile, fun job, and I was making pretty good money. There were a lot of people who tried to keep up with us and either lost their jobs or flunked out of school.

I did experience a relapse and fell back into being the introverted guy I once was before radio. A friend of mine had a plane and invited me to go on a vacation to Cozumel, Mexico. It was a scuba diving club, and I thought, this will be one outrageous party. However, divers are like skiers; they are there for a purpose, and I couldn't find any single girls that weren't attached. I wasn't interested in diving. I once again retreated to my own quiet world. I rented a motor scooter and drove up and down the island every day exploring back roads chasing Iguanas. I went to a couple of town dances, but if I wanted to dance with a girl I had to ask her mother or grandmother for permission. That wasn't going to happen. Two beautiful girls were staying in the room next door to me, but every time I saw them, they were with a guy. I finally talked to them, but it was the day they were leaving to go back to England. They were models on a shoot, and the guy was their photographer, and like me, they had nothing to do. That's what I get for being shy.

I was enjoying my newfound persona as the Prof, but I knew my shortcomings, and I was working on them. I've had a weight problem for years. I always need to lose fifteen to twenty pounds. I'm built like a pear. I was getting my mail at the apartment when a lady I wanted to date gave me a nice compliment. She noticed I lost weight and asked me how I did it. I told her in great detail how I was exercising, cutting way back on my drinking, and now dedicating myself to a healthier lifestyle. She knew my reputation for drinking and partying, and she didn't approve. She was so happy for me. I was just about to ask her out when the Velcro on my weight belt came loose, and the huge belt that was holding in my stomach came loose, slipped out of my shirt, and hit the floor. I didn't say anything; she just shook her head and walked away. We never did go out.

A lot of athletes lived in the Forum, and one of my favorites was Tommy Helms, the Reds' second baseman. He was acting strange at lunch. He had a letter in his hand that he wouldn't look at because it was postmarked "Atlanta." The Reds were getting ready to play the Braves, and he thought Felix Millan, their second baseman who was from Puerto Rico, was trying to put a hex on him. The letter wasn't signed. It was just some symbol on a piece of paper that Tommy really didn't see. He told me that during the game Felix would make a hex in the dirt where he played at second, but Tommy wouldn't look at it. He just kicked dirt to cover it.

Norm Van Lier and the Royals

Norm Van Lier played for the Royals basketball team and was one of the first guys I hung out with. We were both from Pittsburgh and lived in the same building. We were with two nurses in his apartment, and the door was open so anybody could come in. Norm had some marijuana, and we just sat around for a couple of hours relaxing. The next day, a girl I knew confronted me because she heard the girls talking in the hospital cafeteria about getting high with us the night before. I explained we weren't making out, just talking. She said, "What if WLW found out you were smoking dope?" This wasn't a Top 40 rock station. I took my bag of stash and threw it down the incinerator, and that was the last time I smoked.

A sight I'll never forget was watching Van Lier playing catch with a baseball on the basketball court next to the pool. Wayne Simpson was a Reds pitcher who lived in our building and was lights out for the first half of the season. Here's Norm winding up, throwing the ball, pretending to be Wayne saying, "I'm Wayne Simpson." Over the years, I've wondered how many kids on basketball courts shouted "I'm Stormin' Norman" as they stole a pass and hustled to score like the NBA all-star.

Norm was a friend and a great guy everybody liked. Well, almost everybody. One night while he was with a group of our friends in a nearby Clifton bar, a couple of jerks called him the "n" word and started a fight. After they found out his name, they apologized as if that made a difference.

Tommy Van Arsdale was the Royals' captain and his twin brother, Dick, played for the NBA Suns. I was riding in my Corvette with the top down on I-75 when a car pulled up alongside of me, and guys yelled, "LaBarbara, take this!" I looked at the car, and I almost wrecked because I was laughing so hard. I don't think many people can say they were mooned by NBA all-star twin brothers.

* * *

I got some unsolicited press, and I did ruffle some feathers when I had Peter, Paul, and Mary on my show. I didn't know it, but Stan Matlock, the number one radio man in the city, had been knocking them and refused to play their records. The newspaper mentioned they were on my show, and I think everyone was surprised by the letters to the editor: "LaBarbara believes in all people, Martin Luther King and civil rights." I got an overwhelming positive response. I believed in Martin Luther King's message and civil rights. At one time, I wanted to be an inner city church minister. King's message was, "Just give us the opportunity to succeed." Somehow the Jesse Jackson's of the world have turned that into entitlement programs and the "I don't have to work mentality." Jesse may have marched alongside Martin, but he sure as hell never heard what he was preaching.

Morganna

Bud Hobgood was one of my first Cincinnati friends. He was the big, tall, white guy who worked as James Brown's executive producer and right-hand man. He wrote a number of songs with James.

Bud was with me when I visited Morganna at a Newport club to set up an interview for my show. Morganna was a stripper who was later billed as "the Kissing Bandit" or "the Wild One." She would go to the ballpark wearing a bulky jacket to somewhat conceal her identity. When it was time to get her target, off came the jacket, and she'd run onto to the field wearing a t-shirt and gym shorts and plant a harmless kiss on a baseball player's lips. Of course, the crowd would go crazy. She got Johnny Bench and Pete Rose. It all started when another girl bet her she wouldn't do it, and she often joked later that her career started on a bet, and Pete's ended with a bet. She was a voluptuous young lady whose measurements started off at 44-23-37 and later went to an unbelievable 60-24-39. At the club, Morganna invited me backstage. Here's the picture: Bud and I are in this room with five or six naked ladies. Morganna is showing me her signature move, practicing her squats, and then while putting a little makeup on her huge breasts, she was asking my opinion: "Jimmy, how do these look?" Most guys would have done anything to be in my shoes, but I have to say it wasn't sexual. Bud agreed with me—it smelled like a gym, and the ladies, although very pretty, just weren't sensual in that setting. On stage it was a little different story. The next day, she stopped by the station to record an interview. She responded to the first question by saying, "Jesus Christ Jim, I . . ." I stopped her and explained we couldn't say "Jesus Christ" on the air. She apologized. I asked the question again, and she said, "Christ, Jim I . . ." I stopped her again and explained we couldn't say "Christ" on the air either. The third time was a charm, and we nailed the interview.

Bud and I were laughing one day, having a good time, and the next day he wasn't around any of the hangouts. Bud Hobgood died of a cerebral hemorrhage. He was only thirty-four years old, and I found out about it after the funeral. James Brown took his death the hardest.

James Brown's advice on love

Pete called me. "James Brown is coming to the Inner Circle tonight and would like you to join him at his table." This was the first of many times Mr. Brown and I would get together and share stories until well past closing time. James had his entourage gathered at a couple of tables, and he always had a beautiful female protégé sitting by his side. We talked about music, what he was doing, and my radio show. James had a great view of life and shared his philosophy. I told him all about my ex-girlfriend in Cleveland. He gave me his thoughts on love. It was about three in the morning. James Brown had me convinced I shouldn't wait—I should get in my car and go. James said, "Jimmy, just tell her you love her." Susan and I had talked recently and were making plans to get together. I didn't call her, it was late, and by the time I'd get to Cleveland, I would catch her walking into work at Wyse Advertising. It was about a four-hour drive to Cleveland in my Corvette so I had plenty of time to think about what I was going to say. I was so confident on the radio, but off the air, I never learned how to let go and show my feelings because of my fear of getting hurt. That wasn't going to happen this time. I dated several Cincinnati ladies, and I violated rule number one in dating: after a few dates or drinks, I'd tell them my Susan story. One lady told me to go back to Susan: "You're in love with her, but don't call me again." I thought about how dumb I'd been. I was going to ask her to marry me and move to Cincinnati. I got to Wyse Advertising just as people were entering the building for work. One of our mutual friends was surprised to see me: "What are you doing in Cleveland?" I waited and waited, but no Susan. Finally, one of our friends said, "Susan wants to talk with you. Call this number." I called, and she told me she was with some guy and couldn't see me. This wasn't the surprise I had in mind. I didn't know what to do. I felt so many emotions. I wanted to throw up; I wanted to kick his ass; I wanted to—I don't know. I reminded her of our recent conversation about getting back together. She said she was serious about this guy. I just wanted to see her, then I would know for sure, but that wasn't going to happen. I got in my car completely devastated and made the long ride back to Cincinnati. Months later her best friend told me she fell apart and that she loved me and wanted to fly to Cincinnati that day. It never happened, and she eventually married and divorced the man. I saw her three years later, and we both had strong feelings for each other. We've talked a few times over the years. At our WIXY reunion weekends in Cleveland, her name would always come up. Jane Scott, the *Plain Dealer* reporter, remembered her and was surprised I didn't marry her.

In another example of what a small world it is, in the mideighties, Nancy, one of the girls who told me to go back to Susan, called me at the station to say hello and tell me she moved back to town. She was divorced from a sports anchor on a Denver television station. Susan had married and divorced a television news anchor who worked in Denver. I described Susan to her. It turned out they were friends and that both their husbands worked at the same station. I said, "That's the Susan I told you about." Nancy said, "Talk about a coincidence!"

Rock 'n' roll has always been about the guy getting a girl, and I didn't. It wasn't easy to forget about Susan. I had girlfriends, but nothing like this. I could still smell her months after she was gone on my old clothes and in my car. I would see her smile or hear her laugh. I'd wonder what Susan would think about this and then answer the question. She told me her nephew would cry when he saw the Pillsbury Doughboy getting his stomach poked. I remembered every little thing about her, but I have been selective in that I've remembered the good times and not the bad.

To forget Susan, I started to run and, at times, I was disgusted by my behavior, almost always the result of too much alcohol. No I can't explain this paradox of a nice, clean-cut guy who was changing and, occasionally, I didn't recognize him. I was once a lay preacher, and my first paying job in radio was at a religious station. I read the station identification, "This is WAVL Apollo, Pennsylvania," and ran religious shows Sunday mornings. At 6:00 a.m., I had to fill the first fifteen minutes with religious music, and that's when I practiced being a disc jockey: "Here's America's *princess of song*, Connie Francis, or I'd give a little Elvis bio and play one of his religious songs, 'How Great Thou Art.'" The station owner called me one morning and said, "It's okay to have a little dead air between songs, people need to think."

Jimmy, I'm entering the convent

I worked on that religious station between my freshman and sophomore college years. That was the summer I met a very special lady. Patty lived on the opposite side of Pittsburgh, or two street cars away. I met her at the West View Park Ballroom and suddenly my life started to change. I got the call to work the radio job in Apollo, and I made the decision to go back to Allegheny for my sophomore year. She told me she was going to her uncle's for a vacation somewhere in Connecticut. The night before she left, I borrowed my Uncle Sam's car, and we had a wonderful dinner date. On the way home, we talked about her coming to visit me for the big homecoming dance. I asked her, "Patty, tell me again, where are you going to visit your uncle?" She said, "Jimmy, I'm entering the convent." I drove the car off the road and stopped. I'll never forget Brenda Lee was singing "I Want to Be Wanted" on the radio. Patty said she made the commitment long before she met me. I know she had feelings for me, and I was really falling for her. We sat on her couch all night talking. Her dad came home real late but didn't see us. She told me she was holding a rosary in her purse when I first asked her to dance. I kidded her from time to time about becoming more worldly. I was clueless. I asked her for something to remember her by, and she said her favorite saint was Saint Teresa, "the Little Flower." I got a letter from her documenting her trip to the convent in Hamden, Connecticut. She wrote that she was thinking about me at a certain time and wondered if maybe I picked up on it. Yes, I was awake at that exact time because I was thinking of her and couldn't sleep. I went back to college, but she was in my thoughts. One day I couldn't do anything. I was a wreck. I called a Catholic church and talked to a nun. I told her I wanted to talk with Patty, but she advised me against it and gave me all the reasons. She was very comforting and before she hung up, she said, "Today is a special saint's day. Today, we honor Saint Teresa 'the Little Flower.'" I started to cry, and I told her the story. I made a promise to myself, that if I made it through the next three years and graduated I would see her. I know she was praying for me, looking after me. My dad had a friend who knew the family, and the day I graduated, I mentioned her to my dad. He told me she was home a couple of weeks earlier because of a death in the family, but he didn't want to bother me during finals. No, I never saw her again, but I've thought about her often over the years.

Harry Carlson

I had my dream job because I loved being on the radio, but I was also WLW's music director, and that put me back in contact with the record promoters, who in turn got me interviews. One of my favorite people lived in room 105 at the Sheraton Gibson Hotel. It was the office and home of Harry Carlson, the owner of Fraternity Records. He'd call and say, "Jim, Louise [his wife] and I would like you to join us. I want you to hear this record. It's an absolute monster hit." Harry was a very charming man, always attired in a pinstriped suit and a starched white shirt with cuff links. I'd join him for a drink and listen to his fascinating stories. He had a number of hits on Fraternity.

One of his biggest hits, "The All American Boy," was credited to a singer who didn't record it and had a tough time lip syncing it on the *Bandstand* shows. The record label credited Billy Parsons, but Harry told me after Billy was on the road for about six weeks, he started to hear rumors, and then he heard from the real singer, Bobby Bare, who was a close friend of Parsons. Harry said, "The reason they did this, Bobby was going into the service, and Billy was coming out. They were afraid if the record didn't have promotion it wouldn't go anywhere. So they decided Bill Parsons would be on the record label as the artist." Harry got the record from Orville Lundsford. He wanted them to make an acetate—a record—from his tape, because they had just recorded it at King Records, and they wouldn't do it. Harry told me that he went out of his mind when he heard the tape and offered to release it on Fraternity and asked, "How much do you want for it?" He said five hundred dollars. Orville said he was the coauthor.

"Bring in the artist Billy Parsons tomorrow, and we'll sign a contract."

Orville did, and that original investment of five hundred dollars turned out to be a million-seller. Harry later made a number of records with Bobby Bare.

Lonnie Mack got his first guitar when he was six, a Lone Ranger model, and he first plugged in a guitar when he was thirteen. His record "Memphis" became a million-seller for Fraternity. Lonnie told me Carl Edmonson heard him play it at the Twilight Inn in Hamilton. The vocalist who normally sang the song wasn't there, and they made it an instrumental. Carl got him into the studio and produced it. Lonnie said, "It was sort of a freaky thing. I was on the road with another band when the thing hit, and I didn't know anything about it. They told me, 'You've got a hit record,' and I said, 'That's nice.'" His follow-up record was another hit, and Lonnie told me that Harry's wife, Louise, came up with the title "Wham." I was the emcee at a New Year's Eve party, and Lonnie was on stage lost in his guitar, playing right through midnight. The promoter was yelling at me to get out and count down to the New Year. I waited—you don't interrupt a legend. John Lennon once called him the greatest guitarist he ever heard.

At that same party was another former Fraternity Record artist, Carl Dobkins, Jr. He only had one record on the label, and it was his first. The song was one he wrote, "Take Hold of My Hand." Carl told me. "I was a sixteen-year-old scared kid in a studio in Nashville. I was very impressed—the Jordanaires [Elvis's backup group] were on the session." That record didn't make the charts, but a year later, on Decca, he had a Top 3 hit, a million seller with "My Heart is An Open Book." I asked him about the song. He said, "I wasn't really sold on the song. I thought, well, it's OK, but luckily other professionals had an ear for the song." The day after he graduated from Mt. Healthy High School, he made one of his fourteen appearances on a Dick Clark television show. The "Teenage Rage," as he was called, later had another Top 25 hit with "Lucky Devil." Speaking of lucky, Carl added, "When I look back, gee I was really lucky, one in a million, a kid who got to do these things and make these accomplishments at an early age."

In 1967 Harry had a giant hit with the Casinos' "Then You Can Tell Me Goodbye." Gene Hughes, the group's lead singer, told me, "They had cut seven records, and nothing happened." Gene said he heard the song by Johnny Nash on the car radio on the way to Nashville, and he told the guys, "If that's not a hit by him, we'll cut it, and it'll be a hit."

"We started doing it in the clubs. We did it for a whole year before we recorded it."

I was honored when Gene asked me to write the liner notes for an album he had recorded titled *Yesterday, Today and Tomorrow* that included a terrific version of the Five Keys' song "The Wisdom of a Fool."

In the 1970s, Harry Carlson fell on some hard times, and Gene asked me to be involved with a tribute concert and dinner to honor Harry. Gene was grateful to him and got a lot of Harry's former artists and friends to attend. We were all moved to tears at the dinner when Bobby Bare spoke. He told a story about his own father passing away when he was young, and how Harry became the father he didn't have. Everybody loved Harry Carlson.

Neil Armstrong

Everyone from the era remembers where they were when Neil Armstrong stepped on the moon on July 20, 1969—the Apollo 11 moon landing. I was in and out of an ongoing two-day party hosted by twins, two lovely ladies who lived in Clifton. Their television wasn't the greatest, but nobody seemed to mind. It wasn't too many years later that I was standing next to Neil in our WLW VIP baseball box. We were singing the national anthem, and I looked at him and the sky above wondering what he knows that we may never know. It was a special moment for me.

I've been to a number of social gatherings where Neil Armstrong was a guest, and he visited my video store several times. I couldn't help myself at one get-together. No, I didn't ask him for an autograph. There were about a dozen of us gathered in Indian Hill for a

Fourth of July party. I've always enjoyed talking with him, and this time I asked if his watch was an Omega. He laughed and said no, but he knew where I was going with the question. He added, "If I told you the minimal tests we put that watch through . . ." The astronauts needed a watch, and apparently they sent one of the guys to a Houston store. He picked an off-the-shelf chronograph that was in stock. They had enough of this model for all the astronauts. He bought it, and they tested it. Omega has done a terrific job of promoting this watch. They market it as, "the Omega Speedmaster Moonwatch," selected by NASA for all the Apollo missions. I thought Omega would supply him with watches for life. I'm a watch collector and a big fan of the Omega Speedmaster. I've owned three Speedmasters, and I still have two. However, Neil Armstrong left his Speedmaster inside the lunar module *Eagle* during his famous first walk. Buzz Aldrin did wear his on the moon.

Big Joe McNay

Big Joe McNay was a guardian angel I didn't know I had looking over me until one night I slipped out the back door of a Kentucky after-hours club. It was early in the morning, and I was hung over when I answered the phone: "Jimmy, what did you do last night? . . . Don't do that, you could get hurt." It was my new friend Big Joe McNay. I explained that I was hitting the Newport clubs, and when they closed, I found an after-hours joint. There was a jazz organist playing in a dimly lit room with a lot of working girls with older guys. I was enjoying my first drink when I spotted a couple of our company's corporate management with some ladies. Although I didn't work with them, it would be an awkward situation so I slipped out the back door. Big Joe explained that he had guys watching me when I crossed the river. I did stand out with my long hair and beard. I wondered why I was never hassled, even when I got with the strippers. Big Joe was bigger than life, a professional gambler and bookie who made some collections, but I didn't know exactly what he did until years later. His lady was a bunny mother at the Playboy Club, and that's where I met him. He was friends with everyone from Bench and Pete to the big politicians. He lived in a modest-looking house in Taylor Mill, Kentucky, but the inside of his house was fabulous. He told me he couldn't show what he had. "You know, Prof." I think he introduced me to half the people in town, everybody seemed to like him. I do know Big Joe had a dry cleaning business in Northern Kentucky, but he didn't have any dry cleaning equipment. People brought him clothes, and he'd take them to a real dry cleaner. I understand, according to his son Don, that he made his money in the backroom where there was a lot of action with card games and sport betting. This was before the lottery and casinos outside of Vegas. A lot of people knew what was going on, but nobody bothered Big Joe. He was a generous man who liked to pick up the check. He gave me a fancy watch and said, "Professor, you should wear this when you go out someplace nice."

Vegas, Elvis, and Terry Q.

I was invited to see Elvis open in Las Vegas, and Big Joe got me a good price at the Dunes. I planned on spending a week, but I was gambling and drinking and within twenty-four hours, I lost two thousand dollars, a lot of money at that time. I had tickets to see Elvis at the International, but since I was just about broke, I decided to go home. I was getting ready to check out when I got a call from Los Angeles: "Prof, this is Squirrel's roommate, Terry Quatkemeyer. I'll be in Vegas tonight." I explained to him that I was short of cash, but he told me not to worry. I had only met Terry a few times at the Inner Circle. He was a character, a college student who paid people to write his papers and take his tests. He pledged a fraternity and tried to pay somebody to go through Hell Week for him. He always had a fancy car, good-looking ladies, and a wad of cash that he wasn't afraid to spend on a round of drinks. Terry was with a friend, a young guy who just got back from Vietnam. They were in Los Angeles on business and decided to visit me. Terry met a husband-wife act in his motel that opened for comedian Joey Bishop, and in turn, they invited us to see the show and to the after party. There were only about fifteen people at the party. A group of Joey's Philadelphia celebrity friends told some jokes, and I met the man with the sunglasses, Mr. Ed Sullivan, who was three sheets to the wind. The guys said he was always drinking, and when he introduced the Supremes for the umpteenth time on his number one–rated Sunday night television show—he called them "The Girls." He really had forgotten their names. Dave Clark Five's lead singer, Mike Smith, laughed when he told me, "We did eighteen Ed Sullivan Shows and he always said, 'Thank you very much boys that's a great performance and we'll see you soon.' That was the only thing he ever said to us." Joey Bishop was very gracious and agreed to be on my WLW radio show. I asked him if he was still close to his old gang, the Rat Pack: Frank Sinatra, Dean Martin, and Sammy Davis, Jr. He said, "Do you have buddies you were close with who got married, but their wives aren't close to the other ladies? People just drift apart." I later learned what he was talking about. It was a get together I've never forgotten. We saw several shows: Dean Martin, John Davidson, and others. Terry offered to chauffeur Davidson around in his Rolls Royce the next time he was in town.

The place was electrifying. Elvis was the talk of Vegas. In the lobby, Colonel Tom Parker was hawking programs. We were escorted to a front table and about to be seated when Terry's friend handed him a tip. Before you could say "Elvis," we were shoved to the back of the room. I asked, "How much did you give him?" The guy said ten dollars. Terry and I had a good laugh and enjoyed the show. It turned out to be a terrific vacation for me. Terry was picking up the check everywhere. I offered to pay Terry when we got back to town, but he said it was taken care of. Terry had an auto repair shop in the Clifton area and sold some exotic cars. He insisted on giving me a free paint job for my Stingray. It would take a week, and he gave me an old clunker to drive as a courtesy vehicle. I picked up Johnny Bench at the airport, and he couldn't believe I was driving this "junk." We saw Terry at the Inner Circle, and John chewed him out. It was pretty funny, but the next day, Terry had a new car for me. It was a year-old, blue Lincoln Continental Mark 3. A couple of days later, I was driving down Westwood Northern Boulevard, and I discovered I had no brakes. I bumped into the curb to slow the car as I made it down the hill. I phoned Terry, and he said, "Oh, now I remember why we had that car in." I eventually got my car back and a nice bill for my "free" paint job. It looked sharp. I didn't mind paying him because he was such a likeable guy. He'd call: "Professor, what are you doing? I'll pick you up in an hour?" He'd wear his chauffeur's hat, open the back door of his Rolls for me, and we'd be off. I'd put the window down and wave to people. He sure knew how to have a good time, and I traveled like a rock star.

One day Terry disappeared; he was gone. Some people said he owed them money. He reappeared in Beverly Hills with an exotic car shop, became best friends with television's Grizzly Adams, changed his name to Terry Quinn, and bought a big house in Bel Air, California. I was watching *Dorothy Stratten: The Untold Story* on video; she was the Playmate of the Year in 1980 who was murdered by her estranged husband. At the press conference when she was introduced as the Playmate of the Year, Terry was standing next to Hugh Hefner. I hadn't heard from Terry in years when I got a call saying he wanted to meet me at Jim and Jack's Bar. I was greeted by the Vietnam vet who was with him in Vegas. We reminisced about the good time we had. I mentioned that I couldn't believe how Terry kept picking up the checks. He corrected me: "That was my money he used." I had no idea he used this guy's Vietnam checks to party. I asked if I could pay him, but he said no. Terry had never paid him, but he continued to do Terry favors and was sure that someday he would repay him and make it right. Terry showed up and was full of great stories. He married one of Dean Martin's dancers, the lovely Patty from Cincinnati, but they got divorced. I asked him a few tough questions, but he gave me what sounded like good answers. That was the last time I saw Terry, but he would later be front-page news in Cincinnati.

In the 1990s, George Fiorini had the Ten Percent Incentive Plus Plan. It turned out to be a huge investment scandal that robbed lots of mostly elderly investors of their life savings. One of the key players in the scheme, accused of taking over nine million dollars, was the same Terry Quatkemeyer, a.k.a. Terry Quinn.

Commercial endorsements

I've done hundreds of commercial endorsements throughout the years on radio and television. For instance, I would say, "I'm Jim LaBarbara for Joseph Chevrolet," and then I tell you why I've bought cars from Joseph, which I have. I always checked out a product or service before I did an endorsement. I had been offered a lot of money to endorse the Ten Percent Incentive Plus Plan. I never did; it just sounded too good. Troy Deborg and Tim Donovan have taken care of my investments for years, and I'm happy with their work. The late Bob Braun did a lot of Fiorini commercials, and sadly, when Bob's name comes up in print, the writer seems to always attach it to the scandal. I'm sure Bob didn't have any idea it was a scam. Bob Braun gave so much back to the community. It really bothers me that his image is tainted with this, something he had no control over.

I was approached to do commercials for a product called Body Solutions. I tried it for a week and lost weight, so I agreed to endorse it. I lost thirty-five pounds in a month. All I did was drink a table-spoon three hours before I went to bed, and I'd lose weight. The key was, after the tablespoon, you couldn't eat or drink anything until the next morning. I changed my eating habits, and it worked for me. I became one of the company's biggest spokesperson, and I met with the owner a couple of times at his headquarters in San Antonio. He loved the creative way I did their commercials. Weight loss products are easy to attack. One big complaint came from a guy, who accord-ing to sales records, didn't buy the product until after he filed the complaint. He had also attacked other companies the same way. It was bogus, but no one bothered to check the guy. Tom Brokaw on the nightly news did a report and lumped it in with a group using fen-phen—which it didn't have. Our sister station at WGRR was WLWT. One of their reporters called me to do a story on Body Solutions. I politely turned it down several times because I saw the story. It was a set story they would run in various cities; they'd edit to get the story they wanted, and believe me, it wasn't positive. They called our program director, Tim Closson, and he insisted I do the story. I tried to explain, but he wouldn't listen. I did the story and it was edited to make me look really bad. It attacked my credibility. I was asked if I was compensated for doing the commercial, and I said absolutely. I explained that I got paid for every endorsement I did, but I wouldn't do it if I didn't believe in the product. When the story ran, which they did a number of times, the interviewer acted surprised and said, "And Jim LaBarbara gets compensated for this." Mike McConnell mentioned on his WLW radio talk show, "Duh, that's what we do—we get paid for doing commercials." He explained it very well. The reporter also posted it on their website, where it got plenty of attention. It's easy under an alias to attack someone and make up stories. After the fact, I went to our general manager, Jim Bryant, and told him how I was forced to do the interview. He was furious and told me to see him if I questioned something. He was on my side. I watch that channel a lot, but if I see that reporter, I have to switch.

The internet is wonderful, but I hate it that people hide behind fictitious names and slander anyone. When I was on WGRR, the station was getting beaten up on a radio board. Rockin' Ron, our midday guy said, "Look at this!" It was incredible—one guy had five different aliases, and he used his real name. The thread attacking us was the same guy writing and answering everyone. He was a former disgruntled coworker, and when he came backstage at one of our shows, I lit into him. He denied it and instead threw another friend under the bus. I said, "But you used your own name." This was a man I had gone to bat for and asked our general manager to promote three times to program director. Yes, I was hurt more because I really liked the guy and considered him a friend. I've shed my thin skin because I've seen this on all the boards. I don't like it, but I guess it's here to stay. I'd like to have a system where you can find out a poster's real name.

On KFI Radio Los Angeles

I planned a vacation in Los Angeles so I could catch a Reds' game at
Dodger Stadium and visit with my Cleveland friend Jay Lawrence,
who did the afternoon show on KFI, the Dodger station. I was a guest
on his show, and afterward, we had a drink at Martoni's, a restaurant
frequented by showbiz people off Sunset Boulevard. Jay had just
beaten the great Gary Owens in the ratings, but this was his last show.
They rewarded Jay by firing him and replacing him with the former
Today television host Dave Garroway. I felt terrible, but he wanted to
celebrate because he just received a bigger offer to work across the
street at KLAC. That station changed formats, and Jay became a giant
country personality. He took me to the Dodger dugout to meet his
friend Don Sutton, and I introduced him to Bench and Sparky. On
the way to the press box, we stopped in a VIP booth and met the legendary director John Huston of *The Maltese Falcon* and *Key Largo*. Mr.
Huston was with Francis Dale, part owner of the Reds and publisher
of the *Enquirer*, and he recognized me. I caught up with Bench after
the game for a dinner with Tommy Lasorda, a few Dodger players,
and a pretty blonde named Dee. It was a good day in the life of this
deejay.

Rude fans and the Reds' basketball team

Hanging out with Johnny Bench I got to see how nice fans could be—
and how cruel. At a Royals' basketball game, I had the aisle seat, and
John was sitting next to me. He didn't sign autographs while the team
was playing, but during time outs and intermission, he was accommo-
dating. There was a guy who made a few comments about my beard
and long hair, but John was quick to say I was his friend, and the guy
backed off. One man wanted to talk with John. I leaned back in my
chair, as this guy kept sticking his finger at John's chest telling him,
"You lost that game, you know you did." John didn't say anything,
but I pushed the goof away. This was a scene I would see repeated a
number of times over the years. I was used to a few people approach-

ing me, but if we double-dated for dinner, it would take forever because people would hound him for autographs, even while he was eating. In a group, we'd try to sit John where he wouldn't be pestered, but that never worked.

In the off season, the Reds' basketball team would play charity games. The guys said, "Prof, you're the coach. Sit on the bench with us." In the dressing room, before a game with a group of teachers from a middle school in a small town in Indiana, Pete Rose asked me to check out the players and the crowd. The place was packed, but no way did the school have six foot seven to six foot eight teachers who could dunk. Somebody said that a couple of the guys had played on the ABA Indiana pro team. When I came back with my report, Bobby Tolan and a couple of the guys laughed, but they didn't laugh when they hit the floor. These games were always a lot of fun. However, there was always one guy who wanted to push Bench or Rose around and make a name for himself. The Reds were always very gracious. Pete was a great hustler, but not a good shooter. Johnny played some basketball and was pretty good. However, against these giants they didn't stand a chance. We let them run up the score for a few minutes before we put our ringer in, and then suddenly it became a close game. The Reds' ringer was Dick Vories; he could put it in from anywhere on the court, and we kept feeding him the ball. When Dick graduated from Georgetown College, he was the highest scoring player in the history of Kentucky colleges—an NAIA and a UPI All-American basketball star.

The beard stays

The *Enquirer* ran the story as "Hairy Case." Rich King, our afternoon guy, and I discussed my new beard on his show. It was eleven days old, and King made a bit out of it when he heard that one of our company's vice presidents told me to "think about cutting it off." I told Rich, "I'm going to keep it." Rich embellished the story and made it sound like a major event. He compared my beard to Lincoln's and other famous people. WLW was very conservative in 1969, and everybody was clean shaven, but I had a full beard in Cleveland. During my fifteen-year career at WLW, no one ever brought up the subject of shaving the beard again. Since that time, I've only been clean shaven once. My daughter, Shelby, was about four years old, and she cried when she saw me, and my wife, Sally, laughed so much I thought she was going to cry. Sally apologized because I had surprised her.

A bad boy behind the wheel

My public persona was taking shape, and I was pleased with it. I was a bachelor who partied with pretty ladies and athletes. I had entertainers on my show solidifying the Music Professor image. However, I was a bad boy, hanging out in the wrong places, and Steve Hoffman, in the *Enquirer*, told everybody. The story was under the heading, "Good-Will Time." It read, "WLW radio personality Jim LaBarbara rammed his 1969 Corvette into the rear of WKRC radio program director, John Patton's car on Vine Street early Thanksgiving morning. LaBarbara was cited by a Cincinnati policeman for following another car too closely. Besides the $350 damage to his fiberglass body, he was fined $20 and costs in court. Patton insisted on paying Jim's fine although he was the innocent victim. LaBarbara's car had eight thousand miles on it at the time." I can still picture it. I hit his car and ended up on the sidewalk in front of Frankie's Bar. My car was surrounded by scantily clad working ladies. There were a lot of flags that went up that no one noticed. John and I were friends, but we worked for competing stations. I must have been drinking, and what was I doing in this seedy area in the early morning hours? Surprisingly, no one from the station ever said a word to me about this embarrassing incident.

I have to admit my early driving history wasn't very good. I had an accident one of the first times I got behind the wheel. It was a beautiful, new two-tone Chevy that was the school's student driver car. I needed to learn how to drive so I could go on a date alone. I needed to be more worldly. Mr. McFadden, "the Shark," was our vice principal and our drivers' education instructor. He was a very calm, mild mannered guy, but I saw another side of him. A couple of pretty class-mates were sitting in the back when it was my turn to drive. We were near the football field right next to our principal's flower garden that he liked to talk about on the school's PA system. It was protected by a nice, white wooden fence. I must have been distracted because I hit reverse, broke through the white fence, and ended up in the middle of the flower garden. I floored it to get out, and I tore up the garden spinning my wheels. The Shark started screaming at me, using a vocabulary those girls in the back seat shouldn't have been subjected to. He chased me out of the car and around what was left of the flower garden shouting that I was never to come back. The car wasn't badly damaged, but the fence and the flower garden—that's another story. I never returned to drivers' education, but I passed my drivers exam before the end of the semester and got a B.

Jim Gallant

Jim Gallant was one of the best and most beloved program directors I ever worked with, and I was thankful he brought me to WLW and grateful that he gave me the moniker, the Music Professor. Sadly, by the first of the year, Jim would be gone. During the Christmas holidays, he was late for a meeting with our general manager, Charlie Murdock, who called him out for being tardy. Jim, who was normally very quiet, was upset and said something to the effect that Charlie was always late for meetings. Charlie snapped back and fired him on the spot. The whole staff was very upset because Gallant was such a good program director and an even better person. Jim was a good friend. I had just spent Thanksgiving with his family and I was furious, but as a new guy at the station, was in no position to make a scene. Charlie Murdock didn't make many mistakes, but this was a big one.

In my opinion, Gallant was unjustly fired, and I wanted to work myself into a position where I could stand up and say, "This is bull." I did this on occasion, but then you have to be ready for the consequences, because you will have a target on your back. At that time, there were a number of radio companies, not just the three or four that dominate the business today. I was young and single, and I had a number of job offers. When I got married and had children and house payments, I stifled my thoughts. I've really enjoyed working with most of my bosses, but this experience changed me, and I started to share my opinions at meetings, and I didn't always agree with the program director. I always knew who I was talking with when I opened the microphone. I knew my audience. At one station, the program director had life-size cutouts of a man and a woman in the studio and told us to talk to them. I went along with his game but thought it was funny. A WLW program director always had a little sermon for us to start his meetings. He described in great detail a car he saw traveling on I-75. The whole family was packed into the car with all their possessions, and there was a mattress on top. He asked each of us if we were relating to those people. Of course everyone sucked up to him, saying yes, I'm doing this or that.

"What about you LaBarbara?"

I said, "Hell no. First of all, the car probably doesn't have a radio [there was a time when a radio was an option]; he doesn't have any money to spend with our advertisers; and he was traveling south, moving out of our area." He became perturbed and got red as a beet. I explained that was not the person I was thinking about when I was on the air, but he could probably relate to most of the things I was talking about. It was one of the only times I ever sounded off in front of the other jocks.

Some of our group: Me, Herbie Goodman, Johnny Bench, Dr. Luis Gonzalez, Jeff Ruby sharing some laughs.

CHAPTER 11

My Good Friend Johnny Bench

Johnny Bench and I had a great friendship, and we eventually added people to our group. December 7 is Johnny's birthday, and we decided to throw a party. The ladies outnumbered the guys five to one. Although all the girls thought they were John's date, it was still a good party. Jim Stadtmiller, the "Squirrel," a guy I met at the Inner Circle, insisted on being involved. John was protective of who we would hang with, but after that day, Squirrel proved to be a good friend. The next to join our group was an older guy who golfed with John's dad, Ted. Charlie Shank was a lot older than us, and we called him "Cadillac Charlie" because he worked at General Motors and always drove a Cadillac.

Greg Tabor, a local golf pro, came around a lot, and although I broke a hundred and actually got into the eighties a few times, I had to be at my best around them. Our foursome included Bengals' linebacker Bill Bergy. It was a nice relaxing round of golf until I coughed. It wasn't a put-on cough, it was a natural cough, but it happened while John was about to hit his tee shot. Man, did he chew me out. I came right back: "That little ball is sitting on a tee—it's not going anywhere. You have a three-two count, there are sixty thousand fans screaming at you to hit the ball, and a guy is throwing it ninety miles per hour at you, you don't stop and tell them to be quiet, you're concentrating. All I did was cough." The guys all broke up; John's response was, "You jive turkey."

Jeff Ruby

The next addition to our close group was a former football player from Cornell who managed the Holiday Inn where Sparky Anderson and the coaches stayed. Jeff Ruby told Johnny and me anytime we needed a room or food that he'd take care of it. We later found out that he had a small expense account and paid for stuff out of his own pocket. Jeff liked to punch me on the shoulder, and I'd have to get cortisone shots for the pain. I finally asked him to stop punching me. He was hurt because it was his way of showing me he liked me. I asked Jeff to not like me so much. Jeff was a great asset to the Holiday Inns, and he turned their clubs into the places to be seen. Jeff went on to own some of the premier restaurants in the Midwest and to live the lifestyle of a big time celebrity.

Herbie and a lot of laughs

One of our close friends, Herbie Goodman, represented a women's clothing line and had an office in the Playboy building. He later became John's right-hand man. We often called him "the Prince" because of his generosity. On a number of occasions at the stadium, I saw him give a kid an autographed Reds' ball and say it was from John. The kid's eyes would light up like it was Christmas morning. He had a dry sense of humor. He'd walk up to a complete stranger on the street and start up a conversation: "Isn't your name . . . ?" And the guy would say his name.

"You're from Price Hill."

"No, I'm from Milford."

"Oh, that's right. Our kids went to school at . . ."

By the time he was done, they were best friends reconnecting. He was one funny man who had a heart of gold. He left us at such a young age.

One thing we always did was laugh. If we were having dinner at Johnny's Home Plate Restaurant, I might mention how John wasn't just an all-star catcher but that he was brilliant at trivia. The ladies would be all ears.

"The leaning Tower of Pisa, where is it?"

"Pisa Italy."

"What district?"

"Tuscany."

"What year was it built?"

"1173."

"All those are correct answers."

Then I would hit him with the tough one.

"Who is the night watchman at the leaning Tower of Pisa?"

John would think for a minute and say, "Giovanni Genovese." I'd ask him to repeat it.

"That's incredible! One more question: Who is the backup watchman? He works weekends and holidays?"

John would think about it and make comments about it not being a fair question and then answer, "Bernardo Pasquali." I'd act shocked. The girls would ask, "Professor, is that right?" And I'd tell them, "Yes." We had more fun playing that kind of dumb trivia where no one knew the answer, and we'd just make everything up, or almost everything. Sometimes I'd be the trivia expert, other times Cadillac Charlie or Squirrel. We'd laugh so much we'd be in tears.

We never partied at John's Forum apartment, but when he moved into his Mount Adams condominium, that all changed. Sometimes when the guys would see one another, we wouldn't say hi. We'd say "boogie" or a word phrase I invented, "Yucum Yucum."

John had one of the first VCRs, and on a few occasions after a Reds' game, a group of us would check out WLWT for sports. I'd be busy getting drinks for the ladies, John would make popcorn, and somebody would put a porn tape in the VCR. It would play for a few minutes, and we would ignore it. I don't ever remember a girl complaining. They would just sit there stunned. I'd see it playing, and yell, "John, check this out! I've got to call the station. One of the engineers must be watching this, and he threw the wrong switch. It's going over the air." I'd make a call and start reprimanding the guy. One of our guys would switch the button, and WLWT news would come back on. I've often wondered how many girls told their friends about the porno movie that played on television and asked if they saw it.

Johnny had a syndicated television talk show called *MVP* that he started in 1971 with Avco. He was kind enough to tell me he wanted me to be the announcer, but the company wanted Reds' announcer Al Michaels because they would have to shoot some shows when the team was on the road. John did ask me to do his booking and to help him make a record. He said, "I'll give you 10 to 15 percent. Somebody's going to get it." I explained I couldn't take his money. I was busy enough with my own show, but I did take a couple days off to visit Nashville. I hit the publishing houses, and I gave John a couple of songs Troy Seals wrote, but he never made a record. He did sing on a lot of shows, including his own. How would I describe him as a singer? He was very enthusiastic.

Paul Brown

WLW radio carried the Bengals, and with that came a lot of perks for me. During the season, every Friday and Monday, I'd talk with a Bengals' player, and I was given access to the field and players. The Bengals' owner Paul Brown knew of me from Cleveland, so we had an instant connection, and his son Pete and I became friends. The Browns gave me carte blanche. One of the most exciting games I ever saw was on November 15, 1970, when Paul Brown beat his old Browns for the first time. I was standing near the Bengals' bench at Riverfront and, to the man, you could tell they wanted a win for P. B. Standing on the sidelines during a game sounds good, but you really don't see much of the game, but you do see and hear the players up close. On this day, it was the perfect place to be. The Bengals won fourteen to ten, and sixty thousand fans went crazy. I watched Paul Brown as that clock was winding down. I wondered what was going through his mind as he just beat the team that he created and bore his name and what sweet revenge he must have felt to beat Art Modell, the man who fired him. Afterwards, I joined the team at a celebration party.

I thought he was somebody else

Often in radio what happens behind the scenes is more entertaining. I thought the president of Avco Broadcasting must have liked me because he often called me on the hotline while I was on the air. One night right after hearing some complimentary remarks, I went into the newsroom we shared with WLWT television. Gene Randall, one of the television news anchors was laughing. Gene could do a perfect John T. Murphy imitation, and I had been had. The night of a championship fight between Muhammad Ali and George Frazier I kept my audience informed by giving a round-by-round recap off the wire service. I got a phone call from John T. Murphy, our president, correcting me, and I played along for a minute, but then I told him he was crazy because I was looking at the story and to stop bugging me, I was on the air. I slammed the phone down. I looked in the newsroom and told Randall he didn't fool me. He acted like he didn't know what I was talking about. Early the next morning, our general manager, Charlie Murdock called, "Jim, get to the station immediately." Yes, it really was John T. Murphy, and he wasn't too happy with me. I was about to get fired, but I explained everything to Charlie, and he told Murphy. I'm sure Gene heard about it, but he wasn't upset with me. A few days later, he was showing two beautiful ladies in shorts the station and stopped in the studio but whisked them in and out before I could talk. Who were the ladies? One was his wife and the other, her sister, was a Playboy bunny from Boston who had just moved to town. Gene played matchmaker and got the two of us together for a date. The Murphy incident didn't affect our friendship.

I was heard on NBC television every Saturday afternoon right before the baseball game of the week. I was the voice for the Little Sport baseball game that helped kids hit a ball. Buzz Guckenberg hired me to do the spot for the Ohio Art Company, and it aired for years during the seventies.

Play "Misty" for me

I was feeling pretty good about my radio show, and I was flattered that I had a secret admirer who put ads in the papers to get my attention. In October of 1971, the Cincinnati papers carried a little three-inch ad that was addressed to me. It read: "To Jim LaBarbara WLW, please play "Misty" for me. I love you, Evelyn." The ad had a knife going thru a piece of paper. At the bottom there was a "P.S. Meet me at the Times Town Cinema Friday, October 22." This ad ran for three weeks, and I looked through my mail, but I couldn't find anything from Evelyn. The day arrived, and I finally got to see her. She was on the screen in the movie, *Play Misty for Me*, directed by and starring Clint Eastwood. The movie started slowly, but we soon discovered she was a psycho. Eastwood was a disc jockey targeted by an obsessed fan, Evelyn, who would call and request "Misty." He did meet her in a bar, and they went back to his place, and although he told her he was involved with someone, she didn't care, and they made love. Evelyn then started attacking people with a butcher knife and made his life miserable. Did I identify with the movie? Well, besides being a disc jockey, I once had a cool British sports car, except mine was a Jaguar. He had an Austin Healey. Once in Cleveland, I woke up from a nap and saw a girl I was dating standing over me with a pair of scissors. She was upset because she found another girl's phone number in my wallet. She didn't threaten me with the scissors, but I certainly got the message. I had gone out with a girl a few times when I worked in DuBois, and while I was stretched out on the sofa with my head on her lap watching television, she was smiling, stroking my clean shaven face. I felt a sting, and when I touched my cheek, I saw blood all over my hand. She had used her sharp finger nails to cut up my face. She started crying and told me she loved me as I tossed her out of my apartment. She was truly crazy. I never saw her again, but if I look closely at my face, I can see a scar.

Celebrity Night and Sally

I hosted a celebrity table at The Top of The Inn in the downtown Holiday Inn every time they had a new act. Erik Kamfjored, president of the Holiday Inn, hired me to promote it and gave me a free tab for my guests. I always packed the place with Reds, Bengals, and entertainers who were in town. Colonel Klink from *Hogan's Heroes* stopped by one night. The Bengals' backup quarterback, Sam Wyche, worked for the Inn, and I'd call on him to do a magic trick. He was a pretty good amateur magician. In the spring of 1971, my friend Squirrel had a very attractive date, Sally Suttle, a former TWA airline hostess, who was now working for a child psychiatrist in Dayton. I couldn't take my eyes off her. I told her if she lived in Cincinnati, she'd have more dates. What a dumb thing to say. I called Squirrel later that night for her phone number but was told she's not the kind of girl you can call at three thirty in the morning. I never got her number, but I would see her again a couple of weeks later. One of the Reds' television announcers had a party at his Mount Adams apartment after a Sunday game. Johnny Bench said, "I see my date. She just came in." I stopped him, "Wait a second, John. That's the girl I've been telling you about." I was with a cute redhead, and I said, "John you take my date. I'm going after her."

"Sally, remember me?" I talked to her for a minute, and she excused herself, went to the ladies room, and quickly left the party. I went back to my date, but John took me aside. He said, "Have you forgotten she's my date now?" Needless to say, that was the last date I had with that little redhead.

Rod McKuen

A few weeks later, I was asked to be the co-host with Bob Braun for the world premier of the movie *Scandalous John*, and I needed a date. *Scandalous John* was written by Bill Walsh who grew up in Cincinnati and was a well-known Hollywood writer and producer. He produced *Mary Poppins* and developed *The Mickey Mouse Club* and helped create the famous ears each performer wore. Rod McKuen wrote the sound-track for the movie, and he asked me to be the co-host. I first met McKuen several months earlier. I was a huge fan of his and read parts of his poetry as record intros when I did a night show on WLW. I read these during the time when I was thinking about my ex-girlfriend in Cleveland, and I interpreted his work with a lot of passion because I could relate to it. He liked what I did on the radio, and although he was somewhat of a recluse, he gave me his first interview in years. His manager called me a few weeks later and asked me to join Rod for breakfast at the airport. He was having a business breakfast with Irma Lazarus, a local philanthropist, and would feel more comfortable if I was there. We didn't talk much, but he later sent me the entire record collection of his work. Rod McKuen was a poet laureate of his genera-tion responsible for the revitalization of popular poetry in the sixties and early seventies. His poetry books have sold more than sixty-five million copies and songs he has written have accounted for the sales of over one hundred million records.

Sally and her mom

I think Sally's mom talked her into going out with me. I wore a tux, but Sally convinced me not to wear my red, white, and blue tennis shoes in honor of McKuen. We had a light dinner with Bob and Wray Jean Braun before the parade and movie. There was a party with the movie stars afterward, and I was a perfect date. I didn't have the best reputation with the ladies, but I think Sally saw that I was a pretty good guy.

Cash Amburgy, the owner of Cash's Bargain Barn in South Leba-non, had his annual party, and on my way to pick up Sally at her par-ents' home in Dayton for our second date, I got a speeding ticket. A state patrolman stopped me in my yellow Stingray and asked for identification. I never carried a wallet because it caused a bulge in my pants, and he kept pushing me to show some form of identification. I did have an autographed picture. He said, "You make my job very difficult." I followed him to a police station in Miamisburg. The local police were big fans, but I was ticketed by the state police. I always carried lots of cash in my twenty-dollar gold coin money clip, but this time I had less than twenty-five dollars. I called Sally and asked her to bring me money so I could pay the fine. Yes, the first time I met my future mother-in-law, she was bailing me out of jail. I said, "At least the Reds won." They were up by five or six runs, but they lost. My boss was very upset with me because Cash was a big client, and I never called. It was late, so we went to her parents' home. When I was introduced to her sister, Susie, I did a double take. She was a bartender in a Clifton bar that I had a crush on but never talked to because she was still in college. What a small world, and it was about to get smaller.

Sally grew up in Western Hills and rented an attic apartment from her friend Donna. One day she tried to reach Sally, but her mom wasn't allowed to tell her Sally was with me. Donna Perkins, now married to Henry Peters, and I had one date a couple of years earlier. We had double dated, and when I took her drink order in the bar, she asked for a 7 UP. It cost as much as a beer. I half jokingly said, "I'll buy you a beer or a mixed drink, but not a 7 UP." I forgot. I never did buy her a drink, and our date ended very early because her girlfriend had a bad headache. She told Sally that I was, essentially, a selfish idiot. Today whenever we are with her, I make sure Donna has a 7 UP.

Sally and I had been dating for several months when Mary Wood did a feature interview in the *Cincinnati Post*. The November 1971 article had the heading: "There's a 'Lady' in Bachelor Jim's Life." Sally later told me she was excited to see the story and then disappointed. Mary wrote, "The 'lady' in Jim's life is his beautiful Afghan dog named 'Lady,' whom he acquired a year and a half ago. 'Lady' has unusual tastes in food. So far she's eaten two studio couches and an expensive pair of draperies." In retrospect, I should never have gotten a dog. I was a bachelor living in an apartment with a big dog. I let a former girlfriend talk me into buying her, and I eventually gave Lady back to the people who sold her to me. The first day she stayed with me, I did a whole show talking about her. I mentioned that I had a beautiful young lady with long blonde hair moving in with me. I was nervous because I wasn't used to sharing, and now I was going to have a lady living with me. I went on and on before our station manager called to tell me my personal life shouldn't be discussed. It wasn't appropriate. He was upset and hung up before I could explain. During my last half hour, I finally mentioned that my lady was an eight-week-old Afghan dog named Lady.

Bengal friends

I was in an enviable position working on the Bengals' station, WLW, and having a friendship with the Brown family. Pete Brown and the team's strength coach, Kim Wood, got the Nautilus machine franchise and wanted to work me out on the new equipment. I lost more than thirty pounds in a month working out with the Bengals a few days a week. They showed that Nautilus could work just as well for a chubby deejay as it did for a pro athlete. Kim Wood and Pete later created the popular Hammer machines for training. Kim was new in town, and I invited him to meet some ladies at the Inner Circle. I didn't think he was dressed appropriately, so I gave him a suit. It was a small gesture I had forgotten, but he remembered and told several people.

A number of Bengals lived in my apartment building: Doug Dressler, a running back lived across the hall; Kenny Anderson moved in next door; Jesse Phillips was downstairs; and Mike Reid, the all-pro tackle, lived a couple of doors down the hall.

Mike Reid

Mike Reid and I became especially good friends because of our mutual love of music, and he was a frequent guest on my show. He was classically trained, but he loved pop music, and we would spend hours talking about music. A mutual friend recorded a song, but before I played it for Mike, I gave it a big build up: "You have to listen to this." There was a narration in the middle of the record. It was one of the worst records ever, but I played it straight. Mike was very respectful and made some positive comment about the orchestra. I finally broke up laughing. He thought I was serious and didn't want to hurt my feelings. His apartment faced the front of the building, and after a Bengals' game you could watch him unwind in his robe, playing the piano until the wee hours of the morning. He never had anything good in his refrigerator, maybe an apple or an orange, so he was often at my door asking, "What do you have?" as he checked out my refrigerator. He liked to borrow Crazy Jane, a steak seasoning. The strangest request was after an away-game in Washington when he needed to borrow my undershorts because someone had stolen his. I let him keep the shorts, but can you imagine what kind of guy would steal a 255-pound tackle's underpants? We went to a couple of Indy 500s and would catch some of the local races. Our friend Greg Cook, the Bengals' quarterback, invited us to join him for a gourmet dinner he prepared. Here was Greg talking about his paintings and Mike discussing music—not exactly the kind of conversation you'd expect from professional football stars. Greg told me his dad wanted him to play baseball, but he didn't listen. Greg had a 90 mph fastball in high school, and after suffering a career-ending football injury, he was thinking that maybe he should have taken his dad's advice. Bill Walsh, the Pro Football Hall of Famer and one-time Bengals coach, was misty eyed when he said if he hadn't gotten hurt, Greg Cook may have been the greatest quarterback ever.

Mike recorded a song he wrote called "A Song for Peace," and I played the heck out of it on my show. I think it could have been a hit, but Mike wouldn't take my advice. I suggested a cover sleeve with a picture of him in uniform on one side and playing the piano on the other; he didn't want to mix the two. I called my friend, the vice president of Epic Records, Steve Popovich, but Columbia Epic Records had lost a lot of money on Detroit Tiger Denny McLain's album, and there was no way they were about to invest in another athlete. I kidded Steve for years about that mistake. Mike had a great Pro Bowl career but retired because of a bad knee after the '74 season. Members of the Brown family asked me to try to talk Mike out of retirement on several occasions, but he had already made his decision. He started playing and singing the Holiday Inn lounge circuit. I thought it would be easier to go out one Sunday a week and bang heads with a 275-pound lineman than to listen to some drunk yell out, "Play more Elton John!" He paid his dues, and it paid off when he got a Grammy in 1984 for "Stranger in My House," the song he wrote for Ronnie Milsap. He took Sally and me out to dinner after his first couple of hits, and he picked up the check. Mike was very frugal and laughed when he said, "Just don't tell Bob Trumpy" [a former teammate] I bought you dinner."

After a Bengals' home game, most of the Bengals relaxed at Jerry and Greg Scarlotta's Italian Inn downtown. Of course, the place was packed with beautiful ladies. They were two of my closest friends, and I'd watch *Monday Night Football* at their home in Western Hills. I'd eat pizza, drink beer, and enjoy the company of Bengals players. Two of the regulars were Tim Kearney and Lyle Blackwood. It was always interesting to hear their take on the game. I did a number of television commercials at the time, and I always took the heat if one of my spots ran: "Look! I can see your eyes following the prompter," or "Where did you get that outfit?"

I enjoyed the Bengals' press box privileges and especially the free beer and food. I took my high school friend Anthony Crivelli to a Steelers' game, and he introduced me to the Steelers' owner Art Rooney, the old man himself. Art walked around with a big cigar and said he preferred being with "his boys," the writers, rather than sitting in the owner's box. The most unassuming successful man you could ever meet.

Art Rooney may have been the nicest man ever in that press box, but I was about to meet the most obnoxious, loud-mouthed, egomaniac who ever stepped into that room. During the Monday night football game of the week, I was introduced to the most famous sports announcer in the world. At halftime, the Bengals' spotter, business-man Mike Leonard, introduced us. Mike said, "Howard Cosell, this is Jimmy LaBarbara, the best disc jockey in the country." Howard looked at me and said, "If that were true, he'd be in New York." Mike tried to explain, "He's turned down New York; he loves Cincinnati," but Howard walked away. Somebody had punched Howard the week before, and I could understand why. To some people, everything revolved around New York. However, he was true to his character—pompous and arrogant. Don Meredith, the Cowboy great and How-ard's partner on ABC football, was partying with us a couple of years later, and he just shook his head when I told him the story. Appar-ently, he could be very difficult to work with.

Chicken skier award

During the New Year's break in 1973, Ed Podolak, Kansas City run-ning back, invited Bench and I to stay at his condominiums in Aspen. When Ed was in college, his family wisely invested in Aspen land. I bought Podolak a Polish joke book, and while I was laughing, he turned it over and said, "Yes, it's really funny." I didn't notice it had two sides, one Polish and one Italian. We met with a group of Ben-gals—Bruce Coslet, Chip Myers, and Lyle Blackwood. I never skied before, so I rented a pair of mini skis and spent a couple of hours on the beginners' slope with the players' wives and children. I was an ath-lete. I told Podolak I was ready to go to the top of "Buttermilk." The ride up was amazing, but I fell when I got off my seat, and they had to stop the ride. Ed said to follow him and cautioned me not to go down the other slope because it was a drop off. I was right behind him, but I made a wrong turn, and to stop, I reached out to grab a tree. In the process, my skis hit the tree, and I went flying. I was lying on the ground when the ski patrol stopped to help me. I asked him about the covered sled going down the hill, and they explained it was a skier with a broken leg. It then occurred to me that I could seriously injure myself. Step by step, I made it to the next rest area where there was a bar and some of my friends enjoying a beverage before they continued down the slope. I had a number of drinks over the next several hours before I decided to venture back down the slope in a ski chair. I held my leg as if I were injured as I passed skiers on their way up. I caught up with everybody in the chalet at the bottom of Buttermilk, where I thought that maybe no one noticed I took the lift down. Chip Myers got everyone's attention and presented me with the "Chicken Skier Award." I thanked everyone for the award, and they all got a good laugh at my expense. I haven't been on skis since. We took the train back to Denver, and it took forever because of all the snow covering the tracks, but it gave me chance to talk with some of the biggest names in pro football.

I'd golf from time to time with Bengals' Pat Matson, Bill Bergy, and Al Beauchamp. They could crunch the ball, but unfortunately, they putted the same way.

Pat Matson

Pat Matson opened a fitness club downtown, and I was going through one of my healthy stages, working out three days a week. His pretty wife worked the front desk, but she was busy on the phone and didn't see me come in with a huge box of donuts. I started passing them out on the floor, and everyone was eating them. I made it down to the sauna, and those guys took a few before Matson caught up to me. He was really angry that I was passing out this unhealthy food to his clients. He started calling me "Satan." I couldn't help it—I was laughing like crazy. Pat ran a great club, and a couple of years later, he opened the finest fitness club in town in Blue Ash. It was payback time. He sent me an invitation to opening night and even called to make sure I'd be there. I had just finished my first drink when John Stoffa, a former Bengal, asked me to play racquetball. I told him I wasn't interested in playing, but for the next forty minutes, he was badgering me. He said, "I know you have your racquet in the car." I play, but I'm not very good, and I told him that. We warmed up on the court; he kept saying, "Are you ready?" And by this time, he was whipping me. He finally got his wife, who happened to be a fine athlete, to finish the game. When I got back to the bar, Pat Matson was in tears. He had Stoffa convinced that I was a champion racquetball player, but that I didn't want to play him and embarrass him, and I had my equipment in the car, but he'd have to really convince me to play.

What was I thinking?

We all make mistakes, but what was I thinking? In July of 1971, Khan Hamon, a former Drake-format, more-music-less-talk, program director became my new boss at WLW. He wanted me to play two records back to back out of the afternoon news breaks. I pointed out that on the radio clock that was impossible; it was network news at the top of the hour, two to three minutes of local news, a record, and then the ten-after break with commercials, traffic, and weather. He didn't know anything about the station. We weren't a music-intense Drake station; we were a full service radio station, and I had top numbers. He once said to me, "You shouldn't tell jokes; you're not funny." I explained that I just used throw-away one-liners—I talked about what was going on in Cincinnati, artist news, and pop culture. I asked if our number one morning man Jim O'Neill, who did a humor-based show, was funny. Khan said, "No, he's not funny." I asked him, "Who's funny?" He said George Carlin. George Carlin was an old friend who once told me he couldn't make it work on radio, and he turned to stand up. I knew I couldn't please this guy.

I didn't always check my mailbox, and I'd let things accumulate. Harry Martin once told me in Cleveland as he was tossing a stack of memos into a wastebasket, "F—— the memos. If it's important, they'll call you or tell you in person." I cleaned out my mailbox and threw everything into my briefcase. Later that evening, after hitting the clubs and tossing down a few drinks, I decided to clean out my briefcase. I opened an envelope that contained an official memo approving our new night man Dan Clayton's contract. He was making a couple of dollars more than me, and I was number one in afternoon drive three to seven. I started on the early-evening show on WLW, but in less than a year, I moved to afternoon drive when Rich King left for

San Diego. Rich did a humor-based show, and he was brilliant, but my style appealed to a more diversified audience. I increased the ratings and was a solid number one in the ratings survey after survey. I freaked out and called our general manager, Charlie Murdock, at home. It was late, his young daughter had been sick, and he was in no mood to talk. However, that didn't stop me, I continued to tell him what I thought in not too polite language. I should have talked to Charlie the next day when I was sober, but I didn't. I was always getting job offers from other markets, and a few days later, I got a call from Joe Finan, my WIXY friend. He offered me the morning show at KTLK, his Denver station. I flew in that weekend, we worked out a contract, and I gave WLW my two-week notice. In researching the Denver morning shows, no one was doing put-on phone calls. I called Steve Kirk in Dayton and Dick Purtan in Detroit, both masters of those phone calls. Steve and I met for dinner several times, and Purtan sent me ideas.

Dan Clayton was going to take over afternoon drive when I left. He tried to talk me into staying at WLW. I told him about the memo and his salary. He said, "That's right, but that money isn't for doing a night show. I'm going to be the program director because they are firing Khan." No, I never found out who put that confidential memo in my mail box. I should have stayed, but I had already given my word to Denver. It was Christmas week; I was working on a great station in a city I loved, I was falling in love with a beautiful girl, and I had the best friends. I was a total idiot for leaving, but I was stubborn.

The Neil Diamond song "I Am . . . I Said" kept playing over and over in my mind. I already missed Cincinnati, and I was still here. "I keep thinking about making my way back." While I was in Denver, I told Neil how I really identified with that song when I went from Cincinnati to Denver. He had moved from New York to Los Angeles and said he lived it, "Yeah, it's a lot of people's story. A lot of people kind of caught in between things, a lot of people's story."

CHAPTER 12

Denver
What am I Doing Here?

I packed my Corvette, and I was off to Denver. It was a long drive, and I was dead tired when I got to the counter at the Regency Hotel. "I'm Jim LaBarbara with KTLK radio, and I have a reservation." The clerk looked at me and said, "Their credit is no good here." I made him double check because I was sure there was a mistake. It was now after 6:00 a.m., and I didn't have my new boss, Joe Finan's, home phone number. I called the station, and the guy said, "I can't just give you his home phone number. Who are you?" I explained that I was the new morning man and that I was starting on Monday. It was Friday, and the guy was surprised because he was the morning man, and no one told him he was being replaced. I was embarrassed. I went down the street and checked into a cheaper motel. Finan chewed me out for calling the morning man. What a way to start a new job. I should have gone back to Cincinnati that day.

An old friend from Cincinnati, the former Bengals end, Eric Crabtree, lived in Denver and showed me the city. He had a very attractive lady surprise me by saying, "Eric says welcome to Denver." Maybe Denver wasn't going to be so bad after all.

KHOW was the number one adult station in town. KIMN was the big Top 40 outlet, and KTLK, with its lousy signal and little promotional budget, was trying to make some noise. Jim LaBarbara, the Music Professor was a household name in Cincinnati, and I walked away from WLW and all the fringe benefits for this. I must have been delusional to think I could turn this station around. No one was picking up my check in bars. I quickly discovered I wouldn't get free tickets to the Broncos' football games or concerts. I tried to be friends with Bobby Anderson and a few Broncos, but we didn't carry the games, so that connection wasn't there.

Once again, I had to create a new on-air identity. I was anxious to do morning drive. Traditionally, it's the most important shift, and the talent is the highest paid, but it's also the most difficult to get a new audience, because people are set in their ways. I did a prerecorded put-on phone call every day, and I did a celebrity or artist interview. I shared my musical knowledge and continued to use my moniker, the Music Professor.

The radio station had a public service work program set up with Canon City Prison, a federal prison known as the "Alcatraz of the Rockies." KTLK was a Top 40 teen-oriented station with cute high school cheerleaders answering the request lines and tough prisoners working or lurking nearby. I have to say when I was on remotes with these guys, nobody bothered me. I heard the police sirens—they were outside the station. They had us surrounded. One of the guys was on the station's front lawn, showing some kids how to fast draw with a real gun. That was the end of our work program with prisoners.

Moonlighting

I got a nice surprise when the hottest nightclub in town called me to work one night a week. John Lanigan had been the morning man at KHOW, and he was going to Cleveland, and although we never met, he gave me all his appearances. Marvelous Marv's booked great entertainment that I introduced once a week, and of course, they did my radio show—John Denver, George Carlin, Bill Withers, Lily Tomlin, and others. Oftentimes, I'd go out with the performers for coffee or breakfast after the show.

Bill Withers had giant hits like "Ain't No Sunshine" and "Lean on Me." He invited me to go panning for gold like the old gold prospectors, but we couldn't work it out with our schedules. We were backstage talking about his recent success and old friends. He was very grounded and said, "You need the old friends you have, to remind you who you are because careers in music are very short careers." He asked me several times to come to his Friday show because he wanted me to meet someone. I found out why in his dressing room when he introduced me to his girlfriend, "Jim, this is Denise." He was all smiles; his lady and soon-to-be wife was the beautiful Denise Nicholas from the hit television show *Room 222*.

John Denver

John Denver was thrilled to appear at Red Rocks outside of Denver for the first time, and he invited me to the show and after party. It was a night of wine, cheese, and great music. Some people have referred to the Red Rocks Amphitheater as the most spectacular place in the world to see a concert. I was glad that John and his wife, Annie, included me in the celebration.

He loved Denver so much that he adopted it as his surname. When he first started performing, the people he was with said his real name, John Deutschendorf, wouldn't work on a record label or in lights. They threw a bunch of names at him that he didn't care for, and he wasn't sure he wanted to change his name until they came up with "Denver." He told me, "I've always liked the mountains. I've always liked Colorado. And all the connotations of Denver are really nice for me, so I became John Denver. I guess I feel pretty much like John Denver." He laughed.

John told me he was introduced to rock 'n' roll when he was home sick with the chicken pox or mumps, and they were playing Elvis's "Heartbreak Hotel" all over the radio. He met him backstage at the Elvis Madison Square Garden Concert Presley recorded in the summer of '72. John said, "Freaked me out, he's almost bigger than life. I had 'good vibes.' I felt comfortable with him. He doesn't take himself seriously at all. He has so much fun with his show; that was the thing that impressed me the most. I think anybody who has a thing that they do, and they're having a good time, it's impossible for you not to have a good time."

I knew John before he had hit records and later when he was a superstar. Over the years, he remained a very down to earth, unaffected guy who still got excited and appreciative over little things. Sometimes when he stopped by the station, we would just talk about life and meditation without any tape recorder. I still have one of the books he encouraged me to buy, *Yoga, Youth, and Reincarnation* by Jess Stearn.

The shticks

I got pretty good at doing the put-on phone calls. They took a lot of work, and I had my own engineer to edit them. I sometimes used the name Bob Moore. I had to get permission after the call from the caller to use it on the air. Some of them were a little scary. Once, I called a locksmith, and he agreed to meet me at my house and crawl in through a basement window to help me quietly open a safe. Without asking for proof that I lived there, he agreed to meet me at an open basement window. Another call was to a place that sold garage doors. This person agreed to help me get my own opener because I said I didn't want my car sitting outside my married girlfriend's house. All I needed to do was bring the opener in, and they would make a copy for me so that I could enter the garage when her husband left. Other calls found me as Superman's Clark Kent, Batman, and the leader of the Colorado National Guard. I once said I was sending three hundred men to a one-man barbershop to get military haircuts. These were goof-offs with long hair. The barber knew nothing about it and was to charge them only a dollar. He was going crazy on the phone. I also played the head of the "Help a Hippie Have a Happy Home Organization." We called people to tell them we were sending a hippie to live with them for a week. All they had to do was give them shelter and food for a week. Every day, I had a different bit. The station was talking to me about releasing a "best of phone calls" on an album.

The ladies

Two of my closest friends were Pittsburgh guys who were bartenders in my favorite hangout. One had a master's degree, and the other was a lawyer with no clients. They were typical of the people I met, young people from other cities just hanging out for a few years. Some people moved there just to ski. I never skied while in Denver, but I pretended. On Sunday afternoons, my friends and I would go about fifty miles out of town to Georgetown. There were a number of bars in that little city that were always packed with skiers coming down from the slopes heading home. I met a number of listeners there. I got a huge ego boost when a lady every guy was hitting on wanted to go out with me. She was a gorgeous Eurasian who was a number one fan of mine. We dated, but I was afraid to get too involved because I wasn't ready for a steady girlfriend, and she was definitely a keeper.

One attractive lady hit on me in a bar, but I had to get up early for my show, and I had to leave. She suddenly started yelling at me saying I didn't want to be with her because she was a Chicano, a Mexican American. I told my engineer I thought one of the teenage girls who helped out at the station was really cute. He looked at me like I was crazy and said, "She's a Chicano." In 1972 there was this atmosphere of prejudice in Denver, and I didn't know the difference.

I was on the radio, and I think that card helped me get a date with a Denver Playboy bunny who had just been featured in *Playboy Magazine*. This was the most excited I had been about going out since I got to town, but I had a root canal that afternoon, and I was full of medication. She said, "Let's make it another day," but I insisted we go out. I got lost, was late picking her up, and the rest of the evening went downhill from there. I could barely talk because of the meds. It was another life lesson learned. It was our first and last date.

My Denver dentist called to give me a heads up: "There will be a beautiful lady in the waiting room today. You may know her, but don't talk to her. She's living here with her boyfriend, Sam Giancana, and the guy sitting next to her is one of Sam's bodyguards. He's not the friendliest guy." Sam was the Italian-American mobster and boss of the Chicago outfit until 1966. He died a violent death in 1975 at the hands of someone he was friendly with. At that time, he was keeping a very low profile somewhere in the area. Frank Sinatra introduced him to the beautiful singer Phyllis McGuire, and she was his lady. The singing McGuire Sisters were from Middletown, Ohio. I played her records often over the years, and I saw her recently in Las Vegas. I wanted to talk with her, but as I sat in the waiting room, just looking at the burly guy with the sunglasses sitting next to her convinced me to remember the words of my dentist. I didn't say anything, and I tried not to look at her.

Interviews and contacts

Sport magazine was the big sports magazine before *Sports Illustrated*, and as a kid, I'd dream about seeing my name in it. George Vecsey did a cover story on Johnny Bench for the October 1972 edition, and he looked me up in Denver to get a friend's view of Johnny. I was glad to tell him about a side of John not many knew. I said, "People said John had changed after his MVP season; he didn't. He'd join me on the radio, but he wanted to talk about music and not himself. He was against drugs; when someone offered him marijuana at a party, we made a quick exit. He had to keep his hair short because he was in the army reserve, and yes, we double-dated often. He was very respectful to girls. He didn't date much as a kid because he had to work, and in the minor league, he didn't have enough money. John was very careful, but loyal to his friends." The *Sport* magazine interview was an exception; I usually turned down requests because of our friendship.

David Kidder, the head of the Kidder Organization, liked my show and especially my knowledge of oldies; he made me an offer to do a nationally syndicated radio show. Casey Kasem was just getting off the ground with his *American Top-Forty*, and Dave thought a syndicated oldies show would have a market. We did twenty-two, three-hour shows packed with my interviews and artist information. One of the ads he ran in *Billboard Magazine* read, "It took thousands of people almost twenty years to bring you the Music Professor." We recorded it in real time on tape, so if I made a mistake, we went back to the break. It would be so much easier to do it in today's digital era. There was no internet and not many books on artists, but I did a lot of interviews and collected artist information. Instead of a straight salary for doing the shows, I took a percentage of the revenues. I made just a few dollars for all my work. However, I was smart enough to put into my contract that if I would leave Denver, the company would fly me back to record the shows. I think we got into sixty markets, but it was too costly to keep flying me into Denver when I went back to Cincinnati.

KTLK was the number two rock station in Denver fighting against the heritage rocker, KIMN, but without a good signal or promotion, I knew it would be a rough ride. Our general manager hired John Rook as consultant. I was very familiar with Rook from KQV in Pittsburgh and his success at WLS in Chicago. My first meeting with him was interesting. He was consulting WCFL in Chicago, and he gave me an air check of their morning man Art Roberts and one of Larry Lujack. I was told by our general manager that Rook didn't like my name; he wanted to change it to a radio name, and he wasn't thrilled about the money I was being paid. The next day, Rook asked me what I thought of Roberts's morning show. I've always given my opinion when asked and sometimes when I'm not. I was brutally honest. "Art Roberts was a good night jock when he was on WLS, but he isn't a morning man—he doesn't say anything relatable; he has no personality; and he read those fifteen-second public service announcements that are national, not even Chicago." I added, "I'm a big fan of Larry Lujack, but on this tape, you've successfully taken away his personality." Needless to say, I insulted one of the top radio consultants in the country, and he wasn't happy. He ended our conversation by telling me that Art was going to be a top morning man in Chicago and that I was wrong. I wasn't.

I am broadcasting from our WLW studio at 140 West Ninth Street in the Comex Build-ing, a part of Crosley Square. Our hit records can be seen behind me and above those are taped cartridges that we used for station jingles and commercials.

CHAPTER 13

Back to WLW and Cincinnati

I went on vacation to Cincinnati and never went back to KTLK. I had a job offer from the number one rocker in St. Louis, KXOK. King Kirby, my Cleveland friend, was the program director, and he wanted to give me a lot of money to do morning drive. At the same time, WXYZ in Detroit talked to me about afternoon drive. I called my friend Claude Hall, the editor of *Billboard Magazine*. He thought I sounded better in Denver than he had ever heard me. WXYZ was a country station owned by ABC. Claude said, "It's a great station, but there's a stigma in country, and once you're in it, it may be tough to go to another format." It was a different era in country radio.

I didn't know it, but WLW had just completed a survey: What changes would you like to see to make us better? They were bombarded with phone calls and letters to bring me back. It's funny, when I left Cleveland to work at WLW, it was a clean break. However, when I went to Denver, I still got calls from Bench, my friends, and several people at WLW, including our traffic guy, Lt. Jim Stanley. Of course, I was still thinking about Sally Suttle and starting to fall in love.

Dan Clayton, the program director, put the deal together. Charlie Murdock, WLW's general manager, and I came to an agreement—no more misunderstandings. If I ever had a problem or a question, I was to go to him. I still answered to the program director, but we had this unique arrangement.

I didn't have to think about an image because I was established in Cincinnati. I was the Music Professor. I was plugged into the community, and I was still good friends with Johnny Bench and the guys. The put-on phone calls worked well in Denver, but I didn't need them here.

One of the papers reported, "Cincinnati's Prodigal Son Has Returned: The Music Professor was brought back to WLW by popular demand." I came back just as the Reds' season was ending, and Bench was on a tear, hitting seven home runs in seven days. In game five of the playoffs, he led off the bottom of the ninth with a home run over Roberto Clemente's head in right field, and the Reds beat the Pirates. We lost the World Series to Oakland. When I saw John after the game, I had tears in my eyes. He looked at me and said, "What are you crying for? I'm the one that lost. Do you know how much money I could have made?"

My friend, John

He had something serious on his mind, and he wanted to tell me. A month earlier at a team physical, the doctor discovered a spot on his lung. The operation was scheduled for December 9, two days after his twenty-fifth birthday. Barry and Anne Buse threw a great party for him, but I was worried I might lose my best friend. The night before the operation, Mike Reid of the Bengals and I went to visit John. A strange guy from Detroit with a box somehow got into his room. He had a gift for John—it was a dog. He was quickly escorted out. John, of course, jokingly blamed me for the incident. We laughed, and the next day, Dr. Luis Gonzalez performed a perfect operation. The lesion on his lung was benign. During this time, I was John's connection to his fans, and I kept them updated on his progress. John and I kidded about the operation on my show, but it was a frightening situation, and no one knew if he could rebound from this operation. I bought him a tabletop hockey game, the kind with knobs on the side to keep him occupied. He had broken ribs and wasn't to move or laugh too hard, but I played game after game whipping him: "LaBarbara scores again against the All-Star." John laughed so hard he was crying. Dr. Gonzalez called and asked me not to let him laugh so hard, he was worried about his stitches. It was the first and only time I beat John at a competitive game, and I took advantage of it.

We double dated that New Year's Eve and stayed in the presidential suite at a downtown hotel. I found a receipt for a Rolex watch that Sammy Davis, Jr., purchased in a desk drawer. Early the next morning, a very emotional John knocked on my door and woke me. He wanted to talk. One of the networks tracked him down to get his reaction to Roberto Clemente's death. Roberto died in an aviation accident while he was en route from his native Puerto Rico to deliver aid to earthquake victims in Nicaragua. While we were sitting reminiscing about Clemente, I didn't say it, but I couldn't help but wonder what a pretty blonde I graduated with from Stowe High was thinking. Early in his career with the Pirates, she had been his girlfriend.

John invited me to join him at a couple of All-Star games. On the plane trip to Kansas City for the '73 game, I sat near John and Sparky Anderson. They were surrounded by reporters. Just before landing, John asked me about my experience in the Pirates' organization. I went into great detail about how much I enjoyed it, especially since Pittsburgh is my hometown, but I was unhappy that it ended so abruptly. On the front page of the *Kansas City Star* July 23rd edition, above the caption "Here's Johnny" was a picture of Bench at the airport surrounded by pretty "All-Star greeters." If you look over John's left shoulder, I'm the guy with the glasses talking to a reporter. The reporter heard us talking on the plane and was asking me why I left the Pirates' organization. I then described to the writer how I lost my job as a peanut vendor at Forbes Field. Sparky and John got a big laugh.

Bench got me a great seat at the game; Stan Musial sat next to me; Bob Feller sat right in front; and Pete Rose's wife, Carolyn, sat behind me. John hit a home run. The Cubs' Ron Santo stopped by our suite after the game, but the only ladies were a couple of John's dates. We did hit all the great network and sponsor parties.

In 1974 the All-Star game was in Pittsburgh, and my parents invited John to our house for an Italian dinner. I introduced them to my close friends: Squirrel, Ruby, and Cadillac Charlie—the whole gang came over. Bench ate a lot of Italian soup and antipasto salad and left the table. My mother didn't understand why. I said, "John, what are you doing? You're insulting my mom—she's in tears. We still have lasagna, fried chicken, hot sausage, ham, and desert." He ran up and down the front steps of our house a dozen times and rejoined us at the table. We took some fried chicken and Mancini's bread back to the hotel. Reggie Jackson liked the chicken, and Tony Kubek, the announcer, was a big fan of Mancini's bread.

John's ladies

John had a big party suite, and all the guys were in great spirits except me. I was in a bad mood because my new tan suit was wrinkled, and I looked like I was going on *Lets Make A Deal*. It was a linen suit—great for standing up, just don't sit down. One of the guys took it to a one-hour cleaner and saved my day. Our party suite was well stocked with snacks and drinks. The girls started arriving, and we couldn't believe it. One was better looking than the next. One All-Star who stopped by said on a scale of ten, none was lower than an eight. There were at least twenty beautiful ladies. I got a drink for a blonde phys ed teacher who said she was John's date. Cadillac Charlie told me the girl he was with was John's date. Ruby and Squirrel said the same—Bench's date. Suddenly, the happy atmosphere changed, and the ladies who had been talking among themselves abruptly left the party. It was a little after nine, and the only people left were the guys. It turned out, each of the girls thought she was Bench's date for the night.

John gathered his entourage, and we hit all the All-Star parties. I had a chance to talk to one of my Pirates heroes, the great Ralph Kiner. He gave me his autograph when I was a kid. I'll never forget getting the autograph of his first wife, tennis star Nancy Chaffee, because it was the only game my dad and I saw together at Forbes Field.

I was living my childhood dream. John took me to the park to watch batting practice and hang out in the clubhouse. It was a kick to stand around the batting cage with Hank Aaron, Reggie Jackson, Al Kaline, Rod Carew, Frank Robinson, and Mike Schmidt. I don't think many people can say they hung in the clubhouse with Morgan, Rose, Brock, Bowa, Perez, and Garvey.

Bench once said to me, "You never ask me for anything." People were always pulling at him: "Give me tickets," "Give me this . . ." WLW was the Reds' flagship station; I got free tickets to every game. The only time John gave me tickets besides the All-Star games was if I was escorting one of his special ladies. Two of my favorites were Tara Leigh, she was one of the Ding-A-Lings on the *Dean Martin Show*, and Cindy Sykes. I was dating my future wife, Sally, and we both hoped he would marry Cindy. She was a Miss Kansas who had just signed a contract with NBC and would later star on television in *Falcon Crest*, *St. Elsewhere*, *Jag*, and a number of movies. She married Bud Yorkin, the television, film producer, director, and writer who teamed with Norman Lear to form Tandem Productions, famous for a number of shows including *All in the Family*. We still keep in touch. She was a bridesmaid in our wedding.

If I escorted John's date, I would always end up in one of two VIP boxes, Barry Buse's or William Williams's, both part owners of the Reds. I never visited our station's box unless I was invited because I once brought two NBA basketball stars into the booth and was reprimanded the next day. They were friends of mine, and we just stopped to say hello. Our names were not on the guest list.

John called me at the apartment, "Meet me downstairs; we're going to play Santa Claus today in Dayton." His car was full of toys. During the ride, I told John that it was nice that Pete Rose's little boy could appreciate his father. I mentioned that by the time John got married and had kids they would know him as a Joe DiMaggio doing Mr. Coffee commercials. Joe was doing those commercials in the seventies and was out of baseball. He handed me a pamphlet. I recognized Farrah Fawcett, and I said, "You've got a date with her?" He showed me another Ultra Brite girl, Vickie Chesser. A friend fixed him up, and they were going to Vegas for a weekend. When we reached our destination, John introduced me to his little friend Philip Buckingham, a five-year-old who was dying from leukemia. John met him a year earlier and became very involved. He got the family a car, bought him a pony, food, and lots of toys. Philip was more excited to see Johnny than he was his new toys. I stepped outside several times because I couldn't hold back the tears. As we were leaving, Philip came to the car, and Johnny gave him a little Reds' Johnny Bench doll. A short time later, he would be buried with that doll.

John took Vickie to Vegas, and I got a call: "Meet me at Scarlotta's for dinner and bring Sally, I want you to meet her." I think he lost around ten thousand dollars, but he fell in love. After dinner, we went to John's condominium, and we picked out a date for his wedding and mine. He called Bob Hope. We listened and heard Hope say, "Thanks for the tip. I'm going to buy more Kleenex stock tomorrow because of all the ladies who will be broken hearted." John tried to call Bobby Goldsboro, but he was on stage. I asked John three times that night if he was sure about Vickie, and he said yes. It happened so quickly.

Bench and I were the co-hosts for the zoo's second celebrity walk. John, Vickie, Sally, and I had a good time talking with people and visiting the rare and endangered species. They let us hold a few of the zoo's baby animals. One of the baby chimps was fascinated with Sally's hair and started to pull her wig off. Sally was very calm and put it back on. At the last minute, John said we were invited to a dinner party.

William Williams, the head of Western Southern and part owner of the Reds and Bengals, was having a dinner in honor of Vickie and John's upcoming marriage. Everybody was dressed for the occasion except the four of us. We didn't change and had that zoo aroma. I did one of my classic faux pas. The Williams's house was full of beautiful artwork, everything from Russell statues to the finest paintings. I was admiring a painting near the staircase that I had seen many times before. It was a violin and bow on a musical manuscript. It was very old and a little raggedy looking. I said to Sally, "I'm surprised they don't have a newer one. I've seen this everywhere." Mr. Williams heard me and explained that this original painting had been on tour and was just returned. Yes, the print of that was very popular at the time. I felt stupid and didn't know what to say, so I wisely said nothing.

Less than two months after meeting Vickie, they got married. Sally was one of the bridesmaids, and John asked me to stand at the pulpit and read a passage. Dan Ingram, his childhood buddy, was his best man.

John had made arrangements to get some wedding cake to his little friend Philip, but the next morning he got the sad news that he had died. The marriage was almost over by the winter. They separated and were divorced in 1976.

During spring training in '76, the Reds' Bob Bailey and I were riding to dinner with John. He gave us a quote from Dick Young of the *New York Daily News*. Young had a bitter feud with the Mets' Tom Sever that escalated and led Tom to ask to be traded after he wrote lies about Tom's wife, Nancy. Dick Young printed a vicious innuendo regarding John's divorce. He asked Bob what he thought. Bailey said, "he's calling you gay." He asked me, and I said the same thing. John was furious.

Vickie later told a reporter that Johnny spent their wedding night playing a "pong game" with his best man, and that story made the front page of the *Cincinnati Enquirer*. John was best man in my wedding, and a lot of people thought it was me, not knowing that it was Dean Ingram from Oklahoma. When Dean came to Cincinnati for the wedding, Vickie insisted he stay at their condominium and not a hotel. A couple of John's Vegas friends gave them a pong game with their names on each side. So what was a very innocent game with Dean suddenly looked very ugly in print. Sally and I spent the evening with my sister-in-law and her husband, who came in from New Jersey.

Our wedding

Sparky Anderson and I had a serious talk over dinner at Malio's in Tampa during spring training in 1974. He said I was killing myself running around with all these ladies. Almost like a father, he wanted to know what my intentions were for a pretty girl I'd been dating, Sally Suttle. He told me I was crazy if I let her get away: "You should marry that pretty girl, and when you do, I'll be at the wedding."

Bench had announced my engagement December 23, 1974, on the Bob Braun television show that was simulcast on radio. Sally and I were listening while driving back from Pittsburgh. She was really surprised because I hadn't proposed to her. She didn't have to wait long. The next night, Christmas Eve at her parents' house, I asked her to adjust the angel on top of the tree, and that's where she found the ring in a little box next to the angel. I returned Johnny's favor a couple of weeks later by breaking his wedding news on the *Bob Braun Show*. I really caught Bob by surprise when I said, "Vickie is backstage."

In January of 1975 I decided I would buy a house and get it ready to move into after our July wedding. While I was discussing buying a home with Sally and her parents, her dad asked me how much I was going to spend. I said about eight thousand dollars. Sally laughed at me, and I got very upset. I said, "Why don't you marry a doctor or a lawyer?" Her dad had a calming effect and suggested we look at some homes. He said nothing about money, but I quickly realized why she laughed. I bought a home for thirty-five thousand dollars in Western Hills, and the whole family pitched in to get it ready. I got another surprise when I called my friend who was a vice president at Fifth Third Bank. I needed thirty thousand dollars. He didn't think it would be a problem. I got a call back. He couldn't find a credit report on me. I paid cash for everything: new cars, televisions, everything. I didn't know what a credit card looked like. Of course that was a problem. WLW radio came to the rescue. I called my boss, Charlie Murdock, and he talked to our company president who was on the board of directors at Central Trust Bank, and they made the loan. I quickly learned how to charge things.

WLW did a countdown to my wedding. Sparky Anderson showed up as promised after the Reds beat the Dodgers five to three. John Bench was my best man. Gwen Conley from the *Bob Braun Show* sang our song, "The First Time Ever I Saw Your Face" at the church. My relatives from Pittsburgh were told, "Please, no autographs." My favorite aunt, Aunt Dora, had a bagful of balls to get signed by Johnny. She passed away a number of years ago, and I've felt guilty that I never got her those autographs. She was so good to me when I was a kid.

My brother-in-law somehow backed my car, with its soaped windows, into a pole, and I think my friend Arnold Barnett was somehow involved. When Sally and I got to the hotel to spend the evening, we were greeted by about twenty of our laughing friends. How did they find out?

Our honeymoon was a gift from Johnny Bench and bridesmaid Cynthia Sykes. John took care of the first part, Las Vegas. On the plane, we got upgraded to first class and sat with the Pure Prairie League, who played their new RCA single for us. We stayed at the

Bob Braun and Wray Jean (center) at our wedding in 1975.
We were with them on our first date.

MGM Las Vegas and saw all the big shows. Paul Anka gave us a dinner at Caesar's Palace with a special bottle of wine. We spent time with Johnny Tillotson, Lou Rawls, and Roger Miller. Tillotson and I reminisced about the shows we did when he was the headliner over the Supremes.

In Los Angeles, Cindy had just signed a contract with NBC, and she had us stay at the Beverly Hills Hotel. She pointed out Pat Boone's place from our balcony, and we stopped by to see Wayne Newton, who was doing a rehearsal for a *Ben Vereen Special*. Wayne was no longer the chubby kid I interviewed early in his career. At a Hollywood party, a man asked Sally what she wanted. She said, "Coke would be fine." I had a scotch and soda. I got my drink in a minute, but Sally waited and waited. Finally, a guy came over apologizing because they didn't have any coke, but it was on the way. However, he did offer her a number of drugs and marijuana. She declined, and said she just wanted Coca-Cola. They looked at her like she was crazy and walked away. It was too funny. It was an unbelievable honeymoon.

The big guys in Hollywood at that time were Jack Nicholson, Warren Beatty, producer Robert Evans, and screenwriter director Robert Towne. We had lunch a couple of times with Cindy and Robert Towne who had just hit with the movies *Chinatown* and *Shampoo*. Sally was especially interested in talking to Towne because she loved the house and furniture featured in *Shampoo*. She really liked the antique Welsh cupboard in the dining room, and Robert knew all about the place because I think he once lived there.

Sally loves pewter and antique primitive furniture. Once in a theater, during the dramatic part in the *Exorcist* when Blair's head is turning around and the highboy piece of furniture was flying across the room, she suddenly grabbed my hand. She always closes her eyes during the scary scenes, and she had just opened them. Sally yelled, "That's the piece of furniture I'm looking for!" I just about jumped out of my seat.

The Reds

Johnny asked me what I wanted to be when I was a kid. He was surprised by my answer. I wanted to be Johnny Bench. I wanted to be the greatest catcher who ever lived. He just looked at me and laughed. Sparky Anderson and the Reds' PR man, Roger Ruhl, got me an official Reds uniform with the number 700 and my name on the back. I was always at the ballpark. I liked to sit right behind home plate so I could see the pitches. I noticed during one of Johnny's slumps he was doing something a little different. I told him, and he jumped all over me, "Are you crazy?" In the on-deck circle and just before the pitch, he would drop his bat instead of swinging straight. "You do that when you practice, and you do that at the plate." He did break his slump the next day, but I don't know if that had anything to do with it.

In September of 1975, I decided to have minor surgery to fix my deviated septum. It's a common physical disorder of the nose involving a displacement of the nasal septum. Dr. David Zipfel performed the operation and also shortened my rather large Italian proboscis. After the operation, I looked like I was in a fight with Mike Tyson. The operation takes a couple of weeks to fully heal, and the doctor told me to put tape on my glasses to hold them up so it wouldn't press on my nose. I did that, but five weeks later when the Reds beat the Red Sox four games to three in one of the best World Series of all time, Dr. David Zipfel saw me at the victory celebration on television. He wanted to know why I still had the tape on my glasses because I was only supposed to have it on for a week, and I looked ridiculous.

I loved spring training. The Reds asked me to write about my greatest baseball thrill for the *Reds Letter* in January of 1978. This is what I wrote: "I was one of those kids who grew up living baseball. Every spring, I'd find myself daydreaming in a classroom looking out the window wanting to hit a few. I was fortunate enough to play on a little league All-Star team that was just a few games away from being World Champions. I loved baseball so much that when I was in my early teens growing up in Pittsburgh, I lied about my age and worked as a vendor at Forbes Field. I would sell a few bags of peanuts and then swap other vendors for hot dogs, pop, etc. and sit in the front seats and watch the Pirates play. Naturally, I didn't last long as a vendor.

"I have to admit that the little boy in me is still there, and every year at this time, my thoughts turn to baseball. It's funny, but those daydreams have become somewhat of a reality for me. For the past four years in March, WLW has sent me to Tampa to do my radio show with the Reds. It's rather unique, in that I actually do my Saturday show from 10:00 a.m. to 1:00 p.m. from the dugout of Al Lopez Field.

"I leave on Thursday for Tampa along with my helpers, Bernie Kvale, vice president of sales, and Jim Hampton, our vice president of engineering. Although we don't broadcast until Saturday, I'm here at eighty thirty Friday morning with my tape recorders and notebooks to record some interviews as a precautionary measure in case of a rain out. The excitement of walking into Al Lopez Field for the first time each year is hard to describe. You see, for a few days I'll be made to feel like an inside part of the club.

"The first person I look for is Bernie Stowe, the equipment manager. He's the one who can tell me: [Jack] Billingham's riding a bicycle to the park; Morgan's still going to college; Pete got a new car; Lum's doing television commercials in Hawaii. He has the information I can't find in the media guide. Next, I visit Sparky Anderson in his office—this year will be extra special because my friend Alex Grammas is back as coach. Sparky coordinates the interviews, and from our conversation, I'll know which rookies and extras have a good shot at making the club. For most of Friday, I'll be renewing my friendships with the veterans. It's an interesting contrast, the confident veterans and the young rookies pushing to make the club.

"Johnny Bench, my close friend, usually starts off the show with me, and I never know what to expect. One year he's on me about my weight, my clothes, not picking up the dinner check the night before, etc. Anything can happen and usually does for the next three hours. I try to present a personal side of the Reds and talk about things with them the average fan doesn't know. Fred Norman might talk about the time he sang with a group on the *Tonight Show*. Joe Morgan has a music room with an extensive collection of jazz records. John Bench is moving into a new home. Sparky has a pool table and plays golf to relax.

"Well, it's time for me to finish packing for Tampa. . . . I wonder if this year I should take my glove and bat?"

I've socialized with a number of Reds over the years, and one of my favorites was Mike Lum, the first major leaguer from Hawaii and a good utility player with the Reds from 1976 to 1978. As we were standing around my bar in the game room with our wives, he announced he was leaving the Reds. Ted Turner just made him the first one-hundred-thousand-dollar utility player when he signed Mike for Atlanta. He was an amateur magician and part of his deal would include doing a little television. It couldn't happen to a nicer guy.

Malio's in Tampa was the place to go for dinner. I didn't have an expense account, and after a huge dinner with Sparky and a bunch of friends, Bench got up and said, "Thanks Professor," and they walked out stiffing me with the bill. John got a big kick out of that. We always hit the Derby Club to watch the greyhounds chase the rabbit. It was like a who's who of baseball stepping into the elevator. I was standing next to one of my childhood idols, Yogi Berra. A group of us bet on the quinella. The restaurateur Jeff Ruby was given the money, and the list of the dogs we selected, to place the bet. We did it, and we won; we were congratulating each other when Jeff walked back. There was one problem. When Jeff got to the window, he changed the numbers, and we lost. He explained that he didn't like the numbers. We jumped all over Ruby.

The Kid Glove Game was a big event that raised money for the youth baseball program. Prior to the exhibition game between the Reds and the Tigers or Indians, they let the local media play. We were divided into two teams during that era—Bob Braun's and Jim Scott's. Braun was the well-known regional television star with our company, and Scott did mornings on the rock station. I was always the catcher for Braun's team. I was serious—I'd take batting practice at the cages the Sunday before. I was the only one in the Reds' clubhouse changing into my official Reds uniform, number 700. Bench would get me spikes, a protective cup, and one of his gloves. Over the years, I hit three home runs, a triple, and a few doubles. I got at least one hit in every game I played. Okay, maybe Uncle Al wasn't the best pitcher. A hit is still a hit. We never had a serious injury during the time I played, although a couple of outfielders misplayed balls. I remember Bob Shreve having one bounce off his head. When Bob Trumpy did our sports talk show, he decided to bust my chops. He knew how psyched I got, and he took my uniform out of the studio. I went nuts—my uniform was gone. I overreacted, and of course, Trumpy thought it was hilarious. The uniform was found hanging in a clothing store window on the first floor of our building, but I made it in time to start the game. Our morning guy Gary Burbank was pitching. The bases were loaded. I told him, "If the ball comes to you, bring it home." The next batter hit the ball to Gary. I was standing on home plate to get the force out. In the back of my mind, I was thinking I was going to redeem myself for dropping that ball in Williamsport when I was twelve. Burbank wound up and threw the ball over my head and almost over the backstop. I stood there stunned, and he hollered at me, "Why didn't you jump?" I looked at the dugout; Tom Seaver was laughing and yelling, "You should have caught it!" The best pitcher I ever caught in that game was a new talk-show host, Billy Cunningham. He entered the game as a relief pitcher. I gave him the signals and he said, "Four is for a knuckleball; just put your glove where you want me to throw it." I thought he was kidding, but he threw slow knuckleballs, curves, sliders, and he struck out the side.

I have a lot of fond memories of Riverfront Stadium. Sparky even let me shag flies during batting practice. That was me—the guy with the belly and beard running around.

Sometimes I'd wait for Bench in the clubhouse waiting room with the players' wives and children. It's incredible how many of those kids grew up to play in the pros: Ken Griffey Jr., Pete Rose Jr., Eduardo Perez, Lee May Jr., and others.

One of our close friends is singer Bobby Goldsboro. Bobby was with Roy Orbison on the Beatles' last British tour before they came to America, and he was the opening act for the Rolling Stones on their first tour of the States. Bobby had a hit in the seventies with a song he wrote, "Summer (the First Time)."

I mentioned to Bobby, "Bench told me that song was about him. John never went into any detail; we were just sitting around talking." Goldsboro started laughing and said, "It's just wishful thinking on Johnny's part. In a way, it's kind of a personal thing. Something that kind of happened to me but not nearly as romantically as I put it in the song—partly made up."

Pete Rose and Johnny were close friends when I got to town, and we socialized often. Pete and I were talking in a bar when a big guy got all over Pete. This guy was insulting him, trying his best to start a fight. It took awhile, but Pete bought him a drink and won the guy over. Sally and I were on a Reds cruise with Pete and his first wife. It was funny to watch Pete around the pool. He'd wear those old, grandfather cut-off, white t-shirts that later became the rage and his long pants working on his tan.

One night after a celebrity tennis tournament, Sally and I were sitting at a table with Pete, Ted Kluszewski, and their wives. During Ted's playing days, he wore cut-off sleeves because of his biceps and looked bigger than life. They exchanged fascinating baseball stories for a couple of hours while I just listened. Pete can tell you just about every pitch a pitcher ever threw him, and Big Klu had been the Big Red Machine's hitting coach. Pete wasn't with the Reds and was hoping to come back. Marge Schott brought him back the next year.

My son, Jimmy, and I shared the experience at Riverfront September 11, 1985, when Pete Rose broke Ty Cobb's hit record of 4,192. A couple of months later, I was seated next to Pete on the dais at a Marty Brennaman Roast for Cystic Fibrosis. Pete was showing me some pictures. I told him I suddenly realized I was sitting next to greatness. He shook his head and laughed. He was having trouble trying to eat popcorn from a decoration bag that was in front of us. My wife was in charge of decorations and had glued the popcorn to paper on top of the bags because there wasn't enough to fill all the bags. You

*Here I am with Pete Rose in the dugout at Al Lopez Field in Tampa,
waiting to go on the air.*

can add me to that group who think it's a travesty that he's not in the
Hall of Fame.

I played in the last game ever played in Riverfront Stadium—well
the next to last game. Pete Rose wasn't allowed to participate in the
festivities for the Reds' final game at the stadium, so they lined up
some of the biggest retired stars of baseball to play in a softball game.
It was the All-Stars against the Reds. Before the big game, there was a
VIP game. My friend Brian Douglas from Q102 got me into the game;
we were the only radio people invited. Our team had former Bengals'
Anthony Munoz and Jim Breech. In my only at bat, I smashed a line

drive to the outfield, and when I stopped at first base, Johnny Bench yelled, "You're the only guy I know who can turn a double into a single!" After our game, I sat in the dugout for a while, and it was like going back to 1975–76. Griffey was kidding Conception, Perez was laughing, and Bench along with Rose chimed in. The guy I was sitting next to, Joe Morgan, said, "You guys couldn't win it until I got here." It was just the way I remember them, kidding each other in the clubhouse.

I once turned down the opportunity to write for a national magazine. In my single days, I was a patron of the arts, and on a few occasions, I visited the Hustler Club downtown for a drink to watch the dancers. One of the regulars, Speedy, said his boss Larry Flynt wanted me to write a monthly music article for a new men's magazine, *Hustler*. It started as *Hustler for Today's Man*, a small magazine that provided cheap advertising for Larry's strip clubs, but this new magazine was going national. Speedy assured me it would be a good magazine. I wanted to check it out and make sure my boss approved before I committed, but I was interested and flattered by the offer. I picked up a copy—Wow! No way would I ever ask for permission. *Playboy* was modest in comparison, but *Hustler* did get a peak circulation of around three million. I was invited to the Hustler Columbus Mansion, but I never made it for any parties.

In March of 1975, the *Enquirer* did a story that mentioned I had been invited to read for the part of a cop in the proposed movie *The Day after Rembrandt*, based on Jim Haugh's negotiations in the 1973 Taft Museum thefts. Freelance writer Skip Korb was writing the script. A few years later, Skip wanted to write a television series based on my WLW radio talks about the guys in my hometown. He was fascinated by the characters I talked about who hung out at Michael's Lounge in Pittsburgh, Stowe Township. He wanted to do a sitcom based on that bar where everybody knows everybody. Pittsburgh had the Steelers and the Pirates; both were good at that time. He liked the ethnic idea of these Italian friends of mine, with names like: DeArdo, Condeluci, Smarra, Colangelo, Esposito, Mazzaro, Niglio, Masciola, Ficarri, Ciamacco, and Panucci. My high school friend, Anthony

Crivelli was excited, but the guys who hung in the bar were upset when they heard it was a sitcom: "They'll make fun of us—No way!" They wouldn't even talk to Skip. It's too bad, because that same idea became the basis of one of the most successful television shows of all time, *Cheers*, "where everybody knows your name," which ran for eleven seasons, from 1982 to 1993.

Then there's the story of Bill Medley who should have been Bronson. The guy who wrote it and produced it and all the heads of MGM asked him to be Jim Bronson in the television show *Then Came Bronson*. He was still upset just thinking about it and said he had never done any acting, but he was a motorcycle guy, and he had raced motorcycles all his life: "I just put it into the hands of my agent. My agent kept asking for more money, and I wasn't aware of the negotiations because I would have done it for nothing." Medley told me, "It's a real disappointing thing." In the end, they gave the lead to Michael Parks.

I was a happy child.

*I was six years old when this school
picture was taken.*

*From left: Brother, Sam; my mother, Eva; my dad, Jim; and me
at Mom and Dad's 50th wedding anniversary.*

"Rudy" Rudison and me—12 years old and on our way to the Little League Series in Williamsport, Pennsylvania.

"Pinky" Lorenz and me on Junior Prom night.

Ninety-one-year-old "Porky" Chedwick, the "Platter Pushin' Papa" and me.

My first DJ promo picture as Jimmy Holiday, 1963. It caused me pain and later became a joke between my wife and daughter, Shelby.

Top: Bobby Freeman thanked me for play-
ing his record over and over for more than
thirty hours.
Left: August 1964, J. Bentley Starr, the
"Intrepid Leader" WWGO Erie, Pa.

Four Seasons, Tommy DeVito and Frankie Valli, 1964
in happier times before "Jersey Boys."

Top: 1964 Caravan of Stars. By the end of the
tour they were no longer the "no hit"
Supremes.
From left: Mary, Flo, "Bentley," and Diana.

Right: Dee Dee Sharp, the "Mashed Potato
Girl," looked like a little princess, 1964.

Top: Brian Hyland, J. Bent-ley Starr, and Lou Christie, 1964. Yes, that's a cigarette in my hand.

Bottom: Four Seasons, Frankie Valli and Bob Gaudio doing an interview with me from a telephone booth, 1964.

Who, I say, who is Cleveland's most eligible bachelor? And, who is the suave, debonair, dapper, dashing, country-club type pictured on this page? Who posseses more knowledge about the music business and its makers and presents it in a zippy, zany fashion? Who terrifies the citizens of Cleveland with his daily dash for the station in his red fast-back Mustang? Who is 5' 11'' tall, weighs 175 lbs. (around his middle), is 24 years old and dresses in early Goodwill fashions?

If your answer to all the above questions is: Jim La Barbara, WKYC's newest VIP, you're absolutely right! Rush right down to your nearest grocer and award yourself two Snickers bars (pay for them, of course). And, if you're not already a Jim La Barbara fan, we predict you soon will be after catching his nightly show on WKYC Radio, 6:30 to 11 p.m. Give a listen.

KY Sound 11 Survey promoting Jim LaBarbara's 6:30 p.m. to 11:00 p.m. show, September 23, 1966. The number one song was "Cherish" by the Association.

World's first Bed Boat Race, Lake Erie, October 1966.

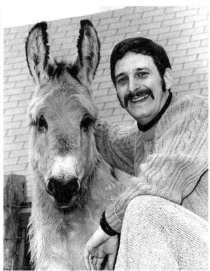

Above: Me on my new Corvette and my WKYC promo picture. I was riding high in 1966.
Right: WIXY promo picture taken at the Cincinnati Zoo. That is me on the right.

WIXY Pop Poster like a scene from Bonnie and Clyde *1968.*
Left to right: Johnny Michaels, "WIXY Pixie," me, the "Duker," Joe Finan,
"Wilde Childe," "King" Kirby.

May 1969 First ad to promote me.
A takeoff of the Man of LaMancha.

Visiting Children's Hospital for the
Ruth Lyons Children's Fund

The Royals' Norm Van Lier and Tommy Van Arsdale were
good friends—both shot better than me.

This was a giant promotion for me.

Stan Matlock, Johnny Bench, Waite Hoyt (Babe Ruth's Yankee teammate and Reds announcer), me, and "Squirrel."

Neil Sedaka wrote "Oh! Carol" for his girlfriend, an unknown singer-songwriter named Carole King.

Ray Charles, the "Genius of Soul" liked a good joke.

This picture was taken with Gladys Knight and the Pips in Greenfield Village, Michigan.

Evel Knievel, Sally, and me at Kings Island, October 1975, checking out the site before his historic jump.

*Jackie De Shannon. I often joked she dated Elvis and John Lennon
and went out to dinner with me.*

Brenda Lee once lived in Cincinnati.

*Bobby Goldsboro had a lot of hit records,
but he really wanted to play second base
for the Reds.*

Rod McKuen drew on his picture because he wanted a beard like mine.
He has sold more than 65 million books of poetry.

Mike Love, the Beach Boys' lead singer, and I discussing Transcendental Meditation.

Top: I emceed many beauty pageants. This picture was on the cover of a 1969 Forest Park program.

Right: Paul Brown, the Coach, let me watch the Bengals' games from the bench area.

Chubby Checker wanted to be a performer from the time he was four.

Davy Jones, everybody's favorite Monkee, dropped out of school to be a jockey.

Roy Orbison with Sally and me. He toured with both
Elvis and the Beatles before they were stars.

Jerry Dowling's Cincinnati Enquirer's *"F. Stop Fitzgerald" cartoon strip*
zinged me for "name dropping" 1979.
COURTESY OF JERRY DOWLING

Left: Sparky Anderson with me in the dugout at Al Lopez Field in Tampa. After the game during dinner he gave me a lecture on why I should marry that pretty girl Sally. Above: Joe Nuxhall, the "Old Left-hander" was beloved by all.

Ben E. King gave me some premarital advice before a concert after a Reds game.

Martha Reeves and Sam Moore (Sam and Dave) with me at the autograph table.

*Tony Bennett. For a number of years he donated money to a charity in my name.
Sinatra called him "the best singer in the business."*

*Tony Bennett drew my picture while I was interviewing him
and he signed his real name.*

Johnny Bench giving me advice during a Reds' Kid Glove Game.

Left: Pete Rose and I relaxing in a restaurant. I never saw him drink an alcoholic beverage.
Above: Marty Brennaman invited me sit in the coveted Reds' broadcast booth for many years.

Joe Morgan in the Riverfront Stadium Reds' dugout September 23, 2002. I got hit in the Celebrity game and Joe was about to play in the Pete Rose all-star softball game. A final farewell to the stadium before it was torn down.

Dion got his start singing doo-wop on the street corners in the Bronx.

The Dave Clark 5's Mike Smith, told me that because of the screaming they never heard what they were singing or playing for four years.

My favorite cowboy—Roy Rogers. I was always Roy when we played cowboys. That's my Dale Evans—my wife, Sally.

Three generations of the LaBarbaras. My dad, my son, and me. Jimmy's son, James, now makes four. Everyone loved my father.

Tony Orlando. He once brought me on stage to sing "Bless You" with him.

Jimmy Webb, me, Paul Williams, and Barry Mann. Three legendary songwriters.

The LaBarbara Family.
On left: Daughter, Shelby, with husband, Danny Tepe and daughter, Colleen.
Center: Sally and me.
On right: Son, Jimmy, with wife, Amy, and son, James.

CHAPTER 14

Drugs, Rock 'n' Roll, and Hanging with a Legend

The story of drugs and rock 'n' roll has been well documented over the years, along with the tragic drug-related deaths of Jimi Hendrix, Janis Joplin, Keith Moon, Elvis, Frankie Lymon, and so many others. In the fifties, you didn't hear much about drugs. I was just a kid playing my trumpet in bands around Pittsburgh when I heard my first tragic drug story. My fellow bandmate Archie Leone and I would visit an older jazz trumpet player, Mike Maracino to talk music and listen to him play a riff or two. Early one Sunday morning, he was upset after answering a phone call from his friend who was strung out on drugs and needed help somewhere on the Pennsylvania Turnpike. I couldn't believe it was Chet Baker, the winner of the Downbeat Jazz Poll in 1954. He was a hero of mine on the trumpet, an icon of the West Coast cool school of jazz. Mike explained that he was sick and broke. I didn't understand because he was the number one trumpet player in the world, and he was addicted to heroin. It controlled his life until the day he died. The older guys would explain that in certain clubs we played to be careful in the bathroom because drug deals we're going down. I wasn't interested in drugs.

Frankie Lymon

One of the big stars at the first rock 'n' roll show I saw was thirteen-year-old Frankie Lymon; he knocked everybody out when he sang "Why Do Fools Fall in Love?" That song influenced so many people. Ronnie Spector of the Ronettes told me she was twelve when she heard it on her grandmother's radio and that's when she knew she wanted to be a singer. Diana Ross recorded the song in 1981, and it sold a million copies. Berry Gordy has mentioned many times Lymon's influence on the Motown Sound and of course Michael Jackson.

Frankie was just a cute thirteen-year-old kid on stage, but we didn't know that since the age of ten, he had been hustling prostitutes. He had a string of hits before he became a slave to drugs. In an *Ebony* magazine interview in 1967, he admitted he had been addicted to heroin since he was fifteen after being introduced to it by a woman twice his age.

In 1968 Frankie was signed by Sam Bray to his Big Apple label. Roulette Records was interested in releasing his records in conjunction with Big Apple and scheduled a recording session for February 28. Lymon was staying at his grandmother's apartment in Harlem where he grew up. This was going to be his big comeback, and he celebrated the night before by shooting heroin. Supposedly, he had been clean for three years since entering the army. He never made it to the recording session. He was found dead of a heroin overdose with an empty syringe by his side. He was only twenty-five.

I asked his close friend, recording star Little Anthony of "Tears on My Pillow" fame, about that tragic day. Anthony told me that Frankie called him the night before he died. He said, "I was out of town and my wife got the call for me to call him, and the following day, he was dead."

"Anthony, I thought he was on top of everything."

"Well a lot of people are on top of everything. Freddy Prinze was too. [Freddy was a stand-up comedian and the star of television's *Chico and the Man*. He suffered from depression, and in 1977 took his own life with a gun.] There are a lot of pressures in the world. We bounce back. It's just that Frankie—violent in the way that he was raised, the problems of the neighborhood that he lived in, the environment, the people that were around him. If he had the influence of people who would have made him think better, he would be alive today, but in fact, Frankie was influenced by the thugs and the guys on the street because he was a street kid. He was raised on the streets, and he was raised in the jungle, and when you're in the jungle, you tend to become an animal of the jungle in order to survive."

Little Richard

I've talked with Little Richard a number of times. In May 1978, we discussed events in his life that had happened a year earlier that made him change. He was heavy into narcotics and said, "I started using marijuana first, and then I went to angel dust, and from there to cocaine. I was paying one thousand dollars an ounce for cocaine. It was just eating up my membranes, and blood was just coming out of my head, and it was just eating me up, eating me out. Then I started using heroin. I started mixing heroin and cocaine together making the speedball. Then I had five deaths happen right in a row. I had one friend that was nineteen years old coming to Magic Mountain to hear me sing one night in Los Angeles. He never did arrive. We waited and waited. My mother was there, my sisters and brothers, but he never did get there. Somebody shot him in the head at the heroin man's home. He died. Then I had another friend named Curly Knight in Los Angeles. He was coming to his car one night. The fellows who killed him were fifteen years old, put him in the trunk of his car, drive him around the city and cut him up with a butcher knife—killed him. I had another fellow I used to get my dope from. I went one night to get a fifty-dollar bag, and he talked to me before I left, and later that night, he had a massive heart attack. I worked in Miami appearing at the Americana Hotel, and after that I came back to LA. My brother had called and asked me for two hundred dollars; he wanted to pay down on a station wagon. He needed two hundred more or something, and I said, 'Okay, I'll give it to you.' When I got to LA, I didn't get in touch with my brother. I was going to go to Hollywood and just live it up that night—to let it all hang out as it were, to have a good time. After arriving there without calling my brother, the next morning, my brother had a massive heart attack and fell dead. I said, 'My God is trying to tell me something. He's speaking to me. He's coming all around me. He hasn't touched me, but he's touching people about me that I love.' I started realizing that there's no secret what God can do, that no man can serve two masters."

The Everly Brothers

There really was a "Dr. Feelgood," years before Aretha sang the song. The Everly Brothers, Phil and Don, were good looking, clean-cut guys, but they had their problems. I asked Phil to tell me about an unethical doctor in New York who treated them. He said, "I often laugh, and I'm surprised we're both still here to have survived rock 'n' roll—the whole psychological, the physical, the life changes that exist with traveling as much as we did, and doing everything else. We're very lucky that we're still around. The doctor you're talking about is a doctor that was treating more people than people suspect. It was rumored that he was treating even the president. He was quite a well-known doctor in New York City. It did not work out well. Usually our lives were about five years ahead of what was going on in society."

Ray Charles

Jamie Foxx won the Academy Award for his portrayal of Ray Charles in the 2004 movie *Ray*. Ray died shortly before the film opened. Audiences were introduced to a side of Ray Charles they had never seen when the movie focused on his drug problems. My audience probably wasn't surprised, because he told me about his problem twenty-three years earlier in a rare interview.

It was a well-publicized story when Ray was busted for heroin in

1965. He ended the tragedy by checking himself into a rehabilitation hospital, and he never touched heroin again. Ray Charles told me that he started using some form of drugs when he was in his late teens. He said, "It was the kind of situation, and I'm not making any excuses for it. I don't recommend how people live their lives. My situation was nobody, and I repeat nobody, nobody that I knew was interested or wanted me in any way to participate in using drugs. As a matter of fact, the people that I was around did their utmost to keep me from this. Obviously this made me more want to do it—like the wet paint, don't touch—that type of thing, plus too, in the early part of my career, I was always the youngest, always. I was always the young kid, and everybody would go off somewhere and leave me by myself. I didn't know what they were doing. So naturally, you want to be a part; you want to belong to the people you're around. Well, they weren't trying to give away nothing that cost money. So it really was a matter of wanting to belong. So it was through my own insistence that these fellas would make me a part of their world because I wanted to be a man so to speak. I didn't want to be set off to the side where I didn't know what the hell they were doing. So eventually, after you keep knocking and knocking and begging and begging and asking and asking, pleading and begging, eventually somebody will say all right just to shut you up: 'Here it is, boom, all right? Sit down.' It was that kind of a thing. A slow process that I got myself involved in. I went through many years of it, and I have to say, I don't recommend it to anybody, okay? I don't tell no kids to go out and get himself on drugs, because believe me, it's a hell of a kind of thing to have to deal with. When you decide you don't want to deal with it anymore, and once you go through the s——t I went through, it can be a very, very bad scene. I'll tell any entertainer or anybody, there's never been, as far as I know anyway, a drug that can make you do what you're supposed to better when you use the drug. If you're good, you're good on a natural high."

B.J. Thomas

My wife and I had dinner with the Maestro Erich Kunzel of the Cincinnati Pops and his wife, Brunhilde, at their home. Erich was not one to throw compliments around, but during a discussion of pop performers, he was especially impressed with B.J. Thomas.

B.J. had a lot of hits, starting with the Hank Williams song "I'm So Lonesome I Could Cry." That song was more than a hit record for him because he told me, "In my family life, there were some problems. I didn't relate to my father, and he didn't relate to me, but I could always communicate with him if I sang a song, and he loved Hank Williams."

Although B.J. had hit records, he also had some big personal problems, and he said that over the years, the people thought he was a John Davidson, but in his heart, he was Ray Charles. He explained, "I had a drug problem from the time I was fifteen years old. It really came from a problem in my family and not having a solid relationship with my dad. I was kind of searching, and when I got away from home and was involved in all this success and money, I think it further confused me. My involvement with the drugs was really rough, and by 1975 I had to drop out. I just couldn't get it together. I was separated from my wife. Through my wife, and the fact that she became a Christian in December of 1975, through her prayers and acceptance of me, I became a born-again Christian myself in January 1976."

He admitted to me that he was taking more than one hundred pills a day. He confessed, "That happened many times. Over a course of weeks, I went through ten thousand pills. I must be honest with you, it really wasn't until 1970 when I got involved with cocaine that I started a real downhill slide. I know I couldn't have made it much farther. It was just a devastating drug that robbed me of everything. I know now it's the rich man's marijuana, and they like to soft pedal it, but in just a month, it can turn a normal person into a neurotic, psychotic person."

He told me he owes his life to his wife: "I was into some real strong narcotics as far as downers go, to get to sleep. Gloria did have to be with me all the time. She did save my life numerous times in the night when I'd be strangling—having problems breathing. If it wasn't for Gloria, I wouldn't be here."

B.J. told me how he met the Lord: "I had asked the Lord to take my drugs. The Lord allowed me to be strong enough to stand up and put them down. Since that day, I've had no problems with drugs—a life of freedom. I don't want to say it's been easier, because in a lot of ways, it's been tougher, but it's certainly been more rewarding, satisfying, and peaceful and secure."

Jerry Lee Lewis

I hung out with a rock 'n' roll legend for a week in October 1974. Jerry Lee Lewis was playing at the Beverly Hills Supper Club. His road manager at the time was my friend Bob Patton. Bob worked at one time for James Brown and was married to a beautiful Cincinnati Playboy bunny. A couple of weeks before James opened in Las Vegas for the first time, Bob was sent in to get things organized. He stayed at the hotel, checked out the restaurants and places James might visit. Bob, a white guy, would tip and be high profile so that when it was time for James to arrive, Bob was a step or two in front of him making sure everything went smoothly. Hey, it was the early seventies, a different era.

Bob got Jerry Lee and me together, and after his shows, we'd sit in his dressing room drinking whiskey out of a bottle. I have a great interview with Jerry, but he could get nasty when he was drunk. Long after closing time, we were sitting at the bar when he started talking about Jesus. The Schilling boys, who owned the club, were sitting near us talking and laughing among themselves when Jerry called them a bunch of "Jews," because he thought they were laughing at him. I calmed him down and explained they were the owners.

He told me before his last show that he had a commitment and couldn't party afterwards. I visited his dressing room to say my good-bye, and after we had a couple of drinks, Jerry Lee asked me if I knew of a place that had a piano. It was late, and everything was closed, but

I called my friend Jerry Scarlotta, who owned the Italian Inn downtown. He had an electric piano in his club upstairs, and he gladly opened the place for me. Jerry Lee wanted to hang, so we took off, followed by his entourage, including his pretty sister, Linda Gail. He sat down at the piano and played every song you could imagine. I sat next to him and listened as he talked about getting kicked out of the Southwestern Assemblies of God University in Waxahachie, Texas, for putting a rock 'n' roll beat to the hymnal. He actually played a boogie-woogie rendition of "My God is Real." He was sure he was going to hell for playing the devil's music. He wished that he could be more like his cousin Jimmy Swaggart, the television evangelist. (Ironically, it turned out Swaggart wasn't so pure when he propositioned a prostitute as reported in a high-profile 1988 sex scandal.) He had tears in his eyes talking about his fourteen-year-old son, who was killed in a car accident a year earlier.

Jerry Lee would bounce back and forth from rock to religious music. He was crying when he played a song about lost love and con-

Jerry Lee Lewis was in a mellow mood when we got together years later when this picture was taken.

fided to me that he was still in love with his third wife, Myra Brown. He was married to another woman at the time. Myra was his first cousin once removed and thirteen at the time of their marriage; he was about twenty-three. A lot of radio stations banned his music when this became public in 1958. He insisted to me over and over that Myra was the only woman he ever loved. Jerry said, in his gravelly, Louisiana drawl, "Jimmy, she wasn't thirteen—she was closer to fourteen." He played and sang everything, even "God Bless America." It was close to seven in the morning when someone reminded him his plane was waiting at the airport. We exchanged hugs and good-byes; he wanted to give me one of his motorcycles, but I couldn't accept it. He did get me a yellow tour jacket, which I still have. It was a night I'll never forget.

Beverly Hills Supper Club

The Beverly Hills Supper Club was the place to be in the tristate area. On May 28, 1977, I was driving home from an appearance about thirty minutes outside of Cincinnati. It was Memorial Day weekend, the weather was beautiful, and my event was a big success. I couldn't believe what I was hearing on WLW. I turned the radio up louder. There was a fire at the Beverly Hills Supper Club in Southgate, Kentucky, just outside of Cincinnati, and people were dead. Every report painted a more devastating picture. An old friend who had been on my show a number of times was the headliner—John Davidson. I thought about all the times I'd been there. Ron and Rick, along with their brother Scott Schilling, ran the place and were always very generous to me. They made sure the entertainers appeared on my show and got me front row center stage even if they had to add chairs and tables to accommodate me. That night, it was the worst seat to be in because you were far away from the exit. If I didn't have a record hop that night, I very well could have been there. I later found out my close friend Jeff Ruby was sitting up front with his girlfriend, Susan Brown, and they just made it out. Only ten other people made it out their door before it closed. The place was always packed because for

$12.95, you got a full dinner, and you saw a Las Vegas show in a beautiful club. The total death count was 167. Everyone in town knew someone who died. Fire code regulations were changed all over the country because of this. Today, it's automatic with me—I always look to see where the exits are when I enter any establishment.

I had seen so many great entertainers at the Beverly. I introduced my wife to Frankie Valli backstage and was surprised to hear that his current wife had also been an airline hostess like Sally. Another time, at a benefit I was involved with, singer Mel Torme told me the story of how he wrote the "Christmas Song" during a scorching hot California summer day. Mel wasn't happy when I referred to him as the "Velvet Fog." It was an endearing label that was given to him years before, but he didn't like it. The Righteous Brothers always packed the showroom. Yes, that was comedian Redd Foxx hanging out in the lounge.

Ricky Nelson

Marty Brennaman, the Reds' announcer, and I along with several Reds' players and their wives took in the Rick Nelson show at the Beverly. We were all pumped to see Ricky. He sang with his Stone Canyon Band, and nobody recognized the songs. He didn't sing his big hits. It was embarrassing because some of our guys started yelling, 'sing "Travelin' Man" or "Poor Little Fool,"' but he just kept singing his new stuff that was unexpected and unfamiliar. People were walking out. My wife is a huge Nelson fan, and she was very disappointed. After the show, I introduced myself to his manager Greg McDonald; I told him what I thought, but he looked at me like I was crazy. He had so many hits that those alone would make a show. My idea was to sing the hits, do a little story intro from time to time and introduce your new music sparingly. Of course a few years earlier, he basically got the same reaction at an oldies show in Madison Square Garden in New York and wrote and recorded his comeback hit the autobiographical "Garden Party." Ricky thought the crowd was booing him, but his manager said the "boos" were directed at a fight that had broken out in the Garden's balcony. He stopped doing the revival shows for a while after that night. He didn't even look like Ricky Nelson with his long hair. It took some time, but Greg did convince Rick to sing the hits, and I had the pleasure of introducing Rick a number of times at the beautiful Murphy Theater in Wilmington, Ohio. Rick was always gracious to me and my guests backstage. He still looked terrific with his hair slicked back, and my wife along with her girl-friends would scream the loudest. One night, I made the mistake of grabbing his microphone to introduce him, and I just about blew everybody's eardrums off. To compensate for his soft voice, they had to crank up his microphone.

I was driving home from a New Year's Eve party in 1985 when I heard on the news that Rick had died in a plane crash. There are a lot of connect-the-dots stories in rock 'n' roll, and this is one of them. I've done a number of shows with Pat Upton, the Spiral Staircase's lead singer. When he sings, other performers stop what they're doing backstage and listen. Sonny Geraci of the Outsiders stood next to me while Pat was singing his hit "More Today, Than Yesterday," and he was hanging onto every note. That doesn't happen very often back-stage. After his group broke up, Pat played rhythm guitar and sang backup for a number of years with Rick.

Pat left Rick in 1983 to open a small club called P.J.'s Alley in Guntersville, Alabama. Rick played his last show at Pat's club before he died in that plane crash. I was under the impression that Rick was doing Pat a favor, but Pat told me: "You know, it was a mutual thing." Rick's manager, Greg McDonald, called him because their travel schedule had them going from Orlando back to Los Angeles and then back in a day or two to Dallas. Pat explained, "So rather than do that, Greg said, 'We'll just work for what comes in off the door, and that way we don't have to make the flight across country and back.' It was just kind of a convenient situation for both." Rick had such a good time performing in front of the club's biggest crowd ever that he stayed over and did an unscheduled show that Monday. He spent the day relaxing with Pat's family. Ironically, the last song he sang was Buddy Holly's "Rave On," and the last words he said on stage were, "Rave on for me." Buddy Holly was killed in a plane crash in February 1959, "the day the music died." The day after what turned out to be Rick's last performance, he headed to Dallas for KLUV's New Years Eve Sock Hop concert. His plane was a forty-three-year-old classic DC-3 once owned by another rock icon, Jerry Lee Lewis. He never made it; his plane crashed northeast of Dallas in De Kalb, Texas.

CHAPTER 15

Am I Dead Yet?

I was going to die a slow, painful death, and there was nothing I could do about it. As a child of the fifties, with the deaths of James Dean and Buddy Holly, I thought I would die young, but this was crazy—I had just turned twenty-one. It happened during my senior year at Allegheny College while I was working in the new freshman girl's cafeteria washing dishes. I was in the deep-freeze getting a dish of ice cream when someone, as a joke, slammed the door. No big deal, there was a latch inside to open it, only it was stuck. I couldn't get out; I started yelling and pounding on the door, but of course no one could hear me. I knew the lights were about to be shut off because everyone was leaving. I had nothing on but a t-shirt and jeans. It was already getting cold. I started stacking up frozen food packages around me in the hope that might keep me warm. The lights went out. I was now all alone. It was a Sunday. I didn't have a coat or books and nothing left behind. The next time anyone would use this freezer would be Wednesday when they got ice cream. I lived off campus, and I had just broken up with my girlfriend who went to another college. I was going to freeze to death, and there was nothing I could do about it. Nobody would miss me for days. It's funny, my whole life flashed before me. I guess that's pretty normal when you know you're going to die. I thought about my family, my friends, and the future I would never see. I said a prayer.

I got angry because I shouldn't have been here. My freshman year, I waited on tables in the dining hall as part of my work scholarship, and I had an accident while I was serving the head table Christmas dinner before break. I hit a Christmas decoration while I was carrying a full tray of eight dinners; dishes and food went flying everywhere. I tried to joke about it, but it wasn't funny to the head table. During desert, I served chocolate pie with lots of whipped cream, and one of the girls turned into her pie as I was placing it on the table. The whipped cream was all over her arm. I didn't think anyone noticed so I scooped it up with my hand and put it back on the pie. That was my last day as a waiter. I was demoted to the "crud room," washing dishes for the next three and a half years.

If I had a few more votes, my college career may have been better. My freshman year, I was nominated for a class office, and I gave a great speech that my classmates loved, but the guys who knew me in my dorm voted against me. They told me, "You are flunking out. It's early November—you've got to study." I lost the election by a few votes. I was a National Honor Society student in high school; maybe I should have known better. My advisor had me carry twenty-one credit hours my first semester. I was only seventeen years old, it was my first time away from home, and I was working two shifts every day in the dining hall. I was overwhelmed. How could they do this to me? I was set up to fail.

I kept busy moving frozen food boxes around. I had to smile when I thought of a study break I took my freshman year to hear Louis Armstrong perform in Meadville, and afterward I waited in the rain to talk with him. Several of us were invited to his dressing room where he signed autographs and regaled us with his stories. He looked at me and said, "You're a horn man. I just entertained you now let me hear you play." He handed me his trumpet and, for a minute, I thought about playing it but didn't. With his openness and engaging personality, it was easy to see why "Old Satchmo" was one of America's greatest ambassadors.

I shouldn't be in this freezer. What was I doing at Allegheny? I flunked out of premed; I was thinking seriously about the ministry, but I was questioning my faith; I wasn't playing baseball; and I was a "GDI." (I was an independent referred to as a "GDI" or "God Damned Independent" by the fraternities.) I was invited to a lot of fraternity parties, but I still had the stigma of being an independent.

I did leave my mark at Allegheny a year earlier when I put together its first rock 'n' roll show. It was the money-raising event for the school's annual fund drive. The appropriation fee was $700.00, and we charged $1.25 at the David Mead Field House. I was the emcee and coordinated the show, which was followed by a Twistathon in the gym until 1:00 a.m. I know the coeds liked it because we got them a 1:30 a.m. curfew. The show was headlined by the Skyliners who had "Since I Don't Have You" and "This I Swear." Andrea Carroll, a television regular from Cleveland, sang "Please Don't Talk to the Lifeguard," the Stereos danced and sang their hit "I Really Love You," and my high school buddy, guitarist Al Masciola led the Bobby Vinton Twist Band and played for the Twist party after the show. Allegheny College had never seen anything like this, and I was happy to be a part of introducing the faculty and students to rock 'n' roll.

Anyway, it wasn't the school's fault I was about to die. My whole life was flashing in front of me. I seemed happiest when I was around music. I remember playing the mandolin with my grandfather when I was four. He had a beautiful pearl inlaid mandolin; mine was an old wooden one. I didn't really play it, of course, but I strummed along. Sundays were great at my grandmother's house. My aunt Dora played the piano, and we all sang along. Sometimes my cousin Joe, dressed in a tuxedo, would play the violin. There could be twenty of us standing around that piano.

My mother took me to my first opera, *Madame Butterfly*, when I was six. She introduced me to the classics and Broadway shows at an early age. My mother played her Mario Lanza records over and over. My mother was an amazing person.

I was getting cold, and my mind was playing games with me. I flashbacked to my house, and I saw my mom working in the yard with Amos. We got Amos as a baby at Easter, and he quickly became a member of our family. He was always right next to mom when she was hanging clothes or working in the garden. He'd wait for me at the gate quacking like crazy when he saw me coming home from school. None of the dogs messed with him. I think they knew better. Amos was the most famous duck in Pittsburgh or at least in our neighborhood.

I wondered if I disappointed my parents by not becoming a doctor. I was one of the good, clean-cut guys in high school, but that image got tainted a couple of years earlier when I was home from college. It was New Years Eve, and I kidded my mom as I left the house with a brown bag that I jokingly called my barf bag. She wasn't amused. I had a date with Judy, the kid sister of my friend Ronnie Miller's girlfriend, Janet. Ronnie's brother Gary was our designated driver because he didn't drink. When we left the party, Judy sat in the front seat with Gary and his date. Ronnie and I were inebriated, so Janet babysat with us in the back. It started to snow on the way home from the party. The roads were icy, and suddenly, just a few blocks from our house, we smashed into a telephone pole. The people in the front got pretty banged up, but I was fine. A history teacher at our high school took us into his house while we waited for an ambulance, and we made a mess of his living room. There was blood everywhere. I was so drunk I was wearing my friend Ronnie's thick glasses, and he had mine. I couldn't see a thing. I missed the ambulance, but his parents came by and gave me a ride to the hospital. I called my mom to tell her, but she knew I was in trouble. She had that great mother's intuition. My brother, Sam, said his teacher told his class about the drunken graduates he encountered. He never mentioned us by name, but everyone knew. Oh, my date, Judy, and I never went out again, but the accident occurred in front of Musmanno's Funeral Home. My buddy Anthony would one day take over the family business, and Judy would become his first wife.

I had some great times at home during college breaks just hanging with my old high school friends. The college crowd partied in the Shadyside section of Pittsburgh, and that's where I was a couple of days before I could legally drink. There was a bar raid with cops all over. I went to the men's room stood on the toilet seat, waited for things to calm down, and climbed out a window.

I was lucky those nights, but sitting in this locked freezer, my time was running out.

My mother went to most of my Little League games, but my father was always working and didn't see me play until we got back from the series in Williamsport when I was twelve. We played on the high school field where there were no fences. I hit one that went between two towers on the football field. It would have been way over a Little League fence and a good hit for a high school player, but the outfielders played me so deep I only got a double. I looked up from second base, and my dad was so excited he fell off the bleachers. He was all smiles, and I was thrilled that he saw me play.

Scenes from my life both sad and happy were flickering by, and I was now shivering. During the summers, I would spend every day practicing baseball at the high school field. Mil Tatala was in charge of the fields, so we always had a bucket of balls and bats. His son Skippy and I would take an occasional break to visit Mancini's Bakery for a hot loaf of bread and a soda pop. Once a week, Mil took us to a baseball camp in North Park run by a former Pirates' pitcher, Joe Vitelli. Joe also picked the Allegheny County All-Star team, ages thirteen to eighteen. Every year the North All-Stars would play the South in a televised game, and I was the starting catcher and got a hit every year from the time I was thirteen.

When a vision of well-endowed ladies popped into my mind, I knew I was in my uncle's garage because those ladies were featured in several calendars hanging in the work area. My uncle Pete owned the Forbes Field Garage right next to the Pirates' home, and that's where some of the players parked their cars. My summer vacation would include a few days in Oakland living above that garage. Gus Bell was with the Pirates, and I'd talk to his dad (he had a Dodge) while he was waiting on his son. Monte Basgell, the second baseman, picked me out from a bunch of kids, "Hey kid, do you wanna see the game?" He walked me in and showed me where to sit. I was like a VIP. I talked with Ralph Kiner and Joe Garagiola (he wore wild clothes and had poor penmanship). The neighbors listening to the game on the radio would yell when a ball was coming over the fence, and we'd run after it.

I got upset thinking about the doctor who messed up the operation on my leg that essentially ended my promising baseball career. I played, but I was limited in my ability.

I was going to die, and here I was thinking about things that happened in high school. The first day of gym in the boys' locker room, we got a stern warning from Mil Tatala, the gym teacher: "Stay away from the keyhole to the girl's locker room," which was connected to ours. He told us about the kid who was caught and expelled from school. Nobody ever found out that kid's name. Some guys looked anyway, but all we ever saw was a towel over the door handle or another eye looking back at us.

One of our classmates, John Seretti, dropped out and joined the navy. Mr. Trapuzzano, our math teacher, would check attendance each day, and every day he'd read John's name. Someone would shout out that he joined the navy, and he'd say, "He's not here. He's absent without leave." This went on for days.

I tried to open the freezer door, but it was still locked, and I had a hard time moving my fingers. I sat on a case of frozen food and tried to make myself comfortable. I was much happier in high school than college. I guess that's why I kept going back there in my mind.

The closest drive-in restaurant was across the bridge in Bellevue. Eat 'n Park is where you went to be seen and meet girls from other schools. Anthony "Stroker" Crivelli had a 1954 Chevy, green roof/ yellow bottom, and Lou Mazzaro had a 1958 Chevy convertible, so they got lots of attention. We'd travel in somebody's family car. I'll be honest, the only time I got to ride shotgun was if I was the first guy picked up. Shotgun was the front passenger seat reserved for the guy who could talk the smoothest to the girls in the other cars. I was too shy. In our group, that seat of honor belonged to Patsy Aluise. He had to be cool—he dated a senior when we were in the ninth grade. The rest of us would argue over who got a backseat window, and then it was understood you had to let Patsy do the talking. Sometimes we'd be cruising the lot, and if a great song like the Drifters' "There Goes My Baby" or "Shout," the Isley Brothers' hit, came on the radio, we'd blast the volume, get out of the car, and dance. Yes, we were cool. We probably cruised that drive-in hundreds of times, and we all agreed Patsy had the lines, but I don't recall us ever connecting with any girls.

I knew a little about hypothermia and that constant shivering and mental confusion are key symptoms. I wasn't apathetic, but I was realistic. I just didn't know how long I had to live. My mind was wandering, but it was still sharp, and that was a good sign.

The toughest teacher at Stowe High was a part-timer who worked after the National Football League season. His bubble gum card listed him at six foot one, 235 pounds, a Stowe High graduate. He would walk into the classroom, and you could hear a pin drop. He knew who the bad ass guys were and would hover over them. Alex Sandusky was an All Pro guard with the Baltimore Colts. His job was to protect quarterback Johnny Unitas, and he did it well. The two years he taught me, the Colts won the NFL Championship 1958 and 1959. He showed us a map and said, "This is Los Angeles where we beat the Rams in our last regular season game. We had to play the Giants in the championship game, but on the way back to Baltimore, a few of my teammates took a detour home and stopped off here in Las Vegas. They spent that championship bonus money before they made it, so they had an extra incentive to win the game." The winners share that year was $4,700, and the losers got $3,000.

Alex Sandusky was one tough guy, and I'll bet nobody ever messed with him. I was never a tough guy. Well, that is until the tenth grade, and then only for a few days. I did enjoy the respect, and I had the swagger that went with it. In the tenth grade, a big new kid we called "Kansas" sat behind me in history class. He acted tough in a leather jacket and rode a motorcycle. He drove me crazy. He would pretend to spit in my hair and laugh. I kept telling him to stop, but he kept bugging me. One day when the teacher left the room, I spun around in my chair and hit him with a right, left combination to the face that bloodied his nose. I turned around, just as the teacher walked back in and asked Charles, Kansas, why he had his head on the desk. He said he had a headache. During the rest of the class, he kept telling me how he was going to kill me after school. This was the last class of the day, and it was also our homeroom. I went to the pencil sharpener, and my friends told me, "You know he's going to kill you." It echoed through the halls: "Big fight after school behind the church across from Stowe High!" I wasn't a fighter, I was one of the goodie academic students, and I was gonna get an ass whipping. The bell finally rang, and everyone left the room except Kansas and me. He kept repeating that he was going to kill me, "You're dead. I'm going to kill you." He said this over and over as he was putting on his leather jacket. He got both arms in his jacket, but he didn't have them all the way in. I whipped into him with punch after punch; he was helpless. As he was lying on the ground, I said to him as I waved my finger at him with a smile, "Not today." About that time, some people came looking for us and saw him lying on the ground. No, he never bothered me again, but I had a target on my back. I got pretty cocky with my newfound fame. Even around my best friends I was obnoxious. Shortly after that at Musmanno's house, one of the guys said, "Do you think you can take Dave Oliver?" Dave was one of my best friends and a big lineman on the football team. We fought in front of our friends, right there. Oh, it wasn't much of a fight; he got me with two punches. None of my buddies felt sorry for me. I deserved it. Within a week, someone went gunning for Dave, and he got beat. That's how it went at our school.

I tried to keep my mind busy. I didn't want to think about where I was and what was about to happen to me in the freezer. I remember marching down a muddy football field in the high school band during halftime when somebody lost a shoe, and our band director was yelling at him not to pick it up. On another occasion, the band was marching in a parade, and as the people starting clapping, one of our members took his hat off and bowed to the crowd. He did this a number of times, and the crowd loved it, but our director went crazy.

I wanted to thank some people who helped me but that wasn't going to happen. It was pitch black in that freezer, and I couldn't see my hand in front of my face. I couldn't stop shivering. One special person was Tony Pasquarelli, my trumpet instructor. He was the top trumpet player in Pittsburgh and taught at Carnegie Tech's School of Fine Arts (today known as Carnegie Mellon University). He was like a big brother to me, and my weekly lessons included his philosophy. He taught me to be self-confident. He later taught my brother Sam, who became a high school All American trumpet player and toured Europe with the All American band. Our family was poor, and my brother and I don't remember ever paying him. He got a special scholarship for me during the summers to study music at Carnegie. The trumpet was a big part of my life. I practiced at least three hours a day, had the first chair in the high school band from my freshman year on, and played in several bands. I was good enough to make the All State band, but when I didn't even make district band my senior year, I quit. One day I put the trumpet down after having played it for well over six thousand hours, and I walked away. Mr. Pasquarelli had a lot of time invested in me, and he deserved an explanation, but I didn't have one.

I wanted a chance to tell my family good-bye. I thought about some of my old girlfriends and especially Faye. She went to Grove City College. We had just broken up, and I wondered how long it would take for her to find out I was dead. I was now moving very slowly, but I was still alert and scared.

All of these thoughts were going through my mind during a period of about forty-five minutes when a miracle happened. One of the freshman football players who said he'd meet me at the Red and White convenience store for a soda opened the door. In shock I threw a carton of ice cream and just missed him. I apologized. He got to the store and asked where I was, and the guy who shut the freezer door said the last time he saw me was in the freezer. That should have been the end of it, because getting a soda was just an afterthought, nothing definite. He kept thinking about that, and he had a feeling I might be in trouble. We worked together, but we weren't close friends. He was a freshman, and I was a senior. He decided for some reason to see for himself. He walked to the other end of campus through a closed cafeteria to the back of a kitchen and opened the deep-freeze. He saved my life!

Lou Rawls, Sam Cooke, and Herb Alpert

I was lucky. I defied death that day. I wasn't alone. I know of two recording stars that stared death in the face and walked away. Lou Rawls was a backup singer touring the south with Sam Cooke in 1958 when they were involved in a horrific accident. One passenger was killed, and Lou told me he was pronounced dead for a few seconds. He had a brain concussion and stayed in a coma for five and a half days. Lou said, "It wasn't time I guess." Sam Cooke defied death and was only slightly injured. Sam wasn't as fortunate six years later.

We were sitting on the deck of a boat enjoying a few drinks and talking about the music business. He was a Sam Cooke prodigy who had several hit records. I told him I never believed Sam died the way the police and the press reported. Sam was murdered in December of 1964 in a three-dollar-a-night motel in south central LA. The manager of the hotel said she shot him in self-defense. It was ruled a justifiable homicide. He was in her office wearing only a sports jacket and shoes but no shirt, pants, or underwear. Cooke was looking for the woman who accompanied him, Elisa Boyer. Elisa said she had taken his clothes by mistake; she ran away because she thought he was going to rape her. Incidentally the cash he had was never recovered.

Sam's friend told me why he was killed and the name of the man who had him murdered. He told me this story a couple of times. The man he accused was a big name in the entertainment business and has since passed away. In the spirit of confidentiality, I won't give either name. Sam was lured to this motel or somewhere and was savagely beaten and his body was dumped there and the story made up. Sam Cooke had gotten too big and uppity. He was set up, and there was a cover-up.

Sam was married, but he was a womanizer, and he had dated Elisa Boyer—the woman he was with that night, three weeks earlier. About a month later she was arrested for prostitution. Earlier that evening, Sam had a business meeting at Martoni's Restaurant off Sunset Boulevard, and Elisa was with him in his red Ferrari convertible when they hit PJ's club later that night.

Sam Cooke was a singer, songwriter, and entrepreneur. He was one of the first black performers who took care of the business side of his career. He had a record label and a publishing company. He was one of the first black performers in the rock era to have white women swoon. That fateful night, some people wanted to buy into his lucrative business. Sam reportedly declined, saying, "I like being my own man." He had recently signed an unprecedented deal, in which he would get his master tapes, site fees, gate revenues for live concerts, 10 percent of all records and singles sold, and back royalties, resulting in over one million dollars a year. He was setting a dangerous precedent, and it could cost the record industry a fortune. This angered a lot of white executives. Instead of recording another vanilla song like "Wonderful World" or "Twistin' the Night Away," a few weeks before his death, he recorded a protest song that sounded like a slave narrative, "A Change is Gonna' Come." Was he sounding like an angry black man?

I believe my friend's story that Sam Cooke was not murdered the way the LAPD investigation reported.

Sam Cooke influenced a lot of people in the business, including recording star Herb Alpert. Herb has one of the best ears in the business for talent and is the "A" in A&M Records.

Herb told me that they worked together, and that Sam was probably the biggest influence in his life in terms of records and how to approach music. Herb said, "He gave me an experience I'll never forget. We were auditioning this singer from Trinidad, and I was really entranced by this approach that this fella had. He was very handsome, and he came in with a box, and he put his foot on a stool, and he started singing and strumming his guitar. I was really sucked in by him. Sam said, 'Turn your back on him for ten minutes and see what you think,' which I did, and I didn't feel a thing. Sam said, 'Look, it doesn't matter if a guy is black or green or red or if he practices twelve hours a day or he doesn't practice at all, because when you're dealing with a record, you're dealing with a cold piece of wax, and that's all there is.' So whenever I hear a group or listen to new material, I keep that in mind."

Set-ups

In the spring of 1975, the *Enquirer* story read, "It's no secret that WKRC has approached Jim LaBarbara who has a binding contract prohibiting him from moving locally." WKRC's general manager, Leon Lowenthal discretely asked me at a radio function to be their afternoon-drive personality. He said they'd pay me a lot more money, and he wanted me to get together with their program director. I knew Taft Broadcasting was very generous to their key people. I met the program director at Grammer's Restaurant. While we were being seated, the *Enquirer*'s radio writer Steve Hoffman just happened to be sitting nearby. A few minutes into our conversation, I realized I had been set up. It's disappointing, but sometimes this is how the radio game is played.

Transcendental Meditation

In 1975 I finally took John Denver's advice, and I began meditating. I was featured in a July 1976 article in *Cincinnati Magazine* titled "Things Go Better with TM." I was a student of transcendental meditation (TM) and the teachings of the Maharishi Mahesh Yogi, the one-time guru to the Beatles and the Beach Boys. I know it sounds weird, but this has nothing to do with Eastern cultures, uncomfortable pretzel positions on the floor, or altered lifestyles. It's a simple relaxation technique where you sit quietly for twenty minutes twice a day with your eyes closed saying your mantra over and over. A typical mantra might be "ommm." This really does soothe your mind and body. For me it offered a sanctuary of silence in a crazy world of noise. I was doing a four-hour afternoon drive show on WLW, taught broadcast-ing at the University of Cincinnati, freelanced for television commer-cials, and carried a heavy load of personal appearances.

My wife stopped by the center because she was a skeptic. I was given my mantra at a ceremony and was told only my teacher and the Maharishi would know it. I was to tell no one. Sally bought a piece of furniture for the same amount of money I spent on TM and said, "Let's see which one lasts longer." We did have dinner with the Beach Boys' Mike Love, a TM advocate, and his girlfriend at the center. It was an all natural, healthy meal—and I wanted to stop at McDonald's on the way home.

When I practiced TM daily, I had a tremendous amount of energy, but I never wanted to advance my meditation to the next level. I only used it for relaxing. I had a guest on my WCKY talk show who wrote a book about everything. I asked him if he knew my secret TM mantra. He asked me my date of birth and quickly told me my secret mantra that was no longer a secret. It's based on your astro-logical sign.

Evel Knievel

The number one daredevil in the world was in town, and he wanted to talk with me. Working on a powerhouse like WLW had its privi-leges. The great Evel Knievel wanted to check out King's Island before his big jump over fourteen Greyhound buses, and he invited my wife, Sally, and I to see his trailer. Howard Cosell did a network Saturday night variety show that Evel was on with Muhammad Ali. Ali admired a beautiful gold necklace of Jesus that Evel was wearing. Evel said it was one of a kind, but he graciously took it off and gave it to Ali. It was a very touching moment. Knievel had a very gentle and giving side. I mentioned this, and he said, "I want to show you some-thing, but if you tell anybody, I'll have to kill you," and he laughed. He proceeded to pull a board off the trailer floor exposing a hidden safe. He opened it and showed me half a dozen golden Jesus necklaces like the one he gave Ali.

"But you said you only had one."

He answered, "Yes, I did say that," with a smile on his face.

There were just a few of us in his trailer. He had a bottle of whiskey he shared, and we talked about his career, the mafia in Detroit, and his upcoming jump. I had to turn the recorder off from time to time. He loved to golf and gamble, but he carried a sawed-off shotgun in his golf bag just in case someone was hesitant to pay up. Yes, he had to show it on occasion. Don Cherry, the singer, saw it up close. Evel made his own money collections.

I wanted to emcee the jump, but that honor went to my friend Cleveland disc jockey John Lanigan who was a close friend of the event's sponsor, a Cleveland car dealer. As I mentioned, when I left WLW to go to Denver for nine months, John was leaving Denver for Cleveland, and he gave me all his personal appearances. I made a lot of extra money thanks to John.

On October 25, 1975, Evel Knievel successfully jumped fourteen Greyhound buses at King's Island theme park and scored the highest viewer ratings in the history of ABC's *Wide World of Sports*. It was his longest successful jump, 133 feet.

After the jump, Lanigan and I had dinner, but we skipped Evel's party and instead had a great six-hour conversation, as only radio guys can have, talking about radio.

John once tried to get me to do afternoons on WGAR in Cleveland when he did mornings. I was tempted, especially when his program director said, "If you ever leave WLW for any reason, I will hire you at whatever salary you were making." Lanigan later moved to Magic, and we got together when they brought me in for WIXY reunions. He is one of radio's great talents. John has pushed the envelope for years on his show and has been on the cutting edge of talk radio.

Personal appearances

It's funny. You could say my radio career started at that first record hop I did at the high school dance with Pinky in the 1950s, and I'm still playing music for events. I've played the music for hundreds of weddings, class reunions, and parties over the years, and I still enjoy it. I don't think there are many guys in the country who have been doing them longer than me.

The hardest part is getting the equipment in and out. I learned the hard way and now do it myself. Years ago I watched an inebriated client drop one of my big speakers down a flight of thirty steps. It wasn't a pretty sight as it disintegrated on the way down.

I've seen a number of wedding crashers. During one reception a couple was pretty obvious—drinking and dancing up a storm. At one point in the evening, I noticed everyone seemed to be preoccupied with something on the outside patio. It was an expensive venue, and the mystery couple finally disappeared. At the end of the evening, I mentioned the couple to the father of the bride. He was very calm and asked if I saw them on the patio. I hadn't. Apparently they were enjoying their lovemaking in front of everyone. They got kicked out but continued with their activities just off the property. This ended when someone called the police.

I had done a number of dances in a particular church basement, but I thought it was a little strange when I was greeted by a police officer. As the evening proceeded, I noticed a few of the guys in the wedding party were sporting black eyes and missing teeth. After the reception, a fight broke out in the church between the two families. The bride's family wasn't happy with the serviceman groom taking their daughter away. Two of the brothers really got into it outside, and when the police chased them, they jumped into a car, locked the doors, and whipped up on each other. In a way, it was kind of funny. The police were knocking on the car windows and couldn't do anything because the doors were locked.

For another event I was playing the music for a wedding reception in northern Kentucky, but no one was on the dance floor. They were all gathered around a table chanting, "Go, go, go!" The table centerpieces were big goldfish bowls, and a couple of the guys were having a chug-a-lug contest. It wasn't long before all the goldfish were in fishy heaven.

During a high school reunion at the Kenwood Country Club, I couldn't help but notice one very romantic couple that really connected with my music because they were so openly affectionate. I later asked the lady who hired me about the couple. Yes, they were married, but not to each other. It was quitting time, and as I was playing my goodnight songs, a few attractive ladies asked me to play longer. I explained it was time to leave when one voluptuous lady said, "What if I show you these?" And she exposed herself to me. Okay, I did play a few more songs.

I had done a number of dances for this group, and it was always a lot of fun, but that changed when I played the 45 record "Gloria" by the Shadows of Knight. A big guy pounded the table and got all over me. He said, "F—— Gloria." I stopped the record, but he kept yelling at me. The guy who hired me just stood there and said nothing. It turned out, the angry guy was once married to Gloria, the sister of the man who hired me, and they had recently divorced. He didn't want to get involved. I never did another dance for them. Life's too short.

It was a snowy winter night and I was booked in a hall I had never worked on the top of a steep hill. I was surprised it was a motorcycle club, and the dance was oversold. They had free whiskey and beer—a lethal combination. I was set up on the dance floor with no buffer between me and the dancers. The ladies' room toilets were overflowing before I played the first song. I learned not to be judgmental. It turned out to be a great night with no problems.

I did a rock 'n' roll dance, and there were only six people. I did my regular routine and talked about the music. The people danced and had a good time. When they paid me, I said, "I'm sorry you didn't have a bigger crowd." They answered, "This was everyone we invited."

CHAPTER 16

Bill Randle
My Friend and Mentor

There have been a number of radio personalities who have had an influence on me. The earliest one I remember wasn't a disc jockey. I couldn't have been older than nine or ten in the early 1950s, when I would hang onto every word sportscaster Bill Stern said. He did a network radio show and would tell fantastic stories of the oddest characters who ever played sports. His stories ranged from horses winning races with dead jockeys on their backs, to legless or armless baseball players, to a blind athlete winning a marathon but losing the only love of his life. He read each story with incredible emotion. It was like a soap opera. A newscaster on his network adopted his style and became a millionaire. Paul Harvey could also paint a great picture with words. Listening to Bill Stern gave me the idea to do my little stories about artists and records. Of course I didn't go through all the dramatics, but I did a lot of research and loved to tell the listener something I didn't think they'd hear anywhere else.

I loved to listen to the radio. I'd even practice introducing records on a tape recorder I got when I was a teenager. Yeah, I could do that, it was easy. I mentioned earlier that I was influenced by Porky Chadwick's honesty and passion on the radio. However, I thought if I'd ever be a disc jockey, I'd be like Clark Race. He did afternoons on KDKA Pittsburgh and had a television bandstand show. He drove fancy sports cars and looked like he had a lot of money. If I got into radio, it would be to make a lot of money. I never planned on falling in love with radio.

On the radio, I always thought I was talking with my friend. I prided myself in being plugged into the community, and I brought that to my on-air work. I'd reflect whatever the water cooler talk was that day and give my observation on things I saw. I was always over prepared. I believe in preparation, preparation, and more preparation. I have a passion for radio, and I love being on the air. I always listened to the personality who would entertain me, not the guy who just gave the time and temperature.

The disc jockey that influenced me the most was a man I never heard do a radio show until years later. I knew his name and reputation. Bill Randle is an important name in the history of radio and pop music. He played an enormous role in my life.

On WKYC Cleveland, I introduced a Bobby Darin song with one of my quick stories, and my engineer yelled in to me, "You sounded like Bill Randle. That's something he'd say." I was flattered, and I said, "I've got to give him a call. I'd love to talk with him." He was Bill's engineer years before, and he laughed at me and added that Randle wouldn't give me the time of day. Bill Randle was one of the most successful disc jockeys of all time. He introduced Elvis for the first time on network television and was credited with discovering Johnny Ray, the Crew-Cuts, the Four Lads, the Diamonds, and others. *Time Magazine* named Bill Disc Jockey of the Year 1955. He was hired by record labels to find new songs and artists. He showed me receipts from Mercury Records for work he had done. Bill made a lot of money. He did the first movie with Elvis, and his weekday radio show was number one in Cleveland. He flew his plane to New York on weekends for his radio program on WCBS. He was a scholarly, well-educated man with a law degree, several PhD degrees, and a number of master's degrees. WERE even answered his request to have a shower installed near his studio so he could freshen up before his program after playing tennis.

I never tried to reach Bill when I was in Cleveland, but my engineer was wrong. He did talk to me. It was ten years later when I called him, and he knew all about me and said he was planning on calling me. Bill was the new head of the broadcasting department at the University of Cincinnati. We had lunch, and he made me an offer. If I would teach two eight o'clock classes, he would give me a scholarship to get my master's degree in broadcasting. With the number of years I had in the business and a master's degree, it would be equivalent to a PhD. Columbia University in New York was already recognizing

Dr. Bill Randle, my mentor, my friend. Graduation day, 1977.

writers with the same background. A master's degree combined with my radio experience would be a yardstick for trading off professional experience for the PhD equivalent. Dr. Randle was putting a master's degree class together, and I was a part of it.

I enjoyed teaching, and I did have a teaching background. I student taught sixth grade for six months and taught at two Cleveland radio schools, including the WIXY School of Broadcasting. I taught a couple of years at the University of Cincinnati and a year at Xavier University. A number of my students went on to have wonderful radio careers. Randi Douglas was the co-host of a top-rated Cincinnati radio show for years, and Jeff Ziesmann bought a radio station and later hired me to do the afternoon show.

I got my master of arts degree in August 1977, and it was the busiest year of my life—my son, Jimmy, was born; I had the highest numbers ever doing afternoons on WLW; I did about one hundred appearances; and my lowest grade was a B. I planned on working on a PhD or getting a law degree, but Dr. Randle left at end of the year.

I just wrapped up a twenty-four-hour documentary of Elvis and rock 'n' roll for my master's thesis at the University of Cincinnati when Presley died. I became a go-to person for a number of interviews about Elvis, and I'm referenced in a number of Elvis books and writings. I called it "The Golden Years of Rock 'n' Roll from Elvis Presley to the Beatles." It included more than 150 interviews that I did, including one from the man who did the first movie with Elvis and introduced him to a network television audience.

Elvis Presley

Bill Randle had a lot to do with Elvis's early success, and he told me in great detail how he became involved with Elvis. "I read about a riot in a small Florida town. Elvis, Scotty Moore, and Bill Black had played a gig in that town, and like most hillbilly or country artists, they sold pictures and records out of the back of their car. Presley had an old pink Cadillac at the time. He had started to get interested in strippers. Most people aren't aware he had dated strippers, and he had seen strippers work. He started to implement some of the bumps and grinds into the act. It just had these kids crazy that night. They had rushed the car. They were breaking the records, and so it made the wires. I thought anybody who could do this . . . and the name fascinated me, 'Elvis Presley.'

"Arnold Shaw, who worked for the music publisher Edward B. Marks, was very tight with the artists and repertoire (A&R) guy, Steve Sholes at RCA. [Steve was the producer in charge of the label's Country and Western Department.] I asked Arnold if he could get me some records at Sun. I had seen some blues records on Sun, but we didn't have access to the Sun Records. Arnold was on his way to Nashville, and he heard Presley work. He bought the one song 'I Forgot to Remember to Forget' for publishing. He brought me the records. At first I didn't play them in New York because of CBS; it would have been unthinkable to play them. I had a free hand. I'd play 'Honky Tonk' by Bill Doggett, but a down-country artist like Presley's 'That's All Right'—the crudity of the record was just too much. Technically the records didn't meet CBS performance sound standards with Al Harris. Two weeks later, the reaction in Cleveland— phones ringing off the hook.

"This was mid-1955, because by the time of the Country Music Convention that summer, Presley records weren't even being played in country. *Billboard Magazine* carried a story. Presley won some small award, 'Even a disc jockey like Bill Randle thinks that Elvis Presley is going to be a big star.' It was an unusual thing to play country music at the time."

Bill was there, and he explained how Elvis went from Sun to RCA: "Okay, what really happened? Saturday afternoon Freddy Bienstock and Gene and Julian Alberbach [Gene and Julian were brothers who owned Hill and Range Music Publishing Company. Freddy was their nephew] came in, and they were signing me to a twenty-page contract on things that later on would have been constituted to be illegal. I had found so many records that they wanted to pay me literally a royalty for X thousands of dollars for anything that I brought to them that grossed over fifty thousand dollars—so in other words, if I gave them the information first. The first piece of information I gave them was Elvis Presley. I said, "There's a kid in the south who's the biggest thing I've ever seen in my life." Two weeks later, I was playing them on WCBS in New York. Freddy Bienstock had a date that night with a blonde lady who was very important to him. Gene and Julian Alberbach, very German, very rich heads of this music corporation, told Freddy, 'You get on an airplane, and you go down, and you sign him as a writer because of this other song 'I Forgot to Remember.'' So, Freddy, grumbling and groaning, goes down, and he signs him as a songwriter. At that time, Presley was managed by a local deejay, Bob Neal. Colonel Parker was with Eddie Arnold at the time. This is how the Alberbachs come in, and the real thing went down. Gene and Julian signed Presley to a publishing deal, but Steven Sholes was a part of their deal. They had contracts with everybody. Who knows what went on under the tables after everybody left? Mitch Miller of Columbia Records had a deal with the Alberbachs. They were very influential people at the time, so they signed Elvis as a writer. They brought Sholes in to make the deal with RCA Victor, and Victor put up some of the money for the buy-out from Sun Records and so did the Alberbachs with some royalties and things from the Alberbachs. So that was the package: Steven Sholes, who had never heard of Elvis until that time; the Alberbachs, the two German heads of a publishing company; Freddy Bienstock, who missed a date with this gorgeous blonde to sign this million dollar thing; and Bob Neal, who was the manager. Then they closed him out with the contract that wasn't up to snuff. Colonel Tom Parker became the head honcho because the Colonel was Steven Sholes's guy, and they were all in bed together, and that was the history of Elvis. Parker did run his career, and it was at that time that I stopped having anything to do with Presley on the level of things we were doing. I did the first concert with Presley at the Arena in Cleveland, but by then the relationship with Parker was very strained. The Colonel wrote me out of the history because he was only interested in Parker [himself]. The previous history has never been told until now—I'm telling you."

Bill Randle told me the deal to get Elvis to RCA went down for forty thousand dollars. Bill added, "We offered him to Mitch Miller at Columbia Records first. I was doing a film called *The Pied Piper of Cleveland* for what's now MCA but was Universal. In the film was Bill Haley and the Comets; Pat Boone; the little girl singer, Priscilla Wright from Canada; the Four Lads; and Elvis Presley, with Bill Black and Scotty Moore [he was appearing at the Circle Theater in Cleveland at the time]. We shot the film on October 20, 1955, at Brooklyn High School and at Saint Michael's Church hall. Pat Boone talked about it in a *Rolling Stone* article where he said it was the first time he ever worked with Presley. We did the film with Elvis, paid him two hundred dollars to do the film. At that time, the Four Lads were managed by Michael Stewart who was the president of United Artists. Mike Stewart afterward came up to me and said, 'You don't want to be associated with that kind of music.' Presley, by the way, had on red suede shoes, red socks, red shirt, red tie, and a red suit. That was it, a little gross for 1955, right?" He laughed. "At any rate, I said, 'Mike, this kid's going to be the biggest thing you ever saw.' Then Mike saw the reaction of the students—three thousand students. He called Mitch Miller, and Mitch got the records and turned them down. So Mitch had the first crack at Elvis even with the Freddy hustling because Columbia was a big record company. That was a little before Freddy went down, so Mitch had a clear shot at him."

Bill said nobody knew Elvis, but when he sang, the kids went wild, "They went berserk; it was just a mad house."

On January 28, 1956, Elvis made his first appearance on national network television, and Bill played an important role on Tommy and Jimmy Dorsey's *Stage Show*. Bill gave me his master of the original recording of that show recorded at CBS. Tommy Dorsey said, "Ladies and gentlemen, I'd like to present one of radio's most listened to disc jockeys, Bill Randle. . . . William?" Bill then introduced him. "We'd like at this time to introduce you to a young fella, who like many performers, Johnny Ray among them, come up out of nowhere to be overnight very big stars. This young fella we saw for the first time while making a movie short. We think tonight that he's going to make television history for you. We'd like you to meet him now,

Elvis Presley, and here he is."

Bill explained to me how he got to present Elvis.

"There are things that have never been told before. They are somewhat conspiratory [*sic*]. It's the way the music business worked then, and now. Tommy Dorsey had a music firm, a business firm, TD Music. Pop music performers make much more from royalties of songs. It's better to have 'Hey Jude' as a copyright than to make a lot of money on one-nighters. First of all, it's a fifty-six-year ownership. If it earns X dollars, it's important. Performances are a part of the ASCAP payoff. Your songs must be performed X number of times a year to keep the catalog active to keep it in operation. Well, Dorsey's catalog was big with a lot of Sinatra songs and stuff like that, but he needed action on it. CBS was one of the areas that gave the Peedmon Sheet enormous input. That's how they rated them. So when you got a song on CBS and Arthur Godfrey, it counted for X thousands of performances. So the deals were always made so that the song plug-gers [*sic*] got close to Godfrey, close to everybody trying to get their songs played. I had five hours on WCBS New York that was logged. I had more power than any single person in the music business total. When I put a song on, it was logged on the Peedmon Sheet, and every-body made a lot of money. I could have made a fortune playing records for people. I did, but not for that reason. I liked the records I played. Tino Barzie was the band manager for Tommy Dorsey, and he also ran his music firm. Tino had a song out that they wanted played, and we were just pushing Presley. I always got a lot of people on different shows. I used to work with Marlo Lewis's brother who booked the *Ed Sullivan Show*. He was moved out when Bob Precht married Sullivan's daughter and became the producer. The business works that way as well. I got a lot of people on the *Sullivan Show*. We made a deal with Tino Barzie that I would plug X number of the Tommy Dorsey things, plugs they called it, and he would give this kid a shot on the show, and I would introduce him. I knew Presley was going to be the biggest thing in the world, and I wanted national exposure for it, and I would get the credit for it. If I didn't do that, you wouldn't have the tape, and I'd be written out of the Presley story. I never cared about it until twenty years later; you and I are in the office, and I gave you the tape. So we made a deal with Tino Barzie, then Tino went to Dorsey. The Dorsey show didn't feature people like Elvis, a totally unknown performer. He just signed with Victor, and they put him on six shows—six shows—six plugs for me, six shows for scale. Well, it got to be very funny, because when he came in, and they took one look at him . . . He had no music, no charts. Here was a big band; they assumed everybody had arrangements. Today, it's nothing, but then you had to have big band arrangements. The band couldn't play for him, and they couldn't balance him. He had an electric guitar, and he moved around a lot, and they couldn't get a camera on him. Well, they didn't want him on the show. Not only that, the star of the show was the beautiful, black singer Sarah Vaughn, and her husband George Treadwell, a very militant kind of guy even for 1956, did not like hillbilly singers, particularly on the show, and Sarah had the biggest record in the country 'Make Yourself Comfortable.' In between was this iconic banjo player, Gene Sheldon. It was a very funny thing. Presley had a terrible case of acne, and he was in front of a mirror squeezing these big black heads. The makeup girl is running around screaming: "I can't do anything!" This kid's face looks like—you know, he looks like he's got leprosy when we get the cameras on him. It was the funniest scene. They finally plastered him with almost, like, asphalt, to at least make him look human. It was gross. He was really . . . acne bothered him, and when he'd get excited, and this was a big show, it made him break out. He went through all these funny things. They didn't even get a balance on him at the rehearsal because Jackie Gleason's producer said, 'Not going on, we're not going to use him.' But Jackie had seen him at the rehearsal, and he liked him. Then George Treadwell said, 'I'm not working with no hillbilly on my show,' and Jackie finally laid the law down. Elvis did go on, but they didn't have time to rehearse them. Elvis got excited when he got on the show, and he did the wrong song. First thing Elvis Presley ever sang on television was the 'Shake Rattle and Roll' and 'I Got a Woman,' both of which contained, for that time, somewhat dirty references. The Presley lyric,

'She's a woman / she's walking the streets,' it was the Ray Charles song 'I Got a Woman' who's a street walker is what he was saying. Gleason's producer is back there saying, 'I told you he'd ruin the show, and the producers are going crazy, and they're calling upstairs, "Are we getting any phone calls?" It was a funny scene, but it was an extremely exciting show, and they did the six shows. Presley took off from there, and then he did *Milton Berle*, the *Sullivan Show*, and *Steve Allen* things, and that was the beginning of his television career per se."

Bill said the girls in the studio audience loved Elvis that first night: "Don't forget the studios then were much more controlled. You literally didn't get out of line, or somebody would throw you out, but they went berserk. They were waiting for him. We had built up a lot of interest in him in New York in that short period of time."

What Bill remembered most about Elvis was that, "He went out of his way to be a perfect gentleman to every single person I've ever seen him deal with. Totally an honest, gentle person, a lovely human being, he really was."

I thought Randle would say something negative about the Colonel. He surprised me: "Presley loves the Colonel. The Colonel made him millions of dollars. I don't blame him; anybody would love him. The best thing that ever happened to Elvis was to be managed by Colonel Parker."

Johnny Ray

Over the years, Bill Randle has been credited with discovering Johnny Ray, but he wanted to set the record straight. Bill said, "I don't think this story has been told. I get a lot of credit for Johnny Ray, but the people who were responsible for Johnny were Phil McLean and Jerry Crocker. Phil and Johnny were dating a couple of dancers at the Alpine Village, which was across the street from the radio station where we worked. They would be up late at night because the girls worked until two. Jerry worked in Akron, and Phil worked in Cleveland. A booker named Sid Freeman, who booked hookers and gross shows, stags, you name it, he booked gay bars that were open really late because they were violating the law anyway and paying people off. So after the girls' club closed, they went to see Johnny Ray play at this gay bar, the Biscayne, and were knocked out by him. He was a tough down-home blues singer. He grew up with that kind of thing. A day or two later, because of Phil McLean, Danny Kessler, the A&R man from the black division of Epic Records, who went to record Maurice King's band, heard Johnny Ray sing. He had heard about him from Phil and Jerry, and he signed him. Two days later they did 'Whiskey and Gin' and 'Tell the Lady I Said Goodbye.' One of the funniest reviews ever, 'Tell the Lady . . .' they reviewed it as if he was a woman because of his high voice. In *Variety*, they thought it was an unusual song for a girl to sing. We got the records, the acetate, from Detroit, and Phil played 'Whiskey and Gin.' On the information, we got Johnny a booking at Moe's Main Street on Euclid Avenue in Cleveland for three hundred a week to break his record. I played 'Tell the Lady . . .' but at that time 'I got a lady who drinks whiskey and gin'—not exactly a family-hour kind of thing. So I didn't play that side for two days until Phil had busted it. I was a bigger name than Phil or Jerry, and I was very good at exploiting myself and the things I did. I did exploit Johnny Ray; I took him everywhere: concerts, shows, every high school, ran his fan club. I did get him booked. I got him booked at the Town Casino in Cleveland and in Pittsburgh with Lenny Littman. I called Lenny because that was part of the thing that I did. I did that because it gave me the kind of power that I had. Mitch Miller took him to Columbia as soon as the record started to break and they did 'Cry,' the song the night watchman, Churchill Kohlman, wrote. [They also recorded the] 'Little White Cloud That Cried' and all the songs that made him famous. Phil McLean and Jerry Crocker in quotes deserve the credit for discovering Johnny Ray."

Bill and I agreed that in doing a history of rock 'n' roll, it should include "Cry" by Johnny Ray. He said, "Oh yeah, those predecessor songs that you talk about, 'Gee' by the Crows, Willie Mabons's 'I Don't Know,' Joe Liggins's 'Honey Dripper' in the forties, Paul Williams's 'Hucklebuck,' 'Caldonia' by Louie Jordan—plenty of black records, plenty of records that had influence in the changes of it. The pinpoint in time, as you say is 'Rock Around the Clock,' which just exploded the thing. The synthetic things were important too, 'Sh-Boom' by the Crew-Cuts, the cover records."

Black artists and getting accepted

Bill was responsible for a lot of giant cover records, including "Sh-Boom" by the Crew-Cuts. He said, "I did probably twenty cover records. Georgia Gibbs would cover everything but the kitchen sink. She drove LaVern Baker crazy, 'Tweedlee Dee.' To this day, if you want to drive LaVern crazy, just mention my name or Georgia Gibbs. We must have cost her a million dollars."

I thought LaVern took Gibbs to court to stop her from recording her stuff, but Bill corrected me. "Not at all. The small independent labels couldn't get credit. They couldn't get a credit line for shipping and pressing records. They didn't have the power of Mercury or Columbia Records. At that time, a lot of stations didn't play black artists. They'd wait until the white cover version came out. Part of that was the sociocultural factors involved—bigotry involved in that, too. That would change as the culture got used to black artists and the distribution systems got better."

In 1954 Bill changed the image and the name of the Canadaires, a group from Canada. According to Randle, "There was a group in Cleveland called the Crew-Cuts. They had been playing at the Pin Wheel Café, and they had just folded. The Canadaires was obviously not a good name for this group of kids—they were following on the heels of the Four Lads. It just made sense to give them a new name. They came in on a bus. Robbie Buckly, a beautiful girl in Cleveland, had them, and we took the boys to the Statler to get haircuts. I've got a picture of them being changed. We got them a record contract with a demo called 'Crazy 'Bout You Baby' that we recorded in our studio at the station and shipped it off to Mercury Records, who I was doing a lot of things for. They signed them. That was their first record. Then we did 'Sh-Boom,' the song that really made them." Bill said he picked that tune: "Yeah I picked all of the songs for them. I picked the first seven hits they had."

I responded, "The Chords did the original 'Sh-Boom,' and then you had the Crew-Cuts record it."

Bill told me "The lines of communication weren't as quickly developed as they are now. There was a lot of misinformation going around—phony hype. The city was so far ahead of everybody—it would be known in Cleveland but unknown anywhere else. So when the Chords had 'Sh-Boom,' and we covered it—covered it like a blanket. Mercury had records on the street in two days when the Chords didn't even know they had a hit. That's how quick it was."

Some people point to that record, "Sh-Boom," as the start of rock 'n' roll. Bill explained, "'Sh-Boom' I'd say broke the odd, black, rhythm-and-blues-flavored novelty, whatever you want, to group together with a fresh-looking group of young people—made it legitimate. I played it on CBS. We got them on all kinds of TV shows. There was no onus, no bad scene connected with it. As you know, later the first rock things—'Rock Around the Clock'—there were connotations attached to them. Look at some of the titles: 'Drinkin' Wine, Spo-Dee-O-Dee' with Sticks McGee, Mr. Blues Harris, Wyonne Harris, Peppermint Harris, Eddie 'Cleanhead' Vinson; 'I'm Stoned.' Those weren't the kind of things that radio stations played. I was fired for just playing a record by a black artist like Nat King Cole as late as 1949. There was an enormous amount of bigotry involved in radio stations at that time. Black music was just not accepted by management."

The Canadian connection

Bill's name was connected to the Diamonds. He said, "They all came from Canada. They all came from those prep schools, and they all came from the Four Lads. The Four Lads, the Crew-Cuts, and the Diamonds are a succession, like a dynasty. Sure," he said, "they knew each other, neighborhood kids—in fact the Crew-Cuts and the Four Lads went to the same competitive prep schools, within a walking distance area." Five years later, another group of neighborhood kids would dominate the charts. South Philadelphia's Frankie Avalon, Fabian, Bobby Rydell, and Chubby Checker all went to the same high school.

I had a feeling that during the fifties there must have been literally busloads of people coming into Cleveland parking at his doorstep to have him listen, to give them the okay sign. Bill leaned back in his chair and smiled, "The funny thing was, you get a weird reputation. I couldn't stand cigarette smoke, and if anybody came into the studio and smoked an hour before, I would still smell the smoke, that kind of thing. I like the studio about 68 degrees. I thought that was very healthy—most people would consider that to be freezing, you know, very cold, to the point of ludicrousity [*sic*]. Some of the legend is true, some of it is not. But there were many people who came to Cleveland to break a record, many people came in to make records, and I was actively recruiting and doing A&R work. I made a lot of records during that period of time. Some of which now, belatedly, I'm getting credit for because they now credit the producer. You get a lot of back royalties and things. For example, in 1962–63 in New York, I did 'Washington Square' with the Village Stompers. I wound up getting a check for that, for thirty-two thousand dollars or something, for work as a producer. I was working for CBS at the time. Those are part of the contracts now that I didn't know much about.

"The Crew-Cuts, Diamonds, and Four Lads are a part of that Canadian first, new mainstream group of artists. The only thing I did with the Diamonds was change their record label. They were with Coral and working for Bob Thiele, and those records were all stiffs, but the sound was great. David Somerville had that high falsetto thing, but Thiele wasn't into the 'Bird' groups and black music, so I just called [Arthur] Talmadge, and Talmadge signed them to Mercury. Their first records, by the way, were with Allen Toussaint, people like that, Fats Domino's people in New Orleans. They did all-black cover records. No question about it.

"Jerry Wexler of Atlantic Records in a recent article [1977] said as much as I, Bill Randle, was a progressive in terms of politics, that I had an enormous negative effect on the rise of black artists during a period of a year and a half because I covered all of their records like a blanket, and it kept back black artists for about a year and a half. Now that's a misnomer. I mean that's an implication of bigotry. What was really true was that the economics of the industry allowed the rapid exploitation of a cover record, and later on, the bigotry of the industry—the broadcast industry—not the record industry. The broadcast industry lessened, and you weren't able to do that. Once you can play an artist, why not play the original artist? But, if a station manager tells you you can't play any of that music, and Georgia Gibbs comes out with it—that's what you're going to play."

Johnny and Dorsey Burnette

"I did have a lot to do with some other young people. Johnny Burnette was on the Ted Mack *Original Amateur Hour*, and my mother called me and said, 'There's two young guys, Johnny and his brother Dorsey Burnette, on the program. They look a lot like that country singer you like, that Elvis Presley,' and she said, 'You ought to hear them.' I found out their names, and they came literally on a truck to New York. They were truck drivers, and they auditioned for Bob Thiele in the hallway at CBS. He signed them, and they did the first records."

Bill confirmed a legendary story about the Burnette brothers and Ricky Nelson. He said, "They had gone to the Desilu Studios where he was shooting the TV show, and they couldn't get in. So finally, they watched him drive out, and they followed him home and found out when he came home. Then they waited one day when he was driving down the street, and Johnny Burnette laid in his driveway, and it flipped Ricky out, and then on his next album, he did three of their songs because they were good writers. You're right; they would come right into your door and knock it down to get to be heard. Why not? That's the story of the music business."

December 1976, Billboard Forum. A hot argument broke out during our discussion.
From left: The Magnificent Montague, me, Jack Lawyer, Bill Randle, and Ted Atkins.

Bill Randle on a personal note

I spent three days with Dr. Randle at the Billboard International Radio Programming Forum December 1–4, 1976, in New Orleans. While we were checking in, I got a nice ego boost when a couple of Cleveland jocks recognized my name and started singing my WLW jingle. However, the buzz was already beginning, and the convention hadn't started, "Bill Randle is here." It was an experience to walk around with Bill. The biggest names were fawning over him. Nobody had seen this icon in years, and people were asking me how I knew him. Chuck Blore, the "color radio" innovator of Top 40 radio programming looked like he'd seen Santa Claus. The Drake program director, Paul Drew, stopped to talk with Bill, and I couldn't help but notice Randle tugging at his ear. Paul finally asked what was wrong with Bill's ear. Bill said, "Nothing, I was just looking to see if you had an ear piece in. Where's your radio?" Drew was notorious for listening twenty-four hours a day to his jocks and hot-lining them on a special studio phone line if he heard something he didn't like. We both thought it was funny—Drew didn't.

I was on a panel that Bill set up discussing what a deejay can get away with. Our room was packed. Randle presented a tape of Cleveland shock jock Gary Dee, the most controversial radio talker in the city's history, to illustrate how the parameters had been pushed. It was tolerated in Cleveland, and soon it would be accepted everywhere. I don't remember exactly what was on the tape, but typically, Gary would do bits like a woman calling to discuss her unwed teenage daughter's pregnancy; Gary would be sympathetic and then hit her with the line, "What can you expect from her when her mother's white trash? Like mother, like daughter." He was driving to work on the Shoreway when an eighteen-wheeler forced him to hit the side of the road, and he lost a couple of hub caps. He said, "You know those homosexual truck drivers, the ones who drive the big trucks? I'm not worried about the hub caps because I'll just call one of my black friends in East Cleveland, and they'll steal me a couple." A black lady calls to complain and call him a racist. He asks her what she does and remarks she sounds like a hooker he knows. A black guy calls to defend her; Gary asks if he's her pimp. It went on and on. That was Dee's act. Randle was showing how five years earlier, he would have been kicked off the air, but today you can get away with it. The Magnificent Montague, a former deejay and then assistant to the president of Motown Records, was sitting next to me on the panel, and he took exception to Gary Dee. He tried to get into an argument with Randle that he couldn't win and walked out with his entire entourage. Ted Atkins, the former KHJ Los Angeles program director and at that time WTAE Pittsburgh general manager, was the moderator, and he had his hands full. Randle put on a memorable show. As much as people were upset with the content of the tapes, Bill was on the mark way ahead of the curve, just as he had been during his disc jockey days.

The last night of the forum was the awards dinner. Bill and I sat with a diversified group. John R. Gambling from WOR New York was dressed in his finest. Buzz Bennett, the innovative San Diego Top 40 program director arrived late with two very young ladies who weren't exactly dressed for the occasion. They didn't have seats, so they sat on the floor on each side of Buzz. Buzz took off his fur coat and was wearing a t-shirt and jeans, and he was sporting a pair of cowboy boots with spurs. Buzz must have been doing some serious partying and was feeling no pain. Now, I've heard of people doing this, but

I'd never seen it. When dinner was served, Buzz fell face first into his plate—that's right, chicken, mashed potatoes, and gravy. His girl-friends just sat there looking at him. Someone eventually helped him out of his plate and wiped his face off. It was a sight to behold.

It was good to see Claude Hall from *Billboard* and so many radio people I read about over the years. This was my first convention, and before we left, I had two offers from major market stations. I wasn't interested; I had a great job doing afternoons on WLW.

The next day, on the way to the airport, Bill informed me that we were cashing in our plane tickets because he made other travel arrangements. He reminded me that he promised to fly us to New Orleans in his plane. The weather was too bad to fly his plane, so we went commercial. The weather cleared, and Randle had his pilot fly his plane to New Orleans from Cleveland just to fly us back to Cincinnati. That must have cost him a bundle, but that was Randle. His pilot made a mistake, and as we were taxiing down the runway, we just missed a commercial jet. The rest of the flight went smoothly.

It was a proud day for me August 26, 1977. I got my master of arts degree in broadcasting from the University of Cincinnati. Dr. Randle invited the masters' graduates to his apartment for drinks. There were seven or eight of us, and he gave each of us a special gift or two. He gave me a set of custom-made silver cuff links, a record with a microphone on it. He also gave me a ticket invitation for the first Beatles party in America. Bill had it framed and matted with a red background because my wife, Sally's, favorite color is red. It's "Ticket #153, Reception 'The Beatles,' Monday Feb. 10, 1964, 530/730 Baroque Room, The Plaza, 5th Ave. at 59th St." The ticket was for his daughter, but she got sick, and he went by himself to meet the guys. It is priceless. Sally and I were the last to leave the party. Bill had a great collection of old radios in his apartment. He noticed I had been admiring an old Erla Radio with a big horn. As we were leaving, he gave it to me to watch for him.

No one ever gave me more inspiration. I believed I could do anything. He had so much energy, and he passed it on. After he left school and went back to Cleveland, we kept in touch, but I wish I had taken his advice. He was pushing me to get a law degree. Bill had passed the Ohio state bar exam at the age of sixty-four and was a practicing attorney. I was a guest on his Cleveland radio show a few times, and he continued to encourage me to write a book. Bill was involved in some radio deals and offered me a tentative radio proposal. In several of those discussions, he would close with, "and I will pay for your education to get a law degree." That always got my attention, but my roots were in Cincinnati.

Bill Randle died of cancer in July of 2004, and I lost a good friend and my security blanket. I thought he would live forever. If I needed advice, I could always count on him.

The Rock and Roll Hall of Fame did a tribute to Randle and I was asked to sit on the dais. Joining me on the stage in front of Randle's family and a capacity crowd, were one of the Four Lads (Randle was responsible for their career); Paul Steigerwald, a former student and voice of the Pittsburgh Penguins hockey team; and Norman Wain, my old boss, the former WIXY radio station owner and now college teacher. We told Randle stories and answered questions for more than an hour.

As I sat there on the stage, I thought about the irony. The one place I knew he had a total disdain for was the Rock and Roll Hall of Fame. He told me that 75 to 80 percent of all the people in there are accused or convicted felons. He certainly didn't like the politics involved with the selection process.

I remembered a conversation we had about Joe Finan, a disc jockey I worked with and later for in Denver. Joe was on KYW in Cleveland opposite Bill's show on WERE. I mentioned Joe's name, and Bill said, "I p——d on him." I said, "You sure did. I read where you had 80 percent of the audience in afternoon drive." Randle said, "Yes, I did, but I really p——d on him." Joe or someone working for him would call the schools and tell them that Bill and Paul Anka, or whoever his guests were, had to cancel the record hop. This happened a number of times. Of course, when Randle would show up, no one would be there. He found out it was Finan and put a stop to it. One night at a Cleveland club, they were standing next to each other at the urinal in the men's room. Bill told me, "I turned around, and I p——d all over his leg." Finan didn't do or say anything, he just stood there, and Randle walked away. Finan never messed with Randle again.

I would bring in local radio people as guests for my class when I was teaching. My friend Marty Brennaman, the Reds' announcer, stopped by, and after class we met with Bill in his office. I was surprised when he told Marty he would "look good wearing this," and he gave him an expensive, vintage, solid gold pocket watch on a chain. Marty didn't want to accept it, but Bill insisted. I later told Randle that Marty was my friend that he didn't have to do that. He liked Marty and his air work. That was Randle.

I thought back to the many nights after class when Bill would take the masters' group out for a drink. Each of us would hang on to his every word. Those conversations were wonderful, and each of us has those memories.

CHAPTER 17

I was Invited to Party with Elvis

I was invited, but I didn't go, and I will regret it until the day I die. On June 27, 1973, Elvis was performing at the Cincinnati Gardens, and his best friend George Klein invited me to meet Elvis at their hotel after the show. Tommy Van Arsdale of the Royals and his wife were sitting in front of us and asked Sally and I to join them for pizza. I thought it probably was going to take Elvis some time to get to his hotel. However, by the time we finished eating, it was late, and I took Sally home thinking I would catch up with Elvis another time. That never happened.

On August 16, 1977, I mentioned on the air a soviet news article describing Elvis as a "broken, forgotten man, a victim of the American system." A few hours later, I was talking about Elvis again and trying to find just the right words to tell his fans that he died. I just turned in my master's thesis, a twenty-four-hour history of rock 'n' roll from Elvis to the Beatles that took me more than four months to complete. Suddenly I became the expert for anyone wanting to know about Elvis and was quoted in numerous articles and books. I quickly put on one of the first Elvis radio tribute shows. I also hosted

WLWT's *Tribute to Elvis* in prime time, beginning at eight and ending in the early morning hours. We featured three of his movies. I told Elvis stories and interviewed several studio guests. On my radio show, I asked if anyone had ever touched Elvis. The lines were jammed with ladies who got scarves from him and a few totally bizarre stories. One girl sounded different, and she called me frequently. Chris Coffey told me she met Elvis after a concert here, he later flew her to Vegas, and they dated. I decided to ask George Klein, and when I mentioned her name, he lit up on the phone. Yes, Elvis really liked her and flew her to Vegas. She introduced herself to me at one of my appearances but left before I could talk to her. She was very attractive in a natural sort of way. We had many phone conversations over the years, and she described Elvis as being a very loving and spiritual man. They talked for hours about religion. She was questioning herself and thought Elvis picked Linda Thompson over her because she wasn't worldly enough. Chris sent a tape to me a number of years ago, and in her letter she wrote, "I received this tape on my fortieth birthday. The person who sent it didn't know it was my birthday—so when I played it, I was shocked because, over and over again, Elvis is singing along with this record 'Happy Birthday Baby!' It was so freaky!! Nice surprise. Almost felt like a message from beyond. (I know that's silly, but it really made my birthday!)" The tape is Elvis and Anita Wood at Eddie Fadal's house singing with the Tune Weavers' record, "Happy, Happy Birthday Baby." When I first played a part of it on my show, not many people had heard it before.

Red West

A few months after Elvis died, his bodyguard and school friend Red West stopped by to promote his TV show *The Wild Wild West*. He was one of the writers of the book *Elvis: What Happened* that was released shortly before he died. The book exposed Elvis's prescription drug use and, supposedly, he was devastated by the book. I was told not to talk about it, but I had to. Red is a giant of a man. I caught him off guard, and he shed a few tears talking about how much he loved

Elvis. Red was honest with Elvis about his medication problems, and that's probably why he got fired.

Memphis

In early 1981 I was invited to Memphis for the movie premier of *This is Elvis,* the documentary, and was privileged to tour Graceland a year before it was opened to the public. What a weekend. I had a chance to finally meet his uncle Vester. I talked with him on the radio many times while he was watching the gate at Graceland. I'd check in with him on Elvis's birthday, and crazy things were always going on. Once he had to stop a couple of girls who were delivered in a box for Elvis. However, I left Graceland very disappointed. I collect jukeboxes, and his was just an ordinary one. He had weights that you could buy at Sears, the cheap plastic ones filled with sand. I asked one of the Memphis Mafia, and he said, "Elvis wanted weights, so that's what we got him." Jerry Shilling was showing me the last outfit he wore. It must have weighed thirty-five pounds. I was told it had to be heavy because Elvis was always splitting his pants, and none of the guys knew how to sew. I got into a discussion with a couple of the guys about his physical condition: "Couldn't you see how overweight he was?" I was told in so many words that I wasn't there, and it wasn't my business. His game room had his gold records and awards, but mixed in were dozens of handmade items fans sent him that I was told Elvis liked to look at. I thought about all those guys living in that area and how Priscilla must have felt with such little privacy. The swimming pool looks huge on film, but you could dive from one side to the other with a few strokes. I just thought the King of Rock 'n' Roll should have had the best.

I spent time with Sam Phillips at Sun Records. He looked like he was thirty years old with his new hair. We listened to the sound track of *This is Elvis*, and when Jackie Brenston's "Rocket 88" played, he raved about recording that with Ike Turner in 1951. Jackie sang the song, but that's Ike's band. The distorted "fuzz" guitar sound was the result of a bad amplifier. Sam explained to me why he sold Elvis's contract to RCA. Sam thought Elvis was going to be a big star, but he knew he had a million-seller with Carl Perkins's "Blue Suede Shoes." However, he needed the money to press Carl's records and get them distributed.

I watched the movie *This is Elvis* in the Memphian Theater he rented when he wanted to see movies. They tried to recreate the unveiling of the giant Elvis they did for *Love me Tender* in front of the theater. It was a terrific weekend for this Elvis fan.

Scotty Moore

Scotty Moore, Elvis's first guitar player, and I were talking about the recording session in July of 1954 when they recorded "That's All Right Mama." Scotty explained to me that it was actually an audition. Sam Phillips had asked Scotty to listen to Elvis at his house the day before. Scotty told Sam what he thought, and then they went to Sun Records the next night for Sam to hear. He just wanted to hear a little music behind Elvis and on tape, because tape was fairly new back then. Scotty said, "We'd run through several songs, and we were taking a break probably after about an hour, just Bill Black and me, because he didn't ask for the whole band. The door to the control room was open, and Elvis just stood up and started to sing and play 'That's All Right.' I had never heard it, and Bill Black had never heard it. We didn't know the song; we just started playing along with him trying to figure out the chords and such. Sam stuck his head around the corner and said, 'What are you guys doing?'

'We're just jamming a little bit.'

'Do it some more; it sounds pretty good.'

"He went back, got on mic—we run through it, figured out what we were doing, and played it four or five times. Of course, he had to change Elvis, 'Back off the mic a little,' a few things like that. I'd say no more than four or five times, and that was it. It just fell in perfect."

Scotty Moore didn't think this new sound was special. He told me, "We knew it was a little different than what we were accustomed to hearing on the radio mainly because there was just the two of us.

Bill and myself, we're both trying to make as much noise as we could. Normally we'd be playing with five or six guys, but that's the way it was."

Scotty became Elvis's first manager, but he told me that was just a smoke screen because, "There were some other guys in Memphis who had been calling after that first record got so hot, trying to sign him. We were having a meeting one day, and Sam was talking to Elvis, and he said, 'Why don't you just let Scotty be your manager for right now until we can have time to find somebody that we all agree on?' because it was a group at the time. I was only his manager for a year."

Mae Boren Axton

Mae Boren Axton wrote Elvis's first number one hit "Heartbreak Hotel." She did a lot of things—a radio show; taught school; and worked promotion for Colonel Tom Parker's shows in Jacksonville, where she lived, and also Orlando and Daytona, Florida.

Mae first heard of Elvis when Bob Neal, a Memphis disc jockey friend, called and asked for a favor. Elvis had recorded a couple of songs, and Bob signed to manage him but needed to get him some exposure. Bob asked Mae to slip him in on one of Tom Parker's tours. Hank Snow, the Carter Family, Skeeter Davis, and others were coming in on a country tour. Mae told me, "I figured out where I could do fifty dollars worth of advertising additional to what the Colonel had given me. It wasn't on Elvis; we didn't even talk about Elvis. It was on the show itself so I could give him fifty dollars to come in. So he had Scotty Moore and Bill Black. They came in on an old battered Chevy as I remember for fifty dollars a night in those three cities. That's how the Colonel met him. He said, 'Who is this Mae?'" I said, 'Don't worry about it. It didn't cost you a penny.'

"Mae Boren Axton reminisced about that night in Jacksonville in 1954. She did a radio interview with Elvis, and she thought he was the fourth act on stage. "Jimmy," Mae said, "Colonel Tom, and I were talking about business—it was at a baseball field, and there were about fourteen thousand people there. All of a sudden I heard this screaming and yelling and pounding. I thought, what in the world? I've got to go up and see this. So the Colonel and I went up, and I saw this young lady. She was just screaming, and tears were rolling down, and Elvis was wiggling and singing. I grabbed her. I had taught her in high school. I said, 'What is it about this guy?'

'Oh, he's just a great big, beautiful hunk of forbidden fruit.'

"I think that's about the best definition I've ever heard of him. I watched him—there was no hype, nobody had ever heard of him. We hadn't played records, except one little station played one of his little records. Nobody knew him. They didn't come to see him. It was just this magic that he had. I told him, 'Elvis, you need the Colonel,' because the Colonel was going to buy up his contract from Bob Neal. 'When you get the Colonel, you need a million-seller, and I'm going to write it.'"

Mae Boren Axton came through on her promise. She co-wrote "Heartbreak Hotel" with Tommy Durden, and it became Elvis's first number one. The song's story involved a suicide note. Mae said, "A man's picture was on the front page of the paper, and Tommy Durden had seen it. He said, 'Have you read the paper?' He opened it up, and it said, 'Can you identify this man?' He had torn out all identification, and he had written one line: 'I walk a lonely street and committed suicide,' and that stunned me. I sat there for a moment, and I said, 'But Tommy, I don't care who you are, everybody, regardless of their status in life, has somebody who cared. When they see this, they are going to be heartbroken, so let's put a Heartbreak Hotel at the end of that lonely street.' He said, 'Let's do,' and twenty-two minutes later, we had it on tape. I called Elvis that night, flew up the next day, and he listened to it—he and Bob Neal, his manager at the time. He said, 'Hot dog, Mae, play it again,' and he listened to it about ten times. I said, 'If it's your first original on RCA, I'll give you a third of it.' The reason for that was that he had said, 'Mae, I love Florida. I hope someday I have enough money that I can bring my mommy and daddy down here.' So, I said, 'That will give you enough money to bring your mommy and daddy to Florida.'"

D.J. Fontana

Elvis's original drummer D.J. Fontana was with him from 1955 to 1969. They met when Elvis appeared on the *Louisiana Hayride*, and D.J. was the staff drummer. He was never on the Sun Records. He and I were talking backstage about some jealous boyfriends who picked fights with Presley. D.J. was smiling when he said, "That was a bad mistake when they did that. Yeah, we had that. Cigarette in his sleeve, a big guy said, 'I'm going to whip you.'

'Oh no, come on sit down, and we'll have a coke and talk about it.'

'Nope, I come here to whip you, and that's what I'm going to do.'

'Why are you mad at me?'

'Well my wife has got a picture of you in her wallet, and she doesn't have one of me.'

He said, 'Go to the dime store.'

Remember, years ago they'd take your picture. Finally, he swung, and Elvis whipped him real good. Then the guy got outside, and he smarted off to the policemen, and they whipped him all the way to the police station. So they called Elvis the next morning and asked, 'What do you wanna do with this guy?'

Elvis said, 'Well, is he married?'

'Yeah, he's married, and he's got three kids.'

Elvis said, 'Let him go.'

The police said, 'Well, he owes so much money because of his fine.'

Elvis said, 'I'll pay for it. Let him go.'"

Scotty Moore, Presley's original guitarist, and D.J. Fontana did that *'68 Comeback Special with Elvis*. I told Scotty that it looked like they were really having a good time. Scotty thought he looked better than he had ever seen him. He was really on top of his game. However, Scotty kidded, "I'm going to tell you one little flaw. If you remember, they told us to just sit down in a kind of circle. Elvis didn't have a strap on his guitar. I didn't have one on mine, so about the second or third song, Elvis stood up and put his foot on the chair, and then a bit later, he reached over to change guitars, so I ended up with his guitar, and he ended up with mine. Go back and look at my expression. You know I wasn't very happy about that, cause he beat the fire out of a guitar."

Tom Jones and Elvis

Tom Jones has an incredible recording career, and he told me he knew Elvis quite well. According to Tom, they first met in 1965 in Hollywood when Tom was doing a song for the movie *Promise Her Anything*, and Elvis was making a movie. He said, "They asked me if I'd like to say hello, and I met him at the studio. I only had two records: 'It's Not Unusual' and 'What's New Pussycat' and one album, and Elvis knew every track on the album. He had the album—he was telling me how much he liked it. We became friendly right from there. In '68 when I first went to Las Vegas, he drove up from Los Angeles because he didn't like to fly at that time. He came to see my show there. He told me that's what inspired him to work on stage again, watching me work in Vegas. So we'd be in Vegas at the same time quite often. We would see one another's shows and get together after the shows. We became very friendly."

After Elvis died, there were stories that he was too protected and that he never got out and did what normal guys do. Tom Jones thought he made his own world and said, "If he wanted to do anything, he did it with a bunch of people. If he wanted to go to the movies, he would rent a cinema after everybody else was gone. In Vegas, he would sometimes hang out. I remember one night when I was working at the Flamingo in 1968, there was a discotheque upstairs, and we would hang out there most of the night, but he would always have bodyguards around him. He would never go anywhere without them, and that's the way it is. I've always got to have somebody with me. Entertainers, you never know what will happen. He always felt more comfortable when he was in familiar surroundings."

CHAPTER 18

A *"Consummate Radio Interviewer"*

I got some nice publicity in the early seventies when J. Raleigh Gaines mentioned me in his book *Modern Radio Programming*. He wrote, "Every trade magazine you read these days bemoans the lack of personalities. I disagree with the idea that there is a lack of personalities. I believe there is just a lack of people willing to dedicate themselves to their chosen craft. Have you ever heard Charlie Tuna, Don Rose, George Michaels, Larry Lujack, Gary Owens, Jay Lawrence, Jim LaBarbara, Harvey Hudson, Pat Patterson, Ty Boyd, Paul Henning, Don Imus, just to name a few of the nation's outstanding personalities? Do you think that they go on the air and 'wing it'? If they did, they would sound just like thousands of other disc jockeys across the country—a pleasant voice giving time and temperature. As it is, they put work into their programs, and you can detect the difference. Their programs are professional, entertaining, informative, and in keeping with today's world. Their programs are alive." I felt as if my hard work was validated. I was surprised to be included with that group of heavyweights.

I've been mentioned in a number of books over the years, but that was the first to my knowledge. My favorite trade magazine story focused on a facet of my craft that I took great pride in doing—the interview.

In the March 20, 1981, edition of *Radio & Records* magazine, Mike Kasabo featured me in an article titled, "The Radio Interview—A Lost Art?" Here's part of what he wrote, "When I was a kid listening to radio, my favorite part, besides the music was when the DJ would have an in-studio recording artist guest and do an interview. It made me feel closer to the artists, almost as if I had something in common with them. The interview also served a personal purpose for the DJ— it made him my direct link with the recording stars that I admired. In my case, the top guy back in the sixties was Casey Kasem on KRLA, who of course is host of probably the most successful syndicated radio show ever, *American Top-Forty*. But Casey isn't the only one who developed a great style and penchant for interviewing. Jim LaBarbara, who has a musical background of his own, is the very popular afternoon drive personality of Cincinnati powerhouse WLW, and is regarded as one of the consummate radio interviewers around. LaBarbara began his interviewing career in earnest during the mid-sixties when he worked as a rock jock in Erie, Pa., using the name J. Bentley Starr. He would in conjunction with his 'countdown' show incorporate background information on the British invasion groups. Over the years, he has interviewed (live or by phone) virtually every major, or passing, recording star from Herb Alpert to the Zombies. LaBarbara has been with the 50,000-watter since 1969, at which time he was given the nickname "the Music Professor" by then Program Director Jim Gallant. With that label, LaBarbara was off and running.

"R&R: How accurate are the bios and other written pieces on artists?

"JL: You have to be very careful, because there are mistakes, and it would be very poor judgment to assume everything you read is true. The main thing is to be prepared and know the performer— know who you are talking with. Don't pursue a line of thinking that has been beaten to death. I do a lot of my own research. I should point out here that it is impossible to be 'over-prepared,' always make sure you have more than enough material. You can always edit as you go along if time starts to work against you.

"R&R: How in-depth will you carry a subject?

"JL: In the case of Bill Medley, there was an obscure situation that happened in 1974 when he went back to his high school choral director and took vocal lessons for the first time in his life. This was apparently because he was losing his voice—that is maybe a sensitive side note to someone's career, but if properly handed, with all due respect, it will turn out as a very human-interest reflection. I got to the roots of Medley: his dad was a police officer and worked in a ballroom in California where he and his dad would go and watch Fats Domino and people like that on stage. These things are not well known and are important to bring out for audience involvement—to make the artist seem more real than his press releases will indicate.

"R&R: Medley grew up in very white Orange County, but spent time trying to listen to the low-power black station KGFJ—and that was a great influence . . .

"JL: Yes, Don and Dewey were early influences that remain until today, and other things like the Righteous Brothers opened for the Beatles during one of their early American tours. You see, it's things like that and the mood the memories recreate that make the difference between a good interview and a great one."

Needless to say, I was very happy to have a featured, two-page story in a major radio publication.

Favorite interviews

I always did my homework. I know the interviewee appreciated it when I asked a question or mentioned something nobody else had. Ray Charles kidded me because I knew so much about him, "Man do you work for the FBI or the CIA?" Shelley Fabares said, "My own mother doesn't remember that I sang 'Johnny Angel' for the first time on the *Donna Reed Show* to a boy in the high school gym and that he was actor Jim Stacy." I asked Gary Lewis if he had a pretty famous drum instructor. He said, "Yes, I did, Buddy Rich. Boy, you are well versed. I was about five years old when I started to take lessons."

One of my most memorable celebrity interviews would have to be my first. I wasn't a disc jockey at the time, and the interview has never been played on the radio. I was home on a break from college, and I heard Joanie Sommers on Clark Race's KDKA radio show in Pittsburgh plugging her hit record "Johnny Get Angry" and her nightclub appearance. I called my high school friend Henry Tumpa and told him, "Tonight, we are going to be with Joanie." I took my giant tape recorder and talked my way into her dressing room after the show. We were single and about the same age. She was really cute and wore a little robe but talked with us for the longest time. She treated me as if I was the celebrity. If I had any doubts, that night convinced me I had to get into radio.

Bill Haley

I have a number of favorite interviews. I think for most of us, the birth of rock 'n' roll music would have to be the number one song, "Rock Around the Clock" by Bill Haley and the Comets, but I don't know if he ever realized the impact he had on pop music.

I mentioned the fan reaction to his music, the miniriots, and the many mayors who banned his concerts. He told me that went on all over the country. Bill surprised me when he said, "We couldn't understand that, because our music wasn't destructive music, it was just happy music, and that's what we intended it to be, and that happened all over Europe. The first trip to London, it was like a hundred thousand people, they just tore up everything at the railroad station there. After we got off, I believe the *Queen Mary*, and we got a special train that got us straight into London. There were riots everywhere. We went to Germany—they brought the tanks out. It looked like World War II you know."

Haley was confused by the fan response because they never had that situation in the beginning here in the states. "But then over there, we found out it was just a rival thing amongst the cities. Like one group would say, well they tore up this town, now let's see what we can do when they come to our town, tear it up even better. That was happening all over. I think a lot of it, too, could have been some of the promoters would book us into an auditorium that holds say five thousand people. Well, to make the money they'd squeeze in seven or eight thousand. So you'd have people on top of people, and they all wanted to get close to the bandstand. I think that's what happened, and a lot of these little groups would break into fights. I think that was the major thing, because it wasn't the music."

Little Richard

The wildest rocker of them all had to be Little Richard. I've interviewed him several times, and each time he was a different person. One day he'd be a preacher, the next a crazy rocker, but he always had a great story to tell.

You might say Little Richard began his career singing on doorsteps in Macon, Georgia. He said, "I would go down to people's houses and would help sing a church song that Sister Rosetta Tharpe had out called 'Strange Things Happening Every Day' and a song she had called 'Two Little Fishes and Five Loaves of Bread.' I would go around and I would beat on the steps with my hand and people would pay me to sing in front of their house like that."

Richard didn't have anything good to tell me about his experience working at the Greyhound Bus Station in Macon for Mr. Wallace: "I was a little fellow. You know how you get mad at home, and I wanted to be my own little man. I started working at the station, but very shortly I was very glad to go back home. I was working from six in the evening until six in the morning. Those hours were jailhouse hours, and they got everything out of me but my bones. It was hard work; I would scrub floors. At the time, it was very prejudice, and you weren't allowed in certain parts of the restaurant. You was allowed in there if you was moppin'."

The name "Little Richard" came about with a group called B. Brown's Orchestra out of Tipton, Georgia. He was the vocalist for his band, and Richard says, "Instead of saying, 'Richard Penniman,' he just said, 'Little Richard.'"

Little Richard was with Don Robey's Peacock Records. Richard and I discussed Don's reputation of abusing his artists. Richard said he never beat him up, but he did kick him. He added, "Willie Mae Thornton had out 'Hound Dog,' Johnny Ace and Gatemouth Brown was on the label. He was really a horrible guy. He never did bother Big Mama Thornton because she was so big she would have sit on him."

Johnny Ace did "Pledging my Love" on Peacock Records, and some say he was rock 'n' roll's first tragic loss when he was killed playing Russian roulette on Christmas 1954. I always thought that he was murdered, but Richard corrected me. "It was really Russian roulette. I think they had done it many times, and he won. You understand me? I think he just thought he could do it whenever he'd get ready, and he was wrong." Big Mama's bass player, Curtis Tillman, witnessed the event, and said Johnny had been drinking and waving the pistol around. He said, "It's okay—Gun's not loaded, and with a smile, pointed it at himself and pulled the trigger—Bang!"

Little Richard's first big record was "Tutti Frutti" and he told me he was singing it in Macon before it was recorded. "It was a nasty song. It was suggestive. I met Lloyd Price. He had a record out at the time called 'Lawdy Miss Claudie.' He had a gold and black Cadillac, and somehow or another, black peoples was really interested in Cadillacs at that time, so most of the record companies would give them just what they wanted and nothing else. You would sell twenty million records, and all you got was a Cadillac and a diamond ring and nothing else. The man would be sitting up on the hill, and you would still be in the valley. He recommended me to Arthur Rupe at Specialty Records in Hollywood. I sent them a tape of my voice, and they didn't get back in touch with me. About a year later, they said they heard a little thing in my voice that was nice, but they wanted me to sound like Ray Charles and to imitate B.B. King. My interest was far from that. I think Ray Charles is a genius in music, and B.B. King is one of the greatest, but that wasn't my aim. So after they sent for me, I went to Cosmos Studio in New Orleans, and I recorded the songs.

After we finished the recording session, I was sitting down playing the piano. They didn't even know I played piano. I started singing 'Tutti Frutti,' and they said, 'Well, that's what you should have recorded,' and they got a girl in to help me clean up the lyrics cause it was kinda' dirty."

"Tutti Frutti good booty / If it don't fit, don't force it / You can grease it, make it easy . . ." Those lyrics were a little too promiscuous for the radio.

"I had that song for about six years, and they brought a girl in, and she started claiming the song. She, Dorothy LaBostre, gave me two lines, and I didn't know no better back in that time."

Little Richard admitted that Specialty Records cheated him out of a lot of money and weren't fair with anyone. He said they didn't pay him properly for the publishing rights to "Tutti Frutti," that "they just took it."

When Little Richard got his first royalty check, he bought his mother a house in West Los Angeles right behind Joe Louis's, the great boxing champion. He said his mother got so excited, "She started crying. Only white people lived in a house like that in Macon, Georgia, where I'm from. Blacks couldn't afford no house like that. The house was pink and white. I always wanted to do that for her and my brothers and sisters."

He was poor growing up in Macon, Georgia. "Very poor, I wasn't poor I was 'po.' There is a difference between being poor and 'po.' I was 'po.'"

Richard described a scene at the Royal Theater in Baltimore one night. He was singing, and suddenly stuff started flying through the air: "Ladies started throwing panties at me. Yeah, they were doing that with me before they did it with Tom Jones. They took 'em off with me, and now they're putting them back on." (He said this laughing.)

We were kidding about the first time he used his trademark "woo woo woo" in a song. Richard said, "I started using it in 'Tutti Frutti,' but I changed it around a little bit in 'Long Tall Sally.'" I understood he got "Long Tall Sally" from a lady named Honey Child, but Richard was quick to correct me, "No, Bumps did all that. Honey Child was a disc jockey; she didn't have nothing. She just had big legs. They lied. It was really my song; they took it. Honey Child had nothing to do with it. All she was, spinning them records with those big old legs."

In 1957 at the height of his career, he left show business. I've heard different stories: He was on a plane, there was a fire, and Richard supposedly said, "If I ever get out of this alive, I'm going to dedicate my life to God." When he landed in Sydney, Australia, he threw all his jewelry into the harbor. Little Richard clarified the story: "The airplane that we were on had beds on it, beds that let down. It was a propeller plane going to Australia—two on each side. The engine would turn real red at a distance, and it shook my mind. I had never been that far from home in my life. We got to Australia, and thousands of people came to see me, Gene Vincent and Eddie Cochran. It was packed. After getting over there, *Sputnik*, the Russian satellite, went up. That's what really bothered me, cause I never heard of nothing going up like that, and it troubled my mind. I made up my mind that I would like to live for God. Now this jewelry bit. I can vaguely think on it. I think we were on a ferry boat going over to someplace to do a performance. I think one of my band fellas asked me to prove that I was telling him that I was going to get out of the business. I had made up my mind to just let it go. I think I told him, 'If I throw this in the ocean in the water, would you believe it?' I think that's where it came up. It wasn't a lot of jewelry, but it was kind of expensive."

He did go to college to become a minister, but not for long, and then he went back to show business because of financial reasons. "After going back into the business traveling around, I made more money when I went back than I had ever made."

I told him that he brought the races together, black and white. Little Richard said, "They would jump over the balcony. We would do shows, and the white people would be upstairs. They called them 'white spectators,' and they would be upstairs, and they would leap over the balcony. They would come down in the audience with 'Tutti Frutti,' 'Long Tall Sally,' 'Lucille,' 'The Girl Can't Help It,' and they would just be all over the place."

The Rolling Stones' Keith Richards said the biggest thrill of his life was meeting Little Richard. He was with the Rolling Stones before they were stars. Richard said laughing, "I was with them when they didn't have no stone to roll."

I asked Richard about his guitar player who went by the alias, Maurice James. Little Richard's voice got higher with excitement, and he said, "Jimi Hendrix was using the name Maurice James. Yes, at the time, because he had ran away from home. He started living with us, but we didn't know he could play the guitar, and then one day we heard that. I said, 'Oh, man.' He started playing on the stage with us, and he was taking over the stage. Jimmy was a phenomenon. He was a genius in his time and out of his time." Richard was with the Beatles early on. "Didn't nobody know them but their mothers. I took them with me to Hamburg, Germany, at the Star Club. They would hold my hands, and they liked to hear me talk about the old days."

The Beatles' manager, Brian Epstein, wanted to give him the group. Richard confirmed that. "He offered me 50 percent of the group to bring them back to B.J. Records. I didn't do it because at the time they sounded like the Everly Brothers to me. Don and Phil were good friends of mine, and I didn't want to mess with them, you know? So that's what happened with that."

He told me he thought that Paul and John had "superstar" talent, but said, "I never felt that about Ringo. They had another drummer when I first met them."

Pete Best and the Beatles

That other drummer's name was Pete Best. He was the Beatles' drummer from 1960 until August of 1962, the eve of Beatlemania in Liverpool. It was a number of years later, but I could still feel the pain in his voice as Pete described the scene when he was called into Brian Epstein's office. He explained that Brian had taken over as manager the year before but that he had been involved with the business side earlier and that it wasn't unusual for them to discuss venues. It was "no big shakes." This day was different. Pete said, "When I got there, I realized it wasn't the same calm and collected Brian. He was agitated and talked around the subject, and then all of a sudden he said, 'Pete, I can't continue anymore. I've got to tell you the boys want you out, and they want Ringo in.'"

Pete Best said, "The way it happened, it just hit me like a bomb out of the blue. I was totally shell shocked—no forewarning. The boys weren't there. They left it up to Brian. There had been no hint of anything. No prior discussion: *'Pete, you have to change your style, adapt a little bit more.'* So when it was delivered to me, and in that manner, it just left me totally dumbstruck. The reason that was given was that I wasn't a good enough drummer, and I've always been adamant about that, and said look, 'I'm better than Ringo.'"

The story that was repeated over and over was that George Martin offered the Beatles a recording contract, but the stipulation was he didn't want Pete Best, he wanted a studio drummer for the recording sessions. Pete threw a new light on this story. "The amazing thing is, Jim, now this is where history sort of differs a little, because he, George, didn't want me kicked out of the band. He said, 'Don't break the group up physically because of the personality and the looks.' He did not have Andy White the studio drummer standing by on that particular occasion as history portrays. Ringo was in. George Martin turned around and said, 'What happened to Pete?' They said, 'Pete's left, this is the new drummer, Ringo,' and it was the week after that, he had Andy White come in, and he did the final takes."

When the Beatles fired Pete Best, all hell broke loose in Liverpool. Pete said, "That's right, there was fan reaction. There were riots outside the Cavern. There were people walking up and down with billboards saying, 'Pete Forever, Ringo Never.' George Harrison got a black eye from an irate fan. Brian Epstein's life was threatened. He had bouncers walking around with him."

Pete and the boys were best friends for years, and then after he was kicked out, Pete didn't hear from them. "No, that was a funny thing, Jim. I saw them three times after that. Once when I went down to the Cavern to watch them when they were getting recorded by the

BBC, and I couldn't take it in view of what had happened, and I walked out. I joined a band called Lee Curtis and the All-Stars. We played on the same bill as the Beatles, once at the Majestic and once at the Cavern in Liverpool. They were top of the bill, and as we were coming off, the Beatles were going on stage, and there was no communication. The Mexican standoff was there, and it's been that way ever since." (That interview took place March 26, 1987.)

Pete Best loved his days as a Beatle and laughed as he recalled John Lennon going on stage with a toilet seat draped over his shoulders: "We were playing long hours and drinking a lot. In the middle of the number, he turned his back to the audience, he dropped his swimming trunks, and there was a beautiful picture of John's backside right in front of the German audience about six inches from them because the stage was about eighteen inches high, and the German audience used to dance about a foot from the stage."

It's well documented that Brian Epstein was gay and had a crush on John Lennon. Peter Brown in his book says they had a one-night stand. Pete Best hesitated, but admitted that Brian Epstein did make a pass at him. "Yeah, that did happen. This was after he had taken over as manager. We were on a drive. He turned around and said, 'Pete, would you spend the night with me?' It was a simple, gentle approach. There was nothing rude about it. I said, 'No Brian, that's not my scene.' He said, 'Okay, well as far as I'm concerned don't feel embarrassed about it; don't hold any grudges against me.' That was the initial proposition. It was never brought up again."

A rejected suitor, could that have been one of the reasons Pete was replaced? Pete Best was quick to respond. "A lot of people have said maybe Brian felt the initial rejection. I don't think so. Simply, the way it was done, he didn't show it. When I was kicked out, I was getting offers from other bands in Liverpool. Brian approached me again and said, 'Pete, I have a band in Liverpool which I want to make into a second Beatles.' So there is evidence he didn't want to lose me from his stable so to speak."

Pete Best was out on the eve of Beatlemania. He told me it naturally caused a lot of heartache and financial embarrassment. He surprised me when he said, "Looking at it from another point of view, it was nice to see that the hard work which had been put in was happening, the faith which we saw in ourselves. It was around me all the time no matter where you looked: television, radio, hairstyle, clothing etc. All I could do was immerse myself into my own music."

So the Beatles turnaround occurred in a period of twenty-four months, they made forty million dollars, and Pete Best became a baker. Pete corrected me: "I wasn't a baker. I was a laborer. I was wrapping bread, and I was slicing it. The reason for that, Jim, was simply I had the educational qualification from school, and I thought it would be easy to get a job. Hell, it wasn't. They said, 'Pete, fill out an application form. Great educational qualification, but what have you done for the last four years?'

'I've been in show business.'

'Pete, we are very sorry, but as soon as the urge comes back, you're going to be off.'

When the bakery said, 'We'll give you a job, I took it for twelve months to prove to people that I'm stable. Fortunately, after that I was offered civil service in England. I joined them."

Pete Best getting kicked out of the Beatles was a tragedy, but for one American singer, getting released from his group was a blessing.

Ben E. King and the Drifters

In 1958 the Five Crowns were working shows at the Apollo Theater with the Drifters when the Drifters' manager fired them and replaced them with the members of the Five Crowns and their lead singer, Benjamin Nelson. Ben would sing lead on some of the group's biggest hits: "There Goes My Baby," "Dance with Me," "Save the Last Dance for Me," and "This Magic Moment." He later changed his name to Ben E. King and had giant hits like: "Stand by Me," "Spanish Harlem," "Supernatural Thing," and more.

Ben E. King left the Drifters after an argument with their manager, not for himself, but for the whole group. Ben said, "When we became the Drifters from the Five Crowns, we were put on salary, and we found ourselves on the road making very little money and got disgusted about that. When we got back to New York, we decided to go to the office and have a meeting with George Treadwell, our manager. They kind of pointed at me, and said, 'You be the spokesman for the group.' I didn't want to do it, but I stood up and made my little speech. He said, 'Well, don't speak for the group. Speak for yourself, and I did so.' After that, he told me, 'Well, if you're unhappy, you can leave.' So, without turning around to look at the other guys, I just more or less walked out of the office, and nobody followed. That's how a solo's career can begin."

Ben told me it hurt because the Five Crowns were good buddies. "At that point, we had more or less hit lotto as far as becoming the new set of Drifters. We had went through a lot to get ourselves established as the new Drifters, of course being booed off stage, and doing all that stuff because people weren't ready for us until we started making hit records. I was hurt, too, because I was not the one who wanted to be spokesman for the group or had the option of saying, 'I don't want to talk about the group.' So when they pushed me into that position, I did what I was asked to do. So it was a little painful for a little while."

Ben said even in the Drifters' prime when they had all those million-sellers, they were making only seventy-five to one hundred dollars a week: "Yeah, that's true."

His first solo hit "Spanish Harlem," according to Ben, "was to be a Drifters record, but they never made it to the studio because of a snowstorm. 'Stand by Me' is the same situation. I wrote it and took it to the Drifters and rehearsed it with them, but George Treadwell was, I guess, angry with me for leaving the group. He said, 'Well, we don't need any more material,' and lucky for me, I kept 'Stand by Me' for my own self."

I was the emcee for a Ben E. King concert after a Reds baseball game in front of about fifty thousand people in 1975, a couple of months before I got married. Backstage, we talked a little about music. I still have the Five Crowns' record "Kiss and Make Up" that he recorded when I was in high school, and we talked about marriage.

Years later, I reminded Ben of the marital advice he gave me. He smiled and said, "Well, it must have worked."

Neil Diamond

I was going to pick up Neil Diamond at the airport, but he was wrapping up his *Moods* album and running late. Early in his career, he was very intense, especially before a show, so we scheduled the interview for afterward. We were backstage on a college campus in April 1972 outside of Denver. A huge tub of Budweiser beer was in front of us. I was surprised because this was Coors country, and that beer wasn't distributed nationally at the time.

We talked about his background and working at a song publishing house, but I could tell that he was uncomfortable, so I broke away from my line of questions and asked something trite. He answered, telling me the most exciting thing that happened to him was "the first time I had intercourse with a woman, or maybe it was the second time."

Neil was clearly disturbed, and called the record promoter to come over. The guy was excited.

"Yes, Neil?"

"Are these people with you?"

"Yes." He had an entourage of several girls with him, and they were busy laughing and drinking nearby.

"I want you to get the . . . out of here and take everybody with you. The only ones who stay are Jim and his engineer."

The record promoter turned around and got the girls. He smiled at Neil and said, "We'll catch up with you later." It was suddenly quiet in the area. Neil popped another beer, and we had a great conversation.

We talked about "Brother Love's Traveling Salvation Show" and Neil unraveled its story. "'Brother Love' came out of an incident that I fell into when I was about eighteen years old. I went up to a church service in Harlem. I'm not sure now why I went there to that service, but I remember I was sitting in the back. I was the only white in the audience. There must have been a thousand people there; it was an enormous church. The music and the feeling of the people and what the preacher had to say, first of all, it was easily the most exciting kind of performance that I had ever seen. It kind of stunned me, and eventually I knew that I would write something about that kind of thing to capture that. 'Brother Love' was originally to be an album. I was going to do a whole album about this lecherous, backwoods revival preacher. But I started to have second thoughts about what these people are and what really they give, and I thought they do have a contribution, that they do give something. So I made the portrait a little more flattering to the preacher. Instead of doing it as an album concept, I felt that after I had finished writing the single that I had said everything that I wanted to say so there was no point in writing anymore."

Four and a half months later in LA, the song became the focal point for his *Hot August Nights* shows.

Neil had recently screen-tested for the film *Lenny*, the Lenny Bruce story, but he said, "I don't know, the motion picture business doesn't excite me too much. It's not nearly as exciting as doing concerts, as making records, as writing songs."

Neil would later star in the movie *The Jazz Singer* in 1980. I thought he was terrific, but he got panned and would never appear in another movie except to play himself.

The Everly Brothers

The world's most famous rock 'n' roll duo, the Everly Brothers, had thirty-five *Billboard* top one hundred singles beginning with "Bye Bye Love" in 1957. Their close harmony influenced generations of groups, including the Beatles. They are members of the first class inducted into the Rock and Roll Hall of Fame.

Phil Everly hasn't done many interviews, but he was relaxed and open with me. His parents were in the business, and his career really began when he was six years old on a radio station in Shenandoah, Iowa. "Yeah, it's exactly right on station KMA," Phil said, "You know, it's kind of funny from this vantage point. You never know what you're doing in life. It doesn't seem to be anything that you can stop or start that puts you where you're at. We were just kind of born into circumstances because we were working every day. So our training was really kind of thorough. It's almost like being an apprentice to be a musician. I never really thought of anything else. Then we only spent a couple of years from the time I was sixteen until the time we were eighteen sort of on the cuff of things in Nashville, which were fairly lean, but the family kept pushing us up and forward, and then it happened. Hard to understand isn't it?"

There were several people who were responsible for the Everly Brothers' early success. I mentioned Chet Atkins and Archie Bleyer. Phil agreed, "Chet was a great musical factor, and Archie Bleyer was a great record president; if he believed in something, he went after it. But I would put primary first, Boudleaux and Felice Bryant and their song 'Bye Bye Love.' It was a song that Archie thought was a hit, too, and the fact that when we sang it in front of him, it came alive. But without that piece of material, I don't believe anywhere near the kind of career that my brother and I had would have been possible. You know that as you tell the story, when you would answer a question like that, and say, 'Well yes, those people are responsible, but there are so many factors that really are involved.' Up to three months before we recorded 'Bye Bye Love,' Don and I were on the verge of leaving Nashville and giving up show business. This is a little 'nobody knows' story because it takes too long to tell. We had auditioned for a television show, and we had a friend who was saying, 'Next week, next week,' and we just kind of hung on for the next three months. We went to see Wesley Rose because a friend of ours made an appointment to pitch our songs there, and it just so happened that Archie was looking for country acts. So many circumstances come into play that I always consider it a real miracle that anything happened like this."

I heard that Archie had a habit of always taking records home to his teenage daughter, Jackie, and she would listen to the songs. She flipped over "Bye Bye Love," and it was her insistence that convinced her daddy to say okay, let's do this thing and release the record. Phil was surprised. "It may be that she flipped over the demo—I don't know. I married her, too, and I should know. She was my first wife. It's funny isn't it? He did play records for her, and whatever ones she liked, that's what he thought would be a hit. I also know, too, that when I put out 'Cathy's Clown,' they didn't think it was a hit, including her. She did have a very good ear, and he was smart in listening to the young ones."

The Everly Brothers were very close to Buddy Holly. Phil was a pallbearer at Buddy's funeral, but Don was so upset, he couldn't get out of bed. At one time, Buddy decided to ditch his trademark horn-rimmed glasses. Phil told me laughing, "Well, what happened was that Buddy had shot an album cover, and we were all in the dressing room at the time. He had taken his glasses off, and it didn't look good. His eyes were all watery, you know how you can get, he kind of look walleyed. We said, 'Buddy, you'd best stick to the glasses.'" That was the picture they used for his solo album *Buddy Holly*, and they were kidding him because he was trying to look cool.

In 1960 the Everly Brothers switched labels from Cadence to Warner Brothers Records. Phil told me they had no regrets and shared an interesting observation: "In looking back, my opinion has always been, what was going on in the fifties with the music was that everybody was of the opinion it was only temporary, and they were treating the acts and the artists as if they were temporary instead of helping it to blossom. It was more a temporary viewpoint about rock 'n' roll. It turned out to not be the case at all, because not only did the audience keep growing up, so did the acts. That was the only mistake that I regret, that that viewpoint was held at that time by others. Don and I went on to do what we thought had to be done, which is what rock 'n' roll is—continual change, progressive. You have to make moves, and some of the moves that we made after the intensity stopped may have been too progressive. When we did 'Lucille,' we put eight guitars playing at the same time the same riff, which had not been done before. They do multiple guitars now. It's quite common, but in those days, the techniques weren't as good. I don't regret anything actually. Even the way all that worked out is still fine with me."

Chuck Berry had once said, "I didn't think that Presley was as good as the Everly Brothers, and the first time I ever laid eyes on him, that's what I thought, and I didn't think the Beatles were as good as the Everly Brothers either." Phil had never heard that and graciously deflected the attention away by saying, "I think probably what Chuck Berry is talking about is to the degree of originality. There are two guitar players in the industry, Chuck Berry and Bo Diddley, who are really primary creators. Bo Diddley is unique; he has that quality, that open tuning, and the beat that has, like, a backbone to rock music. Also, Chuck Berry, the song 'Maybelline,' the stylization, the structure of a basic rock 'n' roll song—you have to attribute to Chuck Berry. Coming from him, I'm much honored, because it is a very nice remark. I have not read it."

Chuck Berry

Chuck Berry and I have been together a number of times, and he always does a terrific show, but he doesn't like to be interviewed. He was in a good mood, and while we were sitting in the seats at the Cincinnati Gardens, he was looking at my notes as I was doing the interview live on WLW radio. "Muddy Waters was a big influence on you . . ."

"Hey Jim, let me get a word in," he said laughing. "Wait a minute, what's this 'Charles Edward Anderson Berry'? You must be a scientist or something—that's me, that's the whole thing, my mama's baby child."

I understood that his first hit "Maybelline" was actually "Ida Red" with different lyrics, but Chuck was quick to correct me: "Well, no, 'Ida Red' has a different progression from 'Maybelline,' but I was using 'Maybelline' in the place of 'Ida Red' in the tune of 'Ida Red' until Leonard Chess, the owner of Chess Records, advised me to write something original. Then I just went on to the blues progression of 'Maybelline,' and I took my 'Maybelline,' and I left 'Ida Red' alone." Yeah, Chuck had a way with words, and that *certainly* clarified it for me.

When "Maybelline" hit, he said, yes, he was into "cosmetology, fixing hair, and beautification in hair styling." He doesn't fool around with hair today. "No way, I hung up my combs when 'Maybelline' hit because I was making about sixteen to twenty dollars a day. Of course, you know I'm making a little more than that here."

Chuck's first contract for Chess Records was for four hundred dollars, and today we hear about megamillion-dollar deals for artists, but Chuck put things into perspective and said, "When an artist starts off brand new, he doesn't get anything in advance. I got a penny a record for 'Maybelline.' It sold a million, and that adds up to ten thousand dollars. 'Ding a Ling' sold a million at I think seven cents a record. So you see, there's a difference." "Maybelline" came out in 1955; "Ding a Ling" was a number one hit years later in 1972.

Chuck Berry has been referred to as "America's first rock 'n' roll poet," and one of his anthems is "Sweet Little Sixteen." He told me about the song's star and said, "Well, I didn't know the name of the child, but the inspiration came in Denver, Colorado, which at that time had a circular auditorium like an arena. The kid never watched the show at all, she just ran around to get autographs. I remember she had on a yellow dress, and the whole song tells what I actually saw there. She was about seven or eight, she wasn't really sixteen, but the average age of my fans was around sixteen."

Chuck told me his "ideal music is in the line of Nat King Cole." I would have never believed it.

Chuck Berry's trademark over the years has been the duck walk that he does when he walks across the stage with his guitar. We were discussing the origin of that move, and in a negative voice he said, "You know, I can't answer that." I looked at him for a few seconds, and then he continued, "It was first done at the Brooklyn Paramount, which is tore down now. In the instrumental part of the song, I had nothing to do, and to stand up there and twist, you know, was not in my bag. So I just started walking lowly on the floor. What I really wanted to do was get my guitar cord away from under my feet. When I went down, there was a cheer that went up in the audience, so I stayed down you know, and as I went across the floor, they continued to cheer, so I said this is one of those good things you can maintain, so I maintained it. So I added to it the split and all the bits you know. So anything the audience actually likes, I try to maintain it."

When I first met the Beatles, they were asked about people who influenced them, and they said Chuck Berry. Chuck smiled, "This is wonderful. I don't know why they chose me. There are a lot of us I feel that participated. I'm only a cog in the wheel that participated in the launching of rock because surely Louis Jordan, surely Joe Turner. They are the fathers who came before me. So we all had a bit in it to launch it, Presley and all of us."

Jerry Lee Lewis told me a great Chuck Berry story.

I told him, "Jerry you are a living legend."

He said laughing, "I'm a living, loving wreck."

"You and Chuck Berry did a number of shows together and you closed. One night he insisted that you go on first."

"Yeah, I did. He insisted that he close the show, and I said, 'Okay, Chuck.' A lot of people say I had some lighter fluid that I threw on the piano and burned it up. Well, I didn't. I had a Coca-Cola bottle with gasoline in it. So when I closed with 'Great Balls of Fire' for a reason, I just drenched that piano with gasoline and threw a match on it. I walked off, and I said, 'All right Chuck—get it.'" Jerry laughed.

James Brown

James Brown was the "hardest working man in show business," the "godfather of soul," "soul brother number one," and I could go on and on. He shaped American rhythm and blues, funk, disco, and more. His father didn't finish the second grade, and he didn't get through the seventh grade, but he made music history. Ninety-four of his records reached the Top 100 charts. I was with James on a number of occasions, and he may not have had classroom education, but he had a PhD in life.

James had to quit school in the seventh grade, and he spent three years in reform school, in jail for automobile theft, breaking and entering. James told me, "That was a turning point in my life as far as getting it through the system and getting it honest. I had a chance to be a professional baseball player. I had three professional fights as a boxer, but the quickest thing for me, and I needed it in a hurry, was music. So I went into music from all aspects, not only to be a singer, but to play instruments as well. I tried to be everything that I could, and I tried to be self-contained by writing and putting my thing together so I'd know how to execute it when the time came. Music was the vehicle that had more speed. I needed to get there yesterday."

In 1966 he moved from Harlem's Apollo Theater to his first appearance at Madison Square Garden. He told me what he was thinking when he walked into the Garden for that first show. James said, "Well, what I remember was from my early childhood days when Joe Louis used to fight there, and the only way we could hear the fight was over a battery radio. No one was able to financially afford a radio with electrical current. We didn't live in houses that had electrical current; we had lamps. When you had two or three hundred people gathered around a battery radio that would probably last for two fights, and it would be through. It reminded me of that, and now, here I am in Madison Square Garden with a total sellout with people turned away. I felt like that I had accomplished a lot and that people had been very good to me and that I owed a lot to the world."

The idea came from a white wrestler, Gorgeous George, who would enter the ring and throw off his robe, but it became a James Brown trademark. It started in 1962 when his emcee, Danny Ray, put a Turkish towel, then a robe, and eventually he draped a cape over him while he was singing his signature song. At the end of his concert, an exhausted James would drop to his knees, drained of emotion while singing "Please, Please, Please (don't go)." Danny would put the cape on him, and James would rip it off and rush to the microphone on stage. His background singers would continually sing, "Please, Please, Please don't go, oh." This ritual with James struggling free of the cape, throwing it off his sweat drenched body was repeated several times. The audience expected it, and felt his pain with him when he lifted himself and recovered.

We were backstage and he had just captured the emotions of a packed crowd with his ritual. I thought there was a religious significance behind it, and James Brown confirmed that it was in part, and added, "Well, it's a religious story, but there's a lot of things that goes behind that. The crying and the mourning and the stamping on the floor trying to get a point across, trying to express your hurt, your deep feeling, that goes far, far back. One of the things yet we haven't been able to outlive and overcome. So I'd rather at this point in this stage of the game, with the country being in such turmoil—I don't think we need to talk about that—I think we need to go further because we need to be as positive and as together as we can, as unified as we can as a people to combat this economical problem, the relationship among people. So they can function as one and not only save themselves but their family and friends." James Brown was a humanitarian, giving away thousands each year to charities. He sang it and lived it: "I'm Black and I'm Proud." He inspired a generation to resist racism, white supremacy, stereotyping about black beauty, and to stand tall in the face of adversity.

In November 1974, James and I were talking about the success he had in show business and if there was anything else he wanted. He said yes, and he asked me for a favor: "I want very much for you to let this answer go on the air. I want America to live to its true meaning that regardless of race, creed, or color; education or no education; a doctor's degree—if I earn it, I can exercise it. If this country lives its true meaning that regardless of a man's bringing up or what he feels or what he's from or what he thinks he feels, that if he earns something, if I work, I want to be paid; if I make it, I want to be able to spend it; I want to be able to keep it; if I prefer giving it away, then I'll give it away, but at least let me have the chance to be what I want to be. If I become a bum, don't label me as a black bum, let me be a bum. But if I do not become a bum, let me be the president of the United States, if I can be that and get the votes. Thank you, Jim, I really appreciate this. You know we go way back brother."

Chuck Berry had his trademark duck walk, and James Brown had his robe, but for another singer, it was his shoes.

Pat Boone

Pat Boone made a career out of covering the original rhythm and blues hits "Ain't That a Shame," "Tutti Frutti," "Long Tall Sally," and others in the fifties and sold close to fifty million records. His trademark was his white buck shoes that clean-cut guys wore. In my neighborhood, no one had a pair.

Pat Boone told me that it was a natural thing. "It was unplanned. I was a high school and college student when I first began to sing on the *Arthur Godfrey Talent Scout Show* and eventually as a professional on the *Perry Como Show*. I wore the only decent pair of shoes I had. They were the ones I wore to school and the ones I wore to church. They were just this pair of white bucks that I kept polished, and they would go with anything. All the other kids were wearing them too, but I was the first one to wear them on television in singing appearances. Without them meaning to be, they became my trademark."

Favorite ladies

Joanie Sommers was my first, but over the years, I've had a number of favorite ladies. I never interviewed her on the radio, but she was one of my favorites. I got the Skyliners to sing at a fraternity party about a hundred miles outside of Pittsburgh. At that time, Jimmy Beaumont, the lead singer, had left and was replaced for a short time by Jackie Gardner, but they still sounded terrific. I rode home to Pittsburgh with them, and we stopped at a truck stop for something to eat. Here we were, five guys and a pretty girl in the wee hours of the morning. Janet Vogel, the attractive girl who hit the high 'C' at the end of "Since" was upset. "Look at them staring at me Jimmy. They think I'm a hooker. I feel so cheap," Janet said as she glanced over at a group of burly truckers. I tried to comfort her. She should have felt like she was on top of the mountain because we just finished a great show where everybody loved her. She'd been on the bandstand shows, was in a movie, and had several hit records. How strange it was that her song "Since I Don't Have You" was playing on the jukebox, and no one knew it was her. In 1980 they found Janet's body in a car in her garage—cause of death, carbon monoxide. Janet Vogel took her own life at the age of thirty-seven, a combination of mental health and family issues.

Kentucky's Jackie DeShannon could write and sing. I've often joked that she dated both Elvis and John Lennon and went out to dinner with me, which is true. She got married three days earlier to University of Cincinnati alumnus Randy Edelman, the songwriter singer, when she stopped by to visit and talk about her hits and the early days when she sang around town under the name Jackie Dee. She began writing songs when she was fourteen, and the first chart hit she had was Brenda Lee's "Dumb Dumb." She laughed, "Jimmy, you have really done your homework." Jackie's signature song is "What the World Needs Now is Love," and she told me the first time Hal David and Burt Bacharach played it for her, she cried. After she recorded it, she didn't think it would be a hit. "I don't think I've ever thought that about any record I've made." Jackie said, "People kept telling me, it's a beautiful record, but you can't dance to it." "Put a Little Love in Your Heart" was a million-seller for Jackie, and she told me she was inspired by and originally wrote the song for Gladys Knight.

Speaking of Gladys Knight, I've interviewed her a number of times, but my most memorable was when Phil Donahue had a private plane fly me from Cincinnati to watch him do his nationally syndicated show from Greenfield Village, Michigan. His staff called me a few times for music information and I think this was his way of saying thank you. Gladys was his guest and I interviewed her after his show. Her first hit with the Pips in 1961 happened when they were working at the Builder, a local club in Atlanta. She said, "The club owner asked us to try out some new recording equipment that he purchased. We did some songs and he asked us if we had any original material and as stupid as we were, of course we said yes. So we did "Every Beat of My Heart" and about a week or two later, our friends in school told us how much they liked our new record. We weren't signed to this guy. He sold the master to Vee-Jay Records and cut the group out of the record's profits. We didn't get a dime from it."

Some entertainers do not want to be disturbed right before they go on. They are getting in their zone, and I totally understand that. Brenda Lee started a conversation with me backstage, and I said I didn't want to bother her. She said, "Jimmy, I've been doing this for so long nothing bothers me." Brenda Lee is a member of both the Country Music Hall of Fame and the Rock and Roll Hall of Fame, and we go way back. I called her one night in November of 1976. They told her Jimmy was on the phone. I could hear everybody screaming and cheering in the background. I had no idea what was going on, and then she got on the phone. I was mistaken for the president-elect, Jimmy Carter, and I'm sure everyone was disappointed it was the disc jockey Jimmy. Brenda later explained with her country accent, "I was so embarrassed. You must have thought we were a bunch of banshees the way we were carrying on. It was election eve, and we were expecting a call from Jimmy Carter. He called and asked me to join him, and I took a private plane at ten that night, and I stayed until about three. We are good friends. I campaigned for him. He was the only one who recognized that I was from Georgia, and his last act as governor was to proclaim it Brenda Lee Day."

Brenda lived in Cincinnati at one time. "I lived in Cincinnati 1955 into 1956 for a little over a year. I used to sing at the old Jimmy Skinner Record Shop every Saturday."

Rita Coolidge, the "Delta Lady," told me she and Brenda Lee were on the same cheerleading squad in school. I would have loved to have seen that.

One of my wife's favorite singers is Lesley Gore. She was a passenger on a flight when my wife was a hostess. We visited Lesley in her room and Sally, totally out of character, took her dressing room sign. Lesley laughed and autographed it. She was always very gracious with me and one of the few who sent a thank you note after an interview. Early in her career her mother traveled with her and protected her from young, lecherous disc jockeys.

Carly Simon, Yoko Ono, and Lesley all attended Sarah Lawrence College. Lesley Gore graduated with a major in English and American literature. I thought that being a recording star would have been a nice advantage when she went to college. Lesley said, "It was difficult because I was then considered a rock singer, and Sarah Lawrence was kind of an uppity school. So it was really more of a disadvantage than an advantage."

Lesley Gore's favorite song is "You Don't Own Me." This song was years ahead of the women's liberation movement. The first time she heard the song was when two young songwriters from Philadelphia, John Madara and Dave White, came all the way to Grossinger's Resort Hotel in the Catskill Mountains in New York where she was performing. Lesley told me, "They cornered me in a cabana at the swimming pool, and one of them pulled out a guitar and played 'You Don't Own Me.' I was just blown away by the song. Even at sixteen, whether I was a girl or a guy or a cocker spaniel, the idea of being able to stand up there and actually shake your finger at somebody and say 'don't tell me what to do' is as appealing to me today as it was then and in many cases more so."

The best seats I ever had for a concert were tickets for a Judy Collins show that Judy gave to a girlfriend of hers, seats one and two, first row. A friend tried to get us together for a date, but she was involved at the time. She had the most beautiful, mesmerizing blue eyes I've ever seen. When she was leaving Stephen Stills for Stacy Keach, the actor, he wrote "Suite: Judy Blue Eyes" about her. Judy has been around music her entire life and told me she

Judy Collins and me.

learned to read music before the printed word. Her dad was in radio, and I think that helped with our connection. Judy Collins loved to talk about her father and said, "He called his show *The Medicine Show* because he did so many things—poetry, music, talk, he interviewed guests, and played the piano on the radio. He was a fascinating guy; he was blind from the age of four, and he got around with no cane or dog. He just walked around like everyone else. He didn't wear tennis shoes because he couldn't hear the 'radar'—the shoes made a sound. He encouraged me, and he had a great choice of music; he really liked Rodgers and Hart."

A young twenty-four-year-old Linda Ronstadt explained to me why she seldom wore shoes on stage: "The reason I don't, believe it or not, is I have an ankle bone in my feet, and it makes it very uncomfortable to wear them. You can't see them unless you have an x-ray. My brother got out of the army because of that. It makes it very uncomfortable to stand up for very long."

Gracie Slick of Jefferson Airplane was attractive, but a little crazy in a nice sort of way. Before Gracie was a singer she was a model; she clarified her transition to me. "I did model because I don't know how to type or do anything else. One night, I went to see Jefferson Airplane, and we said, hey that looks like more fun than starving to death and modeling, which is very boring. So we formed our own group called the Great Society and played with the Airplane a lot. When their girl singer got pregnant and left, I got into the band and got pregnant, but stayed."

Five days after she wrapped up the movie *Grease*, Olivia Newton John told me about the song "You're the One That I Want." "There wasn't a duet in the original *Grease*, and I thought it would be a good idea to sing a song with John Travolta, and I asked my record producer to write us one."

A number one duet in 1976 was "Don't Go Breaking My Heart" that was done by Elton John and Kiki Dee. She told me Elton actually cut the track in Toronto and put her vocals on it in London. They had worked together before this record. In 1970 Elton, "Reggie" as she called him, worked for Kiki when she was doing a television series in England. He was booked as a background singer. Kiki told me, "I don't tell many people this story, obviously, but I remember him really clearly because he was kind of this chubby little guy who came into the studio, and I liked him. He had a big shoulder bag. So actually, he worked for me."

I think every young guy in the seventies fell in love with the voice of Karen Carpenter, who along with her brother, Richard, had hit after hit. She started singing while playing drums and eventually sang in front. Karen became a drummer because she didn't like gym. She explained the situation to me. "When I got into high school, I was in gym class at eight in the morning, and I didn't like running around a track and jumping in a cold swimming pool. My brother, who had graduated, knew the band director and said get out of gym and get into band. I didn't play anything, so I ended up with a glockenspiel, which I really, boy I hated it, hated," she laughed, "but the glockenspiel is part of the percussion section, and immediately, I fell in love with the drums. Luckily, I had a talent for it. It was something that fit me. I never realized I could do anything, because I didn't sing or play until I was fifteen or sixteen years old."

CHAPTER 19

My Obsession with Jukeboxes

Speaking of pretty ladies, I have to describe a situation that took place one memorable night when I was home during a college break. My friend Henry Tumpa and his college buddies took me to visit my first whore house. Keep in mind, this was a different era. We were going to a black whore house in the Hill District, the tough black section of Pittsburgh. We parked at the bottom of the hill in an area that later became the Civic Auditorium. We walked through a wooded area where we were greeted by a little guy with a limp, "Willie the Pimp": "Boys, this is a good night. Frenchie is here; we got China Doll . . ." I was a nervous wreck. These guys were tough, but not in this situation. After the whistle sounded, giving us the all-clear signal, we walked through the woods. We made it into the house where a giant man was standing off to the side, a large woman was taking money, and some very sexy ladies wearing very little underwear greeted us. I used the bathroom, and while I was standing there, a stunning naked lady was combing her hair smiling at me. She was as comfortable as could be. After looking over all the ladies for about thirty-five minutes, we left and told them we'd be back. No one did anything, but something happened in that house that would stay with me for years. In the back of that room was this gorgeous, lit jukebox. That jukebox with its colorful, flickering lights bouncing off the glistening chrome of the box, and the sight of the needle dropping down into the groove of the 45 rpm record going around and around was very salacious. In remembering my innocent youth, I've equated that jukebox to be as erotic as that desirable naked black lady standing next to me in the bathroom.

I didn't realize the connection until years later when I became obsessed with collecting jukeboxes. At one time, I owned one of the largest collections of vintage Wurlitzer jukeboxes in the Midwest. My collection is the Paul Fuller–designed art deco Wurlitzer's; the oldest is from 1940 and the newest from 1948. Over the years, my jukeboxes have been featured in a number of newspaper and magazine stories. I've taken a 1015 jukebox apart and totally restored it. The multi–Emmy Award winner, George Ciccarone did an outstanding five-minute feature on my jukeboxes for the *Inside Edition* television show.

Jimmy and Shelby, my son and daughter, grew up listening to the sounds of those old 78 rpm records as we played pinball games. When Jimmy was three years old, the Cincinnati *Enquirer* did a story in their magazine featuring pinball games and included a picture of me watching him play. Years later, when his son, my grandson, James, was three, he would play those same games with me and beat me just like his daddy. My collection includes mechanical Mills Slot Machines, a pitcher-batter game from the sixties, a Captain Fantastic pinball game, a brass cash register that I restored, and a number of mechanical games from the fifties and sixties. I have a Howdy Doody marionette from when I was a kid. Buffalo Bob Smith once sang "It's Howdy Doody Time" on my radio show, and I helped sing a little background. The room that houses my collection is my room to relax and enjoy the music of my youth.

A few of my favorite Wurlitzer jukeboxes from the 1940s.
PHOTO BY JOEL QUIMBY

A Wurlitzer model 1080 and a 1015.
PHOTO BY JOEL QUIMBY

Life as an emcee and judge

At WLW, I was the one who got the requests to emcee shows. Some radio people would rather have a root canal than stand in front of an audience, but I loved it. I've been involved in many beauty pageants, both as a judge and the master of ceremonies, but one really stands out. I was the emcee for the Miss Cincinnati pageant, part of the Miss USA pageant that was held at the Downtown Holiday Inn. It went on for several weeks with a panel of celebrity judges changing every week. The ladies were judged on appearance (they had several clothing changes) and how they answered my questions. One week I thought I knew who the winner would be because she was by far the best. Carol worked at a local bar and one day would marry Pete Rose. I tabulated the judge's scores, and I said to Jeff Ruby, who ran the Holiday Inn at the time, "I don't believe this." One of the guys had given Carol low scores like a two or a three out of ten across the board. She was totally out of the running. Jeff recognized the writing and was upset, but there was nothing we could do about it. At the time, he was a very well-known, local married personality. We thought he probably tried to ask her out and was rejected. I've judged lots of beauty contests, but I had no idea one person could do this. In hindsight, I should have talked Jeff into throwing out his scores. It was the only time I ever saw this happen.

The Cincinnati Bengals were looking for cheerleaders—the Ben-Gals—and I was one of the judges. The finals were held at Riverfront Stadium and sitting next to me was one of the great characters of Cincinnati radio. Leo Underhill worked for WNOP Radio Free Newport, the station with studios on the Ohio River at the Newport waterfront. It would have been a dream place to work because the jocks sounded like they had total freedom. The only drawback was it had a small signal, no ratings, and didn't pay much. Leo once described the station: "It was utter chaos. I used to give the bar closings rather than the school closings." He called the Bengals' public relations man Al Heim to the table: "Al, LaBarbara says if you don't get us beer, he's leaving, and I'm going with him." I tried to explain that I never said that, but Leo stood up and grabbed me like we were leaving. Al said beer was prohibited on the field, but ten minutes later he came back with beer for us. There was one potential cheerleader who wore a mesh top that left nothing to the imagination. I asked Leo what he thought, and he surprised everyone. "She would be fine at 2:00 a.m. in a Newport motel, but not on a Sunday afternoon in front of mothers with their children." He had us in tears with his comments the whole night and, of course, I edged him on. After a few beers, Leo had to go to the bathroom. He didn't think with the girls auditioning that anyone would notice, so he walked out to right field and went against the wall. Everyone saw him, and a newspaper photographer captured that moment. That picture of Leo hung on the wall at Sleep Out Louie's bar near the stadium for years.

The Palace Theater

One of my favorite venues was the magnificent Palace Theater at 16 East Sixth Street. It originally opened in 1919 but reopened as a concert house, road show venue with a newly decorated interior in October of 1978. Sadly, it was torn down in 1982 for an office building.

I was backstage watching the opening act at the Palace when there was a knock at the back door. One of the stage guys opened the door and told the man he had to use the front door. I went to see what was going on. There, standing bigger than life was our headliner, Bill Cosby. He explained he didn't want the limo and decided to walk. He was wearing a trench coat and had a cigar in his hand. I couldn't believe that he was such an unassuming guy. Later, my friend Bob Shreve came backstage and wanted to say hi to Bill. Shreve was the crazy host of all-night movies on Saturday night. His show had been on channels nine, five, and twelve at one time or another from 1966 to 1985 under different names. He was the bartender host who sang, danced, and made cameo appearances in the movies. Nobody cared about the movies; we waited for him to come back on. He was hilarious, and the show got crazier by the hour. Among his props were a rubber chicken; Spidel, a large, stuffed spider who would swing at

Bob and knock his hat off; and Garoro, an ugly, severed head with a dangling eyeball. I started to introduce him, and Cosby gave him a big hug like they were best friends. Bill had seen his late night show a few times and even surprised him with a visit on camera. It was neat to watch the two of them together. Bob was one of the first people I met when I got to Cincinnati, and for a long time, a group of us would go out drinking with him one night a week. Everywhere he went, he was beloved. He was sponsored by Schoenling beer at the time, and that's what we drank. He was the best salesman they ever had. He was later sponsored by Hudepohl beer. I stopped by his show a number of times; sometimes I'd be on camera, other times I just had a few beers. One Halloween television show, I knocked on his door, hid in a coffin, and when he opened it, I jumped out of the coffin wearing a horrendous mask, but I got no response. I took the mask off, and he screamed, throwing his rubber chicken in the air.

I introduced our opening act, Jose Feliciano, the talented, blind folk singer who had a number of hits including his signature song "Light My Fire." I was looking at the Palace's crowd, when suddenly a man sitting in an end seat slumped over and fell into the aisle. He was just laying there motionless. The lights went on, and an announcement was made: "Is there a doctor in the house?" Jose started singing over and over, "Is there a doctor in the house? Is there a doctor in the house? Is there a doctor in the house?" It was surreal. He's singing, and doctors are trying to revive this poor guy, and the audience is stunned. One of his bandmates finally got Jose to stop singing. It was only minutes, but it seemed like forever. The ambulance arrived, and I later found out the man survived.

Another talented, sightless singer recognized me from a previous interview. Ray Charles had a great memory and a fabulous ear. We were talking about some crazy things he was accused of doing. However, Ray Charles was cautious in what he said, "Well, in my lifetime I've probably done a lot of silly things. I'm kind of an adventurer. The one thing I try not to do is: I would not want some blind person to go out and try some of the foolishness that I did. They might get themselves killed. Not that I'm so smart, and everybody's so dumb.

You better be real sure that you know what you're doing. You don't go off half-cocked getting on a motorcycle; people who can see get themselves pretty mangled up with that. But, I have ridden on motorcycles and cars, and I know enough about an airplane; I won't say I've flown one, but I know enough about one that, God forbid if my pilot became incapacitated, I could get the plane down without killing myself. I can assure you of that."

On December 3, 1979, our headliner at the Palace was the talented songwriter, singer, storyteller, and humanitarian Harry Chapin. I gave him one of my long Music Professor introductions. He gave me a big smile as we passed each other on stage. While I was driving home, the cold December air was filled with the sound of ambulance horns. Across town at Riverfront Coliseum, eleven people had been crushed to death trying to see the Who. It was festival seating, first-come, first-served seats. When one door was opened, dozens of people were trampled by the crowd. It happened very quickly. The show went on, and the Who didn't find out what happened until after the concert. Some of the concertgoers never found out until the next day's newspaper.

I wanted to interview Harry Chapin before the Palace show, but because of his crazy schedule, we didn't connect until a few weeks later. He apologized and said, "I live a life like a political campaign—I'm not running for anything, I don't play the role of the delicate artist, it wasn't because I was sleeping in some motel room." He made a commitment to end world hunger, and it wasn't just for guilt benefits, he was working it. Harry and I talked about his songs and his childhood when he sang in the Brooklyn Boys Choir with Bobby Lamb of the group Chicago. He recorded some nice hits: "Taxi"; the disc jockey song "WOLD"; and his number one hit in 1974, "Cats in the Cradle."

"Cats in the Cradle" is the story of a father who is too busy to spend time with his son, who grows up to be just like him and then has no time to spend with his dad. Harry's wife, Sandy, wrote it as a poem, and he told me, "Sandy had been zinging me about running around the country not spending enough time with the kids. It scared the hell out of me if you want to know the truth. I'm still traveling maybe a hundred nights a year out of two-hundred concerts I do. I get home somehow—charter flights or early morning flights in time for breakfast." Sandy later explained that the song's story was partly true. She had written the poem, inspired by her first husband's relationship and a country song she heard on the radio, but it did hit home with Harry. Awhile after we talked in July of 1981, Harry was killed in a car crash on his way to perform a free concert. He may have had a heart attack.

I put Harry Chapin in a category all by himself. He donated an estimated one-third of his paid concerts to charitable causes. After his death, Sandy told a reporter, with "only a slight exaggeration," that "Harry was supporting seventeen relatives, fourteen associations, seven foundations, and eighty-two charities. Harry wasn't interested in saving money. He always said, 'Money is for people,' so he gave it away."

After his death, I reflected on something Harry told me, and I felt better: "I got the best job in the world. I get a chance to sing my own music where I want, when I want, for thousands of people, and make thousands of dollars, and I'm able to apply that to things I believe in, and I couldn't be happier. It's an amazing feeling to have a chance to do what you love and get paid for it."

※ ※ ※

That was me, working in a business I loved and getting paid for it. I sat around with Cheech and Chong, the stars of those seventies and eighties marijuana-themed movies. They lived in California mansions and didn't sound at all like the druggies in their movies. Jack Lemmon described the pain women must go through everyday wearing those high heels. He experienced it firsthand wearing those shoes in the movie *Some Like It Hot* with Marilyn Monroe. Raquel Welch was one of the sexiest women in the world when I interviewed her, and I'll admit I was nervous just talking with her. Peter Nero, the pianist, and Wolfman Jack both had ladies sitting on their laps during our interviews. I was a little distracted by what was going on.

I was on a movie junket in LA in 1980 to see a preview of *The Coal Miner's Daughter*, the Loretta Lynn story. Sissy Spacek won an Academy Award for her role as Loretta. When I interviewed Sissy, I couldn't concentrate because there were red drapes in the room, and all I could think about was her horror film *Carrie*. I kept seeing those drapes catching on fire and me going up in flames just like in the movie. One of the film's outtakes was at Loretta's daddy's funeral when everyone was singing "Amazing Grace" around his casket. While they were singing, Levon Helm, of the Band, who played her father, started singing and sat up in the casket; of course, everyone cracked up.

My TV pilot

My WLW boss Charlie Murdock shot a television pilot with me for a half-hour show with interviews and music videos. Don McLean, Cliff Richard, and Bill Haley were a few of the guests on my show. It was a good idea because singers were just starting to make music videos. Timing is everything, and just as we pitched the show in 1981, MTV, the cable television network that featured music videos with VJs, or video jockeys, introducing the videos, debuted. No one was going to pick up our show when there was a whole network doing something similar.

I was later approached to be part of a show for BET, Black Entertainment Television. A group of local entrepreneurs were putting the show together. No one said it, but I was going to be the token white. I was going to interview the stars. I still have the first features I wrote, but for whatever reason, the show never happened.

WLW and shifting priorities

When I started on WLW in 1969 the lineup was Jim O'Neill in the morning, Joe Kelly and a simulcast of the Bob Braun television show middays. Rich King was afternoon drive, I was early evenings, followed by Bill Myers. JFPO "the Morning Mayor" did a humor-based show and scripted most of it. O'Neill even had a daily soap opera, "As Your Stomach Turns," where he voiced all of the characters. Jockey Joe possessed one of the deepest voices in radio and had a wonderful connection with the housewives. He referred to little children as "poopsies" and would ask about their poopsies and talk about his own poopsies. Rich King wasn't really a deejay; he was more of a standup comedian. His bits were local and he made sure to toss in a number of German words. He was funny, but to really understand him, you had to know Cincinnati and the people. He had a loyal audience. When I moved into his afternoon shift, I made no attempt to do his style. He was one of a kind—an incredible talent. Bob Braun gave me good advice and said to just be myself. I was told I picked up the ratings by six points. I did my artist interviews and talked about the records. I interviewed movie and television stars and newsmakers. My approach was different—I called Miss America's mother who assured me that her daughter was a "good girl"; President Ford's teacher described her one-time grade school student; and the mother of Lee Harvey Oswald, President Kennedy's assassin, proclaimed her son's innocence and claimed the FBI tapped her phone. I created local "water cooler" talk and was plugged into the community. My Reds and Bengals friends were always stopping by. I shared my daily adventures with my listeners and did a lot of name dropping. I may have used a few double entendres from time to time, but all-in-all, it was a clean family show. It was a different era.

During the years I was on WLW we had Chuck Daugherty, Jim McKnight, Bob Beasley, Bob Martin, Mike Weber, Debbie Conners, Bill Gable, and the talented Gary Burbank who did mornings for three years. The all-night shift had the most movement and a few stand out: Joe Martelle became a morning star in Boston for years. Pat Rogers became the program director at WTMJ in Milwaukee and WOAI in San Antonio, and Jack Reno played country music and had a few national hits as a singer. Nick Young went on to become a CBS radio network news anchor for many years. The most successful of that group was Harry Smith, who went on to become a star news anchor on television's CBS *This Morning* and other shows. He spent four months doing our 2:00 to 6:00 a.m. shift in 1975. He was doing his CBS TV show from Cincinnati in October 1990, and the *Enquirer's* John Kiesewetter asked me what I thought of him on WLW radio. I was quoted: "He was very nasal sounding. He was very nondescript. We didn't think he'd go on to anything." I was being honest, but I was embarrassed I said that. He is a good guy, and we talked often about our Denver connections. In my opinion, he wasn't a good disc jockey, but he became a wonderful television anchor/reporter who has become a multimillionaire. Two of my favorite behind-the-scenes guys were Cameron James and Greg Picciano. Cam was a comedic college student who worked as my traffic producer and later became a page at the NBC studio in New York. Johnny Carson frequently used him in his on-camera bits. Cam is the co-owner of Mills James, a creative media production company known all over the country and based in Ohio. Greg was a production assistant who wore many hats and was my right-hand man. During the seven years we worked together, he helped me line up guests, took pictures, and engineered recording sessions. He loves radio and went on to become an on-air star in Atlanta.

Joe Scallon bought WLW and was running it into the ground by 1983. I was giving away Arby's coupons while our competition, WKRC, had a million-dollar contest on the air. Every payday we rushed to the bank to cash our checks. The station was being sold, and I wanted the right people to buy it. I contacted some friends and put a deal together. Alfred Nippert's family was part owner of the Reds. He was a lawyer, and he got all the paperwork from WLW. Johnny Bench and his business partner Dean Ingram from Oklahoma were in on it. John had other investors ready. I met with Craig Lindner at American Financial, and if I had X amount of money, I could get the rest. I wasn't looking for anything, just job security. Dean knew the figure they wanted, and late the night before the bid was to be submitted, he called me. He asked what I thought. I looked at the contracts and obligations. We were paying an enormous fee for the traffic helicopter. I was honest. As much as I wanted this to happen, according to my paperwork, it didn't work out. Dean agreed with me. He called me the next day. What did I think of the sale? It sold for around the figure we were told, but it wasn't just for WLW; they included the FM. I screamed, "What?!" It was a hell of a deal, and we were misled. To my knowledge, only one person at the station knew of my involvement. Bench has mentioned in several interviews that he almost bought a radio station. Alfred Nippert gave me the contracts, and I still have a lot of the paperwork. Gary Burbank's contract was the best—he couldn't be fired unless he committed a felony. The new owners somehow got out of the helicopter contract, and the network deal was changed.

There were several program directors whose work I admired, and I saved articles about them: Ken Draper, Cleveland and Chicago; Tom Parker, Hartford; and my new boss, Randy Michaels.

WLW let me go and I was on the front page of the *Enquirer's* Metro Section, September 17, 1983. The heading read, "WLW Fires It's 'Professor.'" I was surprised, because my show was the only day shift to beat WKRC in the latest Arbitron rating, and I had the highest daytime numbers. Just a few months earlier, Randy Michaels gave me a hug and kiss and told me how we were going to make a lot of money. I was in Randy's office because we were going out for drinks. I didn't sense anything. His buddies John Phillips and Dan Allen were hanging around, but I thought they were going with us. Bobby Lawrence, the new sales manager came in, looked at me, and asked Randy, "Did you tell him yet?" Then I knew. Randy said something like, "I may be making a mistake, but it'll be a front-page story." He was right, it was. He gave me no reason for my dismissal. Driving home that night, I decided I was going to make a career change and do a talk show.

CHAPTER 20

Reinventing Myself
Talk Show Host/Entrepreneur

A few weeks later, I was the new talk show host on WCKY, doing a noon-to-three show. Talk radio in 1983 was not the modern talk radio of today; it was in its infancy. I thought about creating a new identity. In the past I was Jimmy Holiday; J. Bentley Starr, the Intrepid Leader; and Jim LaBarbara, the Music Professor. I couldn't be the Music Professor because I wasn't playing music, but over the last fifteen years, a lot of people called me "Prof" or "the Prof." It would be fine if a listener used it, but I never did. I was just referred to as Jim LaBarbara. My first week on WCKY, my boss Jim Glass said no phone interviews. That was what I did best. He wanted open-line talk, just me and the callers. That was the hardest thing I ever did in radio. I fell on my face, but I got up and adjusted. Unlike other talk stations, WCKY never fed shows with fake callers. I might do a put-on comedy bit with a guest but not random callers. Jim Glass worked with me, and I quickly got into a groove and felt comfortable. My deejay radio shows had featured polite but in-depth interviews with the stars of the entertainment world. I always prided myself in that I had something to say as a disc jockey. I tried to have a warm, storytelling approach that people could relate to with an interview mixed in. As a talk show host, I was taking on local political issues and criticizing local politicians and anybody else who was in the local news. Suddenly I'm talking about the person who lives down the street, not in Hollywood. My wife was very cold to me for a few days. She told me she had no idea I felt that way about a certain subject, and she was upset. I explained I didn't and was only playing devil's advocate. Of course, callers who didn't agree with me would give me the line: "Why don't you stick to playing records?" I didn't agree with the station policy of changing topics every hour, but I played the game. Everybody in town was talking about it, but I couldn't carry the hottest topic over to the next hour. As per Glass's memo: "Guest duplication is not to be permitted within program day parts inside a ninety-day period. Guest duplication from one day part to another is not permitted within sixty days. Topic duplication from one day part or from host to host must be approved in advance. Complete weekly advance schedules are due to the programming office by 3:00 p.m. each Thursday afternoon. These procedures apply to breaking as well as generic topics." In my opinion, these restrictions made it difficult to ride the big local stories and encouraged the booking of authors. WLW just had to say call me, and they got callers we really had to work the phones. I did an enormous amount of show prep and read an average of six books a week. In college, I was tested as a speed reader at a rate of close to a thousand words a minute with a comprehension of 80 percent. This skill was very beneficial to me. Every week I would present my show outline for each hour to the program director along with five ways to present the topic.

I knew I had pushed somebody's button when I got off the air. The chief of police was waiting for me in the lobby. He was really upset, but I don't remember why. I know I didn't back down. I did take my calls personally, and after a heated argument with a caller named Phil who had frequently argued with me, I was glad I was done for the day. I was so mad I was shaking when I answered the phone. "Jim, this is Phil. We really had them going today, great show." This was just a game to him. I learned that day—get your message across, but remember, it's still entertainment.

Randy Michaels invited me to breakfast about a year after he fired me. He wasn't happy with his WLW midday host and asked if I was interested. He had already introduced me to the lady who would be my producer. I considered it, but it never happened. He was especially complimentary of a recent interview I had with John DeLorean.

DeLorean

DeLorean was famous for developing the Pontiac GTO muscle car, the Firebird and the DeLorean DMC-12 sports car later featured in the movie *Back to the Future*. I was very familiar with that car. I did a television commercial for Sight N Sound, the audio store chain, in one of the first DeLoreans in town. The commercial was for a car stereo system, and at the end of the spot, I closed the gull-wing doors and sat behind the wheel. The crew was closing down the set when someone finally realized I was still in the car. I didn't know how to open the door. In 1982 John was arrested on charges of drug trafficking while trying to raise money for his struggling company. He successfully defended himself and was found not guilty due to entrapment in August 1984. He was the top story of the day and just as we were finishing, I surprised him by asking what happened to the cocaine. He got a little nervous, and I asked, "Okay, tell me which bank in Sweden is laundering the money. Where's the money?" He laughed, and the interview ended with our good-byes.

Not all my interviews ended so smoothly. Timothy Leary was best known as the spiritual proponent of the therapeutic, spiritual, and emotional benefits of LSD. He coined the phrase "Turn on, tune in, drop out." He had almost single handedly turned on the sixties generation to drugs. I did my hour interview with him, and he was very calm, very good. There was about ten minutes left when I hit him with a tough question. I said, "Jimi Hendrix, Janis Joplin, Jimmy Morrison, John Belushi . . . turn on, tune in, drop out. Do you feel any responsibility, any guilt for their deaths?" He totally lost it and started to swear at me, and I purposely didn't push the delay button so it went over the airwaves. He finally collected himself and accused me of taking a cheap shot at him. He said it wasn't his fault. I lived through it—I thought it was.

Of course local issues took up most of my air time, but I felt comfortable talking with anyone from the head of the KKK, porn star Marilyn Chambers, to the Rev. Robert Schuller. The reverend had a habit of giving me a signal to cut the caller off. He did this a number of times until I just quit looking in his direction. I talked with UFO experts, lesbian nuns, transvestites, along with the top authors of the day including Judith Krantz, William Shirer, Irving Stone, and Dr. Lendon Smith. Dr Ruth Westheimer, the sex expert, was always a hoot, and I'm sure some of the callers were just putting her on. Janet Leigh, the actress, described in great detail her nude scene in *Psycho*. She was wearing a body suit. Dignified actors Peter Ustinov and Anthony Quinn guested with me. Tony Bennett drew a picture of me during our interview and autographed it, signing his real name, "Anthony Benedetto." During my deejay years, I'd often get a Christmas card from Tony with a note saying he donated a gift to a charity in my name. He is very humble. When I mentioned to him that Frank Sinatra said, "For my money, Tony Bennett is the best singer in the business." Tony simply said, "I've been very influenced by him. He's the master and he's taught us all how to perform." I found out years later that my childhood friend Archie Leone wove his wigs.

Mary Wilson of the Supremes reminisced about the first time we met. It was on one of her first tours as the girls became stars. I embarrassed her by talking about a former boyfriend, Tom Jones, because she didn't realize he was married when they started dating. I asked her about the Supremes' Florence Ballard, who was kicked out of the Supremes for being overweight. I had a crush on her when I worked with the girls. Duke, of the Four Tops, Mary's one-time boyfriend, teared up when we talked about Florence's death. He told me, "It was senseless, and the situation with Paul Williams of the Temptations was mishandled." Paul died of a self-inflicted gunshot wound to the head. Mary said Florence was drinking and had put on weight. They were close friends, but Flo was always arguing with Berry Gordy, and she wanted out of the group. At the time, Diana Ross became difficult to work with and was Berry's lover. After leaving the Supremes, the money Flo thought was sitting in a bank turned out to be a pittance. The Supremes' expenses were all deducted from royalties. She had financial problems; she lost her house and her car and suffered the humiliation of going on welfare. She received a nice insurance settlement and was getting her life back together when she had a heart attack and died at the age of thirty-two, leaving her three children behind. Mary Wilson and her mother attended the funeral. Diana Ross was booed when she arrived with her entourage. The Motown record family was portrayed as one big happy group, but like any family, they had their problems.

I always enjoyed talking with Mary Travers from Peter, Paul, and Mary, and if I got her into one of her political rants, she'd go on forever. I asked her a question, and I shocked my producer by going down the hall to get coffee. Five minutes later, Mary was still going strong when I changed the direction of the conversation.

No longer a solo act

I was on WCKY for five years. For four of those five years, I did a solo act and then eleven months as a co-host of the titillating and ill-fated *Bailey and LaBarbara Show*. I was excited the station wanted to move me to afternoon drive, but the catch was they wanted me to have a partner. Rosemary Haddad, a local lady, would go by the name Bailey. We met one night at the station, and the second time I saw her was when they announced the new show. They never heard us together, and the deal was we each had an equal say. When they put the two of us together, they wanted us to be like Howard Stern: Say anything but the "F" word. It was "shock" radio, but it wasn't working, and I didn't feel comfortable. We just didn't have the "chemistry," and that is essential for a two-person show. We were told to be provocative and push it to the limit. We talked openly about the newest scandal and the nude photos of the latest downtrodden celebrity. I may have been able to pull it off by myself but not in this situation.

The day I knew for sure it wasn't working was the day we interviewed Sydney Biddle Barrows. She was a Mayflower descendant from an upper-class family who ran a high-class prostitution service in New York from 1979 to 1984. She had mega power customers, business executives, and foreign diplomats. When she got busted in 1984, she wrote her autobiography, *The Mayflower Madam*. She was big news, and we had her for an hour. In the first two or three minutes, Bailey referred to her as a "whore" or "hooker." I just remember throwing my hands in the air. Sydney was livid and wanted to end the interview. I tried to calm her down while I watched Bailey leave the room because I hurt her feelings. I had to pick up the pieces, but the madam gave me short, abrupt answers. I tried to comfort her by taking her side against an ex-boyfriend who had just sold naked pictures of her to an adult magazine. My interview technique was to ask the soft questions or something that showed I did my homework and make the person feel comfortable before throwing a tough one. I had no problem with her calling the madam a "hooker," just do it at the end of the hour to get her reaction. Don't start off the hour calling her a "whore." Sydney denied it because she didn't do tricks, only to have my partner say something like, "You're still a hooker." I can tell you she was in no mood for a semantics discussion.

Eleven months after the show started, I gave up all hope. I walked into the station manager's office where he proudly displayed a prototype of a billboard campaign featuring "Bailey and LaBarbara." In two weeks, the billboards would be all over Cincinnati. I told him, "Save your money. It's not working." I said, "I'll do any shift. I'm not going to quit. I have a wife and two kids. You'll have to fire me." Two weeks later, they did. I thought they might keep me because I was successful on my own. Basically, I cut my own throat.

"My daddy got fired, but maybe now he will be in a good mood," my daughter, Shelby, then seven, wrote in a school journal. There were times when I didn't like to look in the mirror. I was a former religion student who once gave sermons. I didn't like me. I didn't have any regrets about standing up for my moral convictions. I told a reporter, "I think somebody has to take the responsibility, and that responsibility has to go to the person behind the microphone."

KMOX St. Louis calls

As a solo talk-show host, I had success. I didn't know how well until Christmas Eve 1984. The latest Birch ratings had me at number one noon to three and the highest numbers at WCKY. I had actually taken it from a 3.6 to 9.4 in about six months. I had been doing talk for about a year when Bob Hyland, the senior VP of CBS, called me twice on Christmas Eve to talk about my doing the afternoon show on KMOX in St. Louis. Charlie Murdock, my former boss at WLW, called me on Christmas Day to congratulate me. Hyland had called him and said they wanted me. It was the number one rated station in the country at the time. A few days later, I flew into St. Louis after my show and met with Bob at 5:00 a.m. in his office. He knew everything about me. He had lots of tapes, and he mapped out what I'd be doing three to six on KMOX. The salary was more than I ever imagined. Bob even gave me suggestions on where to look for a house. I called Sally on the way home and told her to put the house up for sale, and then I tempered my excitement and said let's wait a few days. Mr. Hyland called and made arrangements for me to fly back and meet with Dan Dierdorf. He was an all-pro Cardinal football star who had just retired. The day before we were to get together, Bob called to cancel because Dierdorf's child had suddenly died, and we would have to reschedule. Bob Hyland and I talked back and forth sometimes three times a week for about a year. He was always very positive—they were trying to bring me in. It was crazy. I was never hired. Months later, during a phone conversation with Pat Rogers, a former WLW jock who was the program director of WTMJ in Milwaukee, it became a little clearer. Pat said, "You know Jonathan Green, our afternoon guy, isn't leaving to work with you. KMOX wants to team him up with you to do the afternoon show." That was the first I'd heard of it. Green is a terrific talent, but we never met.

Doing a talk show, I interviewed so many people who gave advice on how to get rich. All you had to do was read their book or go to their seminar. After getting fired from WLW, I knew I'd have to make an investment to supplement whatever I did in radio. I discovered several times that there is no security in radio. It doesn't matter if you have the ratings and bring in the revenue. It didn't concern me early in my career, but that changed when I had a family. There are no big retirement plans waiting for disc jockeys when their careers are over. I looked at rehabbing some homes on River Road that overlooked the Ohio River. I was going to buy several and upgrade the neighborhood. I checked out a restaurant that would feature my name. In 1986 a guest on my WCKY show, Patricia Mischell, a well-known local clairvoyant, told me I would have a successful business in Kenwood.

Billy Meister was in jail for a ticket-scalping scheme. He pulled off a Ponzi scheme. It's a fraudulent investment operation that pays returns to separate investors from their own money or money paid by subsequent investors, rather than from any actual profit. He offered very high, short-term returns. He was out of jail for a few days and was my in-studio guest. The lines lit up with people hoping to get their money back. During a commercial break, he showed me a pamphlet with items of his they were auctioning off and suggested I buy his Excalibur car. I said, "I'm interested in buying your video store."

The Video Sound Stage

I followed up, won the bid, and got the store. However, I moved the equipment and inventory to a new location. The Video Sound Stage opened in April 1986 in the Kenwood Towne Center across from the Kenwood Mall. I was officially testing the entrepreneurial waters. I'd put in eight hours a day for my talk show on WCKY and spend mornings, evenings, and weekends running the store. I was used to working on very little sleep, but as time went on, I became a slave to the store. I never took a penny out of the store in the ten years we were open.

I hired a wonderful store manager, Kathleen Ryan, who had worked with me at WLW and later WCKY. We were named "Video Store of the Year" twice by *Cincinnati Magazine*, who described us by writing in October 1987: "The Video Soundstage: Exceptionally good service. It's like being in a fine restaurant with a maitre d' hovering over you. Staff tells you about the movies, helps find them, and does everything but pass out Milk Duds."

Our employees consisted mostly of high school girls entering the workforce for the first time. The store was decorated like a sound stage, and the employees wore director's jackets. My wife and her mom took great pride in decorating our windows. In the back of the store was my elevated office, which looked like a radio sound booth complete with a microphone stand and an on-air sign. In front of the window was a 1940s Wurlitzer 1015 Bubbler Jukebox. I would get on the mic and announce what movies we had and talk about the specials. We even gave away free popcorn. We were also a Ticketron outlet, and we were consistently one of the top venues for major concerts. We'd sell thousands of dollars worth of tickets for the Rolling Stones and only make a few dollars. It was easy to lose money if a ticket didn't come out. A few mistakes like that, and you've lost your profits. One Saturday morning, we had a packed crowd for a teen boy group, and the machines went down all over town. I walked into the store, and I thought it was a battleground because teenage or preteen girls were lying on the ground crying, and their mothers were screaming at me to get them tickets. At one point, I couldn't afford Kathleen, and my wife, Sally, gave up her volunteer work and was thrown into the store to be the manager. (A side note—guys, do *not*, I repeat, do *not* go into business with your wife if you care about your marriage.) I don't know how we survived. I was really rough on Sally. I paid her minimum wage for eighteen months, and then like me, she got no salary. If you walked into our store on a Friday or Saturday, you probably thought I was a rich man because the place was always packed. I bought out my silent partner and moved it around the corner on Kenwood Road across from Graeter's Ice Cream. I spent ten thousand dollars on the giant sign above the center that you could see for miles: "Jim LaBarbara's Video Sound Stage."

My worst business experience was about to happen, and I never saw it coming. I had an accountant from Kentucky who would stop by once a month with his computer and do all his work in my office. He was a radio fan, and he became a trusted friend. His wife baked cookies for me, he gave me a collectable Casinos' LP, and he even had dinner at my house. I'd sign a few blank checks and he'd do the paperwork and send it out. I had asked him several times if he needed more money, but he was happy. One day right before tax time, we were cutting it short, but he told me not to worry. The next day, my box with all kinds of paperwork was missing. I thought he must have been running late and took it to his home in Kentucky. I tried to call him, but he wouldn't return my calls. I got a call from Columbus: "You owe us money." I said, "I'm so glad you called. My accountant stole all my paperwork." The reply I got was, "Mr. LaBarbara, we don't care. That's your problem. We just want the money." I called the county prosecutor in Kentucky. A year earlier, I had helped his office prosecute a man they were after in Kentucky who passed bad checks to me in Ohio. He said, "You know, we like to think we're one big family here in Cincinnati and Northern Kentucky, but that Ohio River is like the Atlantic Ocean." I tried everything to get those papers, but his family wouldn't help. I called a former police officer who was a private detective. I did a free benefit for him when he had problems, but I guess he forgot. I couldn't afford his services, and he wasn't about to give me a break. I shake just thinking about that time in my life. I couldn't sleep; I thought I was going to have a heart attack. I was working the store and doing my radio show. I did hire someone to recreate everything, but it was difficult, and my late tax fees just kept mounting. We had late fees going back a couple of years, and it just about wiped me out. I was going broke. The local Kentucky county sheriff tried to get the papers. I wasn't this accountant's first victim. He did a similar number to several businesses in Ohio. He slipped up when he pulled a stunt on a Kentucky resident. It was about a year later when they called me to pick up my papers that he surrendered. There wasn't much in the box. I have no idea what he did with everything. I never saw his name on a cancelled check, so I have no idea why he would do this. I thought that he may have had a mental breakdown.

Blockbuster Video had three stores that surrounded me. They played by different rules. I paid fifty-six to seventy dollars for a single rental movie. Blockbuster cut special deals with distributors. They would keep two stores and then only one after I closed. I probably should have filed for bankruptcy, but by the time my lease was up, I had been in business ten years, paid back all my creditors, and could sleep at night.

During that ten-year period that I owned the business, I lost more than $250,000 of my investment and I never paid myself. If someone gave me a business today, I would say, "No thank you." I really liked our employees. They were terrific, and I learned a lot from them. They were fun to be around. We had great customers, and over a period, it was interesting to watch their families grow.

I have to tell you about a great business deal that I passed on. In 1981 Jeff Ruby offered me the opportunity to be a partner in a restaurant he was opening on Delta Avenue in Cincinnati. It was a disco. The parking lot was small with no lights. It was on one of the busiest streets in town, and it was in a fairly rough neighborhood. He wanted ten thousand dollars. My friend Squirrel and I were the only partners without big money. Jeff was a good friend who had recently spent a few days sleeping on my couch when he broke up with his girlfriend. Six years earlier, I was invited in on a partnership for five thousand dollars in a friend's Italian Restaurant. The restaurant didn't make it, and I saved five thousand. If that didn't happen, I probably would have invested. I didn't invest with Jeff, and I've kicked myself often. Jeff Ruby's Precinct Restaurant became one of the best steak restaurants in the country and the anchor of a group of restaurants and clubs Jeff would own. A friend who invested told me his investment made him nicely over two hundred thousand dollars.

CHAPTER 21

Radio Flimflam

It took less than two weeks for me to land a job after WCKY. I was new Program Director Drew Hayes's first hire at WKRC. He really wanted me to be a part of his team. I wasn't crazy about the offer, but he said, "Trust me. Good things will happen." Taft Broadcasting's national program director, Larry Anderson, called me and convinced me to take the job. Larry left the company shortly after I came on board, but I didn't know that until years later. Larry was one of the good guys in the business. I was to do a Sunday night oldies show and be WKRC's super sub, filling in for all the shows. I didn't want the oldies show, but I took the job because I knew Alan Browning, the evening talk show host's contract was coming up, and the rumor was they weren't going to renew him. I just demonstrated I could do talk. I was confident I would get the job. If a day shift opened, I had proven for fifteen years I could do the same format at WLW, where I was number one almost every rating book. I was as big or bigger a name in the market than anyone on the station. Drew didn't keep his word to me, and with the exception of a few shows, I only did Sunday nights. They didn't renew Alan, but I wasn't given a chance to audition.

They gave it to the morning man's brother from the last station the general manager worked. The guy had never done a talk show. Sometimes the business works that way. This is an example of "radio bull," and I would soon experience more radio bull—— from the guy in the big office down the hall.

One day the general manager, Dave Milner, stopped me in the hall to tell me how much he enjoyed hearing me on Saturday nights. I corrected him: "I'm on Sunday." I decided to talk with him, and I showed him my resume. He was familiar with Allegheny College in Meadville, Pennsylvania, because he went to nearby Edinboro College. I was an announcer for the radio broadcast at their football games when I worked in Erie. I don't think he knew I did fifteen years on WLW. He closed the office door and asked me if I'd be interested in doing afternoon drive.

"Yes, when do you want me to start?"

He looked at my resume, and then he said, "How would you like to be the program director?"

He wanted my ideas by Monday. We shook hands, and I put together a long proposal detailing what we could do. I did this in-depth presentation without changing any of the on-air talent. He was busy when I delivered it to his office, and I don't think he ever looked at it, because before the week was up, we were introduced to our new program director.

Gary King was our new WKRC program director, and I would be the first person he would fire. His first memo was a new policy: "Announce. No Artists. No Titles. Be Local. Be Happy. Thanks." I did a five-hour oldies show, and this is what he wanted. I did it. He called me into his office: "I'm letting you go. You sound too old on the radio." I wanted to yell, "Age discrimination! Are you crazy?" He made a big deal out of firing me, but I pointed out, "You do realize it is an oldies show and that I'm only on one night a week?" He didn't keep his job very long. I never talked to the general manager again. I went from him talking to me about doing afternoon drive, to being asked for a program director presentation, to being fired in less than two weeks.

WSAI

My next stop was WSAI. Jim McKnight, a former coworker at WLW revived my career by taking himself off the air and putting me in morning drive six to nine. He was operations director for WWNK and WSAI, and all I had to do was play good old rock 'n' roll.

Early one morning in 1990, I got an interesting request. Gregory Hines's assistant wanted to know if Gregory could stop by and visit with me. He had just wrapped up a late night shoot in town for the movie *A Rage in Harlem*, and he was driving around listening to my show. He was anxious to talk about the movie. I was an extra in the Tom Selleck movie *Innocent Man*, and we were told not to talk with Tom. My friend Jon Warden was also an extra, and when we saw Selleck, he introduced himself, and Tom was happy to talk with us. Warden had pitched on the 1968 World Series Tigers team, and Selleck is a huge Detroit fan; he wore a Tiger cap on his *Magnum PI* television show. Nobody said anything to us. F. Murray Abraham, the Academy Award-winning actor, did turn around after one scene, shook my hand, and said, "Good shoot." I told Gregory what the rule was on *An Innocent Man* and asked if the extras were allowed to talk to him. He laughed and explained that he talked with everyone, even the people watching the filming: "I'm in your town disrupting your street. That's the least I can do."

Gregory Hines was a talented actor, singer, and dancer. His idol and friend Sammy Davis, Jr., had died recently, and he shared his thoughts with me. He visited with Sammy shortly before he passed, and although he was dying of throat cancer, he knew Hines was there and communicated with hand signals. Ironically three years later, Gregory would lose his life to cancer. If you were a fan of Gregory Hines, you picked a good one.

Sports talk

WSAI was about to change to a standards format, and I was helping select the music. I had just presented my recommendations, when suddenly there was an abrupt switch. General Manager Jim Wood stopped in the studio during my show to tell me about the new lineup and format. We were going sports talk, and he just hired former sports anchor Don Burrows, but he never mentioned the morning show. It wasn't until Jim McKnight stopped by that I found out he and I would do a two-man morning show along with newsman Fred Slezak. Our show was set up like a magazine, and I enjoyed it, because I'm a big sports fan.

I really got on the Reds' Paul O'Neal for not hustling. A couple of days later, he was in my video store asking for me. I thought, *I'm going to get an earful*, but he was into laser discs, and we were one of the few stores renting them. We talked about the Reds, and he explained what he was going through, but we never discussed my remarks. Paul went on to have an incredible career with the Yankees.

One of our WSAI sports talk hosts was the former first-round draft choice of the Colts, the great Ohio State quarterback Art Schlichter. His compulsive gambling problems got him kicked out of the NFL. He was the quarterback for the Cincinnati Rockers of the Arena Football League in July of 1992 when he was arrested for passing a bad check. I watched him play for the Rockers, and he was fantastic. He could have made a lot of money as a backup quarterback in the NFL. If you listened to him on the air when he'd come out of a commercial break, you would hear the instrumental music bed, that he talked over to start each segment, go on for what seemed like forever. He probably was in the bathroom on the phone with his bookies. He never tried to borrow money from me. I think he knew I was in a tight financial situation with my store. He burned a lot of people, and a bunch of guys covered for him, but you can only do that for so long. He was a sick guy; during the years 1995–2006, he served the equivalent of ten years in forty-four various jails and prisons. It got so bad he had his public defender smuggle a cell phone into prison so he could place bets. In 2004 he was caught gambling in prison and placed in solitary confinement for four months. He had so much talent that he wasted. The last time I saw Art, he was fighting his demons but still having major problems.

CHAPTER 22

WGRR Calls

Oldies WGRR's new program director, Marty Thompson, called me in 1993. He was taking himself off afternoon drive so that he could devote full time to programming, and he wanted me to do afternoons. I found out later the sales staff and other employees had war games. They had created teams complete with jocks, music, and contests that would attack WGRR. I appeared on every team, either in the morning or afternoon drive. It took a couple of months for the official offer. I had lunch with the general manager and the owner's daughter, Diane Dalton. She didn't even order. We talked for about fifteen minutes, and she got up and said, "What the hell's taking you so long? Hire him."

The irony was that in October of 1989, I called the station's owner at his home in Washington, D.C. I told Bill Dalton I had an idea to make a lot of money, but he had to switch WBLZ, an urban contemporary-formatted station to oldies. Bill said the Fox was already playing oldies. I pointed out that they played a few, but I was talking about Elvis, Buddy Holly, the Everly Brothers, the early Beatles and songs like "Wooly Bully," and "Louie Louie." He was very nice and said he was going to do a conceptual study because WBLZ was doing well financially. Two months later, WBLZ's general manager, David O'Donnell, asked me if I would be interested in doing morning drive. This was all confidential, and only three people knew that he wanted to go oldies. I was excited to get a chance to do morning drive. Dave said he was going to work with the consultant E. Alvin Davis. I wasn't excited to hear Davis was involved because I met with him a couple of years earlier. At that time, he suggested I get out of radio because the business had passed me by. A few weeks later, in January 1990 WGRR, with an oldies format, went on the air but without me. I did get a call from Steve Allen, the program director, but he wanted me to do a special Sunday night show. I said, "I'll do it if you let me be the fill-in guy for other shows, because I want you to hear me do the format." They didn't have a set lineup at the time; he was just moving people around, but he said, "No, you'll just do Sunday night." I wasn't interested.

It took almost three years for me to get on WGRR, and then things got really crazy. I was suddenly on three stations at the same time. I was doing the morning sports show on WSAI and the Saturday morning 6:00 to 10:00 a.m. show on easy listening WWEZ. A few weeks earlier, Tom Severino, the WWEZ general manager and I discussed the possibility of me doing a personality morning drive show and adding vocals to the instrumental-based format. This was being done successfully at WQAL in Cleveland. Tom asked me to check it out. My WIXY buddy Larry Morrow was their morning star, and as I watched him do his show, I had a flashback. Walt Tiburski, our WIXY intern entered the studio and asked if we needed coffee or donuts, only now he wasn't an intern—he was the owner of WQAL. I did the research for Severino, and I agreed to do Saturday mornings and fill in for the morning show with the understanding I would get the show. He was going to move the morning host to their sister station WCKY. I was working live on the air at three different stations owned by three different companies at the same time. I did this for two weeks while WSAI looked for a replacement. Incidentally, WSAI gave me permission to explore other options because I needed to make more money. I was on 6:00 to 9:00 a.m. on WSAI, 10:00 p.m. to 2:00 a.m. on WGRR, and 6:00 to 10:00 a.m. Saturdays on WEEZ. This predated the massive voice tracking of radio shows.

I started on the 10:00 p.m. to 2:00 a.m. shift on WGRR. I air checked every show, and for the first couple of weeks, I met with Marty every day to listen to my tape. We then went from three times a week to once a week and then, after two weeks, I was doing afternoon drive. I wanted to master the basics of the format and gradually work my personality into its context. The Music Professor image was a perfect fit; I received immediate acceptance from our core audience. Marty told me he hired me because he was taking the station to the next level. A lot of the oldies stations around the country had laid back jocks and very little, if any, personality except in the morning. We were high energy with a lot of personality every shift. It was the beginning of fifteen years of the most fun I ever had in radio. The nucleus of that staff was Chris O'Brien, who later was joined by his wife, Janeen. I did a number of bits with them and became very good at using self-deprecating humor, which our audience identified with me. At this point in my career, I learned to laugh at myself. Of course, my buddy Rockin' Ron Schumacher was on midday. I admired Ron's work ethic since our days at WKRC, and I often said if I ever became a radio boss, he would be on my team. Ron has a stuttering problem, but only his close friends knew it until the 2010 movie *The King's Speech* came out. Ron publicly announced that he had a similar problem to King George VI in the movie. On the radio or on stage behind a microphone, he's fine. It occurs during normal conversation and not always. Tom Cat Michaels, a guy who really did have more than twenty-five cats, did nights, and later Joe Demma and Steve Mann did that shift. We all liked Steve so much we pushed for him to be our program director when there was an opening. Tony Michaels did the news and played the accordion on the air, but took his playing seriously. Bobby Leach, J.C. McCoy, and Maverick did traffic over the years. Toni Mason, Meme Wagner and Tracy Sunderhaus, our promotion directors, made sure we had WGRR stuff to give away. We had a terrific weekend lineup led by Dusty Rhodes, but the guy who was at the station longer than anyone working nights and weekends was J.D. Hughes. He did more record hops than anybody in town. If I had a busy weekend doing more than two appearances, I would laugh and tell my wife I was having a "J.D. weekend." We set the standard for remotes with our "Traveling Oldies Parties." Our promotion assistants helped make them happen and became well known. Most of them were named after records—"Help Me Rhonda," "Good Golly Miss Molly," "Corrina Corrina," and "Louie Louie." Two used their real names—Captain Bobby Paul and Andrea "Crash" Taylor.

We knew what our audience wanted, but there were occasions when I had to scratch my head. I did a regular Friday night club appearance, and I called in my commercial, but after I finished, I was told to just say, "On Christmas 103.5." Our program director got the brilliant idea to go to twenty-four-hour Christmas programming at 9:00 p.m. that Friday, November 16 before Thanksgiving, and we were now known as "Christmas 103.5." The rating trends had me on track to be number one or two in our key demo. The station was doing well, and we upset a lot of our listeners. To make it worse, we played a number of country artists that didn't fit. This format is actually a good move if you have a struggling station or you're going to flip the format.

Freddy Cannon and I were driving back to the station after a store appearance when he realized he left something behind. He was working out with the Jazzercise ladies and left his workout shorts and top in a brown paper bag. I told him not to worry they'd keep it for us, and he could get it later. He was concerned about the bag and I decided to edge him on. "You know Freddy, those are collector's items because you wore them. They are valuable to your fans." I thought it was funny but played it straight. His mission the rest of the day was to get that bag back. He didn't want to see them on eBay.

Tommy Boyce

I got a note to call Tommy Boyce. He was passing through town and had heard me play a song he wrote, "Action," for Freddy Cannon and wanted to say hello. Boyce and Hart wrote the Monkees' hits, but I hadn't seen him since Cleveland. The next day he stopped to visit.

He was funny on the air. Tommy told me, "The Boyce and Hart hit 'I Wonder What She's Doing Tonight' was written about a lovely girl named Nancy Jane Hecklefinger. I should have married her. I'm still in love with her. She lives in Burbank, California."

Tommy and Bobby wrote a number of hits for the Monkees, including "Last Train to Clarksville" and the "Monkees Theme." Tommy said, "We were contract writers for Screen Gems, and the show was coming on in six weeks, and no one would produce these records. Boyce and Hart were definitely not the first, second, third, or any choice to produce the Monkees, but these executives said to us, 'We're in a jam—we're going on national television in six weeks.' The first album they did, we did the whole thing—wrote all the songs, produced it, mixed it, got the singers Mickey [Dolenz] to sing and Davy [Jones] to sing the slow songs."

One day I was walking into the station when Tommy pulled up in his big green Cadillac to give me a ride. He wanted to cruise the station parking lot in Hyde Park like we did when we were kids. For the next twenty minutes, we drove about 10 mph in a circle around the lot laughing and exchanging stories. He insisted I take an Elvis pillow he got from Memphis. I thought he was kidding, but I didn't want to hurt his feelings so I finally took his goofy pillow with me to the studio. That was the last time I saw him. A few days later on November 23, 1994, he shot himself to death. He was supposed to start working with us as a weekend disc jockey. His wife, Caroline, told me his health had been declining. A few years earlier, he was devastated when his best friend, Del Shannon, committed suicide with a rifle. I have the Elvis pillow in my office. I look at it often and think about my friend Tommy.

Outdoor venues

Music fans over the years have loved the big outdoor concerts.

Michelle Phillips of the Mamas and Papas told me what she remembered most about the Monterey Pop Festival in 1967 that they helped put together was their lousy performance. Jimi Hendrix and Janis Joplin were there, but she loved Otis Redding.

The Byrds sang at Monterey, and Roger McGuinn agreed with Michelle that Otis Redding really came into his own that night. Roger said, "I thought he stole the show. I was sitting with Paul Simon, and I remember going, 'Man that guy is scary,' and Paul said, 'No, he's not scary; he's great.' I said, 'Yeah, yeah, that's what I meant.'"

The most famous of the outdoor concerts was Woodstock. I've kidded Tommy James because he turned it down. Tommy's explanation was, "In 1969 I was invited to Woodstock. Here's how it was put to me. My secretary called me from Roulette Records in New York: 'A farmer rented his field in upper state New York, and a couple of local promoters are putting on a show. They're going to have Joplin and Hendrix.' Here I am lying on the beach at the foot of Diamond Head, and my biggest decision of the day was whether to go into the ocean or the pool. I really wasn't thinking about anything."

John Sebastian of the Loving Spoonful did play at Woodstock and told me it was a terrific moment in his life, although it was quite accidental. "I went there as a spectator never intending to perform, and they had some trouble with electricity on the second or third day. I was backstage hanging out with some friends, and they said, 'Look, we need someone to hold them with an acoustic guitar while we go fix things.' So that's exactly what I did, totally unprepared. I didn't have a guitar. I had to borrow one. I wasn't on the bill or anything, but it ended up being one of my highest visibility performances, although not by any means one of my best."

We put on a lot of great shows, but the biggest were our WGRR Oldiesfest concerts. The first was in 1994 at Festival Park in New Richmond. Standing on stage looking out over a sea of people was a thrill. I don't think any of us expected that big of a crowd. These shows would draw around thirty-five thousand people. Our station consultant, E. Alvin Davis was backstage and made it a point to tell me how good I sounded. "I'm telling you, you really sound good."

This was nice to hear from the same guy who told me to get out of the business a few years earlier because it had passed me by. I was looking forward to hearing the Loving Spoonful's John Sebastian, but he just didn't get it. He sang unfamiliar jug band music peppered with a couple of his hits. When "Flo and Eddie," Mark Volman and Howard Kaylan, of the Turtles came on singing their hits, a light must have gone on, and Sebastian joined them on stage singing rock 'n' roll.

Flo and Eddie of the Turtles had worked as disc jockeys and were always fun to interview. The Turtles did a party for Tricia Nixon, the president's daughter, and the guys actually did drugs at the White House. Mark Volman said he felt no pain and kept falling off the stage.

Tommy James, our headliner, stuck around signing autographs for everyone, and when it got dark, someone moved a car over by the autograph table and turned its lights on.

In 1995 our Oldiesfest star was Frankie Valli, and it was great to renew our friendship. The Casinos' Gene Hughes and our production director, Jim Blommel, were with me in his trailer and heard Frankie praise Eric Carmen. He loved his voice and thought he should have been a major star. We called it the "World's Largest 'Louie Louie' Sing Along" and it was led by two singers who recorded it—Mark Lindsay of the Raiders and Jack Ely of the Kingsmen. It had to be in the nineties, but Brenda Lee was singing "Rockin' Around the Christmas Tree." I can still see her with her granddaughter sitting on her lap signing autographs for everybody. Our WGRR listeners at this time were the most passionate anywhere. At one point during the show, our midday guy Ron Schumacher and I tried to walk across the field. We couldn't walk three feet without getting stopped to sign autographs and talk to fans. Rockin' Ron often reminds me that I said, "There is no way anyone can have low self esteem after experiencing this."

In 1996 our headliner Chuck Berry didn't show, so Jan and Dean went back on to do another set. Our program director told me to go to the front gate and thank people as they were leaving. I was in a golf cart when I heard on the two-way: "There's a black man here at the gate in a Ford Escort who says he's allowed to come in." I started yelling, "It's Chuck Berry—let him in!" He was on Indianapolis time, an hour behind in those days. Chuck's deal was fresh musicians, no charts—we are playing Chuck Berry music—oh, and I believe thirty-five thousand dollars cash. He doesn't rehearse and tunes his guitar on stage. I was standing next to the Outsiders' Sonny Geraci when Chuck hit a chord in a song that was so off, and he looked at one of the band guys to blame. Sonny and I both laughed; he did it on purpose because he loved to mess with the band. Chuck's show was worth the wait.

The 1997 show we refer to as "Mudfest." It had rained, and our headliner, Neil Sedaka, took one look at our muddy shoes as we entered his trailer and said, "I can't go out there like that." We made sure he got to the stage without a spec of mud getting on his "neon" blue suit or Italian shoes. After the show, we had tow trucks pulling cars out of the mud. I know they got me out. Our listeners were soaked and muddy but had a terrific time. I run into people all the time who tell me, "Prof, I was with you at Mudfest."

In 1998 we brought Johnny Rivers back as our headliner, and man, did he get upset with me. I've introduced hundreds of entertainers, and I take pride in working the audience. Just as I was walking on stage, his manager told me to say, "Here's the Johnny Rivers Band." I couldn't help myself. I thanked the crowd for coming, and I went into my Rivers rap—he owned his own record label, publishing company, his hits . . . I pumped my hands in the air and shouted, "Johnny 'Go-Go' Rivers!" The crowd went wild, but Johnny and his manager both said to me as I walked off, "You had to do it didn't you?" My boss loved it. I've known Johnny from the sixties, and I've interviewed him several times. I was always one of his biggest fans, and when he hit with "Poor Side of Town," I started playing a song off his album called "By the Time I Get to Phoenix." I played it like a single on my show in Cleveland. I told his label to release it, but they let Glen Campbell take it, and he had a million-seller with it. We helped Johnny get a guitar once when his didn't arrive. It wasn't even our event. Johnny had been arrogant the year before, refusing to sign

autographs. This was the only time I ever went against an entertainer's intro request. I felt badly, and a few months later, I mentioned this to my friend Peter Noone of Herman's Hermits. Peter
told me they were sharing the same dressing room, and as Peter was
coming off stage, Johnny was going on. Peter then discovered that
Rivers had taken all of Peter's clothes and put them outside the room.
Peter is not a big Rivers fan.

Little Richard was the headliner at our final Oldiesfest show in
New Richmond. It was the only time I've ever blown out my vocal
chords. I revved up the crowd with a long dynamic intro: "Not the
duplicator, not the imitator, but the emancipator, the originator from
Macon, Georgia—Little Richard!" After shouting out "Little Richard," as I was walking off stage, I knew I was hurting. It happened that
quickly. I couldn't talk for four days.

Bobby Vee and Bob Dylan

I had a chance to renew an old friendship with Bobby Vee at that
show, and he set the record straight for me. I heard that Bob Dylan
once played in his band, but he fired him, and Bobby wanted to clar-
ify that. "The truth is I didn't actually fire him. I couldn't afford to
keep him in the band. We were paying him fifteen bucks a night. It
was shortly after 'Suzie Baby,' and we were looking for a piano
player. My brother Bill was in Sam's Recordland in Fargo, and this
guy came up to him and introduced himself as Elston Gunn and said,
'I just got off the road with Conway Twitty playing piano, and I hear
you're looking for a piano player.' Bill took him over to the local
radio station. There was a piano in the studio, and he said the guy
played pretty good. We hired him and bought him a shirt like ours
and went out and did a couple of shows with him. The first venue we
went to, they had a piano that was terribly out of tune. So after a couple of nights, he realized that it wasn't going to work out, and he left
Fargo, and he went to Minneapolis and rolled up to the University of
Minnesota. It was a short time after that, maybe a year or two, I was
in Greenwich Village, and I was in a record store, and I saw a face that

looked a lot like Elston Gunn, and of course, it was Bob Dylan."

Bobby told me Dylan didn't play with Conway Twitty. "He was in the audience at a Conway Twitty show, and he just made that leap to the stage. He used to make up a lot of stories."

One of the craziest name stories involves the leader of the Byrds. In 1967 I was calling him Jimmy McGuinn on the air when a record promoter said, "No, it's Roger McGuinn." Roger laughed and said I could call him Jim if I wanted to. He said, "I did that Eastern religion thing back in the sixties. I've gotten out of it since then, but I changed my name to Roger. I still go by Roger today. I thought it would be too confusing to change it back."

In 2000 we moved Oldiesfest to the Butler County Fairgrounds with Dion as our closer. We were backstage, and he must have gone to the Port-O-Let six times. I later found out that he hadn't performed rock 'n' roll in three years, and this was his first time working with his band, and he was nervous.

At that show, the Monkees' Davy Jones drove security crazy when he jumped into the crowd. The Monkees were America's answer to the Beatles, and they still have their fans.

Where did the money go?

Davy Jones had the television show and sold millions of records and merchandise, and the guys were a cash register for Screen Gems. Davy was a bit irritated when I brought up the subject of money. He surprised me when he said, "I don't know. How much are you supposed to get? We signed a contract. We made four hundred dollars a week doing *The Monkees* television show; it's gone on to profit lots of other people and reruns. We don't get paid, not a penny."

It's hard to believe the Monkees got taken advantage of that way, but they signed a contract. So many entertainers I've known were cheated by unscrupulous people.

What's even worse is the story of "America's Band." Brian, Carl, and Dennis Wilson's father would never be named "Father of the Year." The Beach Boys wrote most of their songs, and their song catalogue was massive. Mike Love, the Beach Boys' lead singer, told me: "Murry Wilson totally disenfranchised his sons. He was a very abusive person, and I couldn't say enough bad about him. He really hurt us financially and emotionally. I didn't get the brunt of it because I was the nephew. He sold the Beach Boys' song catalogue for a little over $750,000. It's worth 30 or 40 million today. [That was in 2000] That's pretty disgusting when a father does that to his sons and his nephew." Mike was agitated but continued, "We were represented by an attorney who had a conflict of interest. The attorney who represented us also represented the company that bought the publishing."

On their fortieth anniversary, Mike said, "We loved singing. It was a hobby that miraculously became a profession." The group's masterpiece is "Good Vibrations," a song that cost Brian Wilson a reported sixteen thousand dollars to record, more than most albums at the time. The session took place in three major studios over a period of several months. I thought it was funny when Mike Love told me, "I wrote the words to 'Good Vibrations' on the way to the session. I dictated them on the freeway. It has the element of spontaneity as well as the structure of a highly developed track. It's been voted the number one single of that era in some trade magazines."

One of our last Oldiesfest concerts was in West Chester, and Tim Closson, our program director, selected as a headliner KC and the Sunshine Band. The only problem was, at the time, we didn't play any records by KC. This marked the end to Oldiesfest as we knew them.

Clubs and shows

We did the regular club appearances at the Drawbridge and Jim and Jack's. Jim and Jack's on River Road had the best bands—the Avenues; Ritchie and the Students; my close friends, Oo La La and the Greasers; and I even did a video with my boys, the show band Hot Wax. The Van Dells travel a lot, but they got their start in Cincinnati, and I was emcee for some of their first shows in the early seventies.

We presented our regular concerts—Jingle Bell Rock at Christmas and the popular Let the Good Times Roll. These shows featured six or seven acts from the fifties and sixties and were almost always sold out.

Chubby Checker

I was backstage with Chubby Checker watching David Somerville, the Diamonds' lead singer, do "Little Darlin'," and I found myself taking a walk back through time to Stowe High School almost forty years earlier when I was onstage emceeing another show. It was our weekly Friday assembly, and they were always incredible. Dolores Masciola and her girls in tight sweaters would lip sync. She did the talking part in the Diamonds' "Little Darlin'," and the place went wild. "My darlin', I need you to call my own and never do wrong / To hold in mine, your little hand / I'll know too soon that all is so grand / Please, hold my hand." Dolores got a standing ovation to do an encore, and they did the only song they knew, "Little Darlin'." The real singers were a group of pretty girls, the Promises led by Betty Barnes. I was their manager, and every deejay in town wanted them for their hops. They were good enough to make records, but a couple of the girls were headed to college. Betty did sign with RCA Records. William Manz was a quiet kid, but all that changed when he went onstage and sang just like Ricky Nelson. The best was guitar player Al Masciola. He sounded like Duane Eddy, maybe better. Al plugged in his twanging guitar, and his sound was so full that guitar should have burst. The gym vibrated with every chord he played, and no one wanted the assembly to end. Al and a drummer from our school, Lou Carto, played in Bobby Vinton's band. Lou was Bobby's bandleader for many years. In high school, Bobby and his dad's band was good, but I decided to play trumpet in a hip band called King George and his Knights. Well, not many people remember King George, but everybody remembers Bobby Vinton.

I couldn't imagine that any school was rockin' more than Stowe High in 1959. I told this story to Chubby Checker. He smiled and said, "I was a junior that year at South Philly High, and Fabian was walking the halls like a tiger in his white buck shoes." Fabian had big hits with "Turn Me Loose" and "Tiger," but I knew Chubby had a few records. Chubby jumped in: "Not like Fabian. I only had one record and two bombs. The 'Twist' is on its way, but it hasn't been born yet. Fabian's walking the halls and getting mobbed, and he's on magazine covers, his books under his arms and his cool walk. I was looking at him going—wish it were me." He laughed.

"Then you had it."

Chubby said, "I was out of school when I had mine. He was in school; all the girls were going crazy over him while he was in school. I graduated and then it started to happen. I missed all the other stuff." He told me Frankie Avalon was burning up. "When he stepped outside his car, the neighborhood stopped; the cars stopped. If they knew he was in the neighborhood, they just screamed. They were mesmerized."

I said, "Now wait a minute Chubby, Fabian is getting mobbed in the school hallway . . ."

Chubby stopped me. "This is even worse, and when they both got together, we just watched. Frankie wore white shoes too, and he had his little movement. He and Bobby Rydell and Fabian, they're all making the same moves. They have a little twitch in their step when they're singing their song. All the girl's liked it."

Chubby had a singing group when he was twelve called the Quantrells. They tore the school up when they sang, but he wanted me to hear another story. "We used to go to these talent shows—we were hot. There was one group that we couldn't beat, and they were called the Ballards. We could beat everybody but them. About forty years later, we played in Philadelphia in front of like fifty thousand people, and who's in the audience but the leader of that group. His name is Church. I made him come onstage, and he did that Little Richard song 'Miss Ann' all by himself. I watched him sing with my band. This guy who had never made it in the big leagues, but that day in front of fifty thousand people, I made him sing a song. Isn't that awesome?" He was so proud to share that with me, and only Chubby could have made that happen. I've always enjoyed being around

Chubby, and we've had a lot of laughs. Chubby would say my last name over and over sometimes real fast; he thought that was funny. One thing I don't think is funny is the way Chubby has been ignored by the pompous selection committee at the Rock and Roll Hall of Fame. It is a travesty that he is not in the Hall.

Chubby mentioned his schoolmate Fabian. Fabian was discovered crying on his front steps after his father was rushed to the hospital. Fabian told me: "Bob Marcucci, who at the time managed Frankie Avalon and owned Chancellor Records, thought the commotion was about a man he knew who lived next door. He liked my name, 'Fabian,' because it's my real name, and we later got to know each other. Bob kept asking me if I'd like to record. After I found out my dad was going to be okay but he couldn't go to work again, because of economic reasons I said yes. That's how it all started, and I wasn't quite fifteen years old."

If you were to take a quick look backstage at a WGRR show you might see Freddy Cannon, a former yo-yo champion, playing with a yo-yo; Mark Lindsay of the Raiders practicing his high kicks he did on stage; or Lou Christie reminiscing with me about our old neighborhood. The acts we worked with were old pros, and with the exception of a couple, were very relaxed. My friend Tony Orlando caught me by surprise and had me join him onstage to sing his 1961 hit "Bless You" in front of about twenty-five thousand people. I love that song, but I couldn't remember the lyrics. I just smiled and faked my way through it.

Scott made my day

It was bring-your-daughter-to-work day, and my teenage daughter, Shelby, was in the studio with me. I answered the phone, and she heard the conversation. The guy said, "I've wondered what happened to you, and I read in the trades that you were at WGRR. I just want to thank you because you're the reason I'm in the business."

I laughed and said, "Please don't put that blame on me."

"No, I really want to thank you." I thought it was somebody

from a little station in Kentucky. I asked him his name and where he worked.

"Scott Shannon. I'm here at WPLJ in New York. I'm the program director, and I do the morning show."

I was stunned. It was the Scott Shannon who brought the *Morning Zoo* to New York in the eighties, invented Pirate Radio in Los Angeles, and initiated Mojo Radio in the nineties. He added, "I used to listen to you when I was a kid growing up, and you were on nights at WKYC in Cleveland." That call totally knocked me out. I later saw something similar in print when we were both listed in *Rock Jock Hall of Fame: Radio's Top 40 All-Time Best Deejays* by Decalcomania (1996). I'm number thirty-seven, just after WABC's great morning man Herb Oscar Anderson, and Scott's listed at number nineteen. Shannon once wrote, "I remember when I was a young man, during the winter the WKYC signal would boom out of Cleveland and Jim's warm voice would sound so good while the snow was coming down and Christmas was approaching. He was the very best. He used to talk about all the women who would come by the station in the middle of the night and drop off gifts for him, made me wanna do the all night show."

Alcohol and a wake-up call

One of the first things I did when I was hired by WGRR was to get myself back in shape. I was working to recreate my Music Professor image from WLW. No, I'm not talking about exercising. During the ten years I owned my video store, I seldom had an alcoholic beverage because I never knew when I'd have to go to the store if there was a problem. Before starting at the station, I bought several six packs of beer and reacquired a taste for alcohol. I was right back where I was in my single, carefree days working the clubs and drinking with the gang from the station. I didn't have a drinking problem. A few drinks, and I was a lot less inhibited and relaxed. I had everything under control. I knew I could keep up with these younger people.

April 30, 1997, I got a wake-up call. It was one of the best days of my life, but it turned out to be one of my worse. Bill Dalton sold the station and had a thank-you dinner for us. We had drinks and dinner. It was a fantastic night. They presented me with a glass-cut star that was embossed with "You're a Star With Us, WGRR, the Daltons 1997" and a nice five-figure bonus check. There aren't many people like the Daltons in broadcasting. After the party, a group of us went to a downtown bar for a drink. I didn't have any alcohol in over an hour, so I thought it was safe to drive home. I missed a turn, and I went the wrong way on a one-way street. I was unfamiliar with the area and tried to find a driveway to pull in. I saw one, but suddenly, my little red Miata was surrounded by police cars with flashing lights. One officer asked me if I'd been drinking, and I was so embarrassed that I said something dumb like, "I must be stupid or drunk to be driving here." I then explained that I hadn't had a drink in over an hour. They gave me a breathalyzer, but it didn't register. I took the field sobriety test, and I flunked. With flashing lights in my face, and my bad left leg there was no way that I'd pass it even if I didn't have a drink in a month. They took me to the station and gave me the breathalyzer test three or four times before it registered a little blip. The Cincinnati police drove me home to an unsympathetic wife. Sally was disgusted with me because I had been staying out late after appearances, and now this. Sally and my daughter, Shelby, had to drive me around. I pleaded no contest, guilty and got a six-month license suspension. I told my bosses at the station. I wasn't trying to hide anything—I couldn't. It was a very expensive experience: lawyer, fines, and penalties. However, it may have saved my life and my marriage. Alcohol suddenly didn't taste the same, and I stopped running around and staying out late. Today I seldom have a drink, especially if I'm driving, and then only one. If I'm on my Harley, I won't drink at all.

I thought I'd be an example to my fellow workers, but it didn't change anything, and they continued to drink and party. I was surprised at the number of people who told me they had also received a DUI.

The Reds' Marty Brennaman

John Allen became the Cincinnati Reds' chief operating officer in 1996. He was a big fan of our station and gave me a Reds press pass every year. I was the only nonsports-radio personality who received this perk. I love baseball, and I sat in the press box and watched every pitch. I quickly learned press box etiquette: the first row, home team reporters; second row, visiting team press; no cheering and no loud talking. I wasn't an outsider for very long. Hal McCoy, the Hall of Fame writer, talked with me and sat next to me occasionally in the press dining room, and that was my validation. That meant a lot to me. Ken Broo and several others liked to talk with me about music and my jukeboxes. I became the go-to guy in the press box for music trivia. I liked sitting next to Gary Shatz in the press box because he logged every pitch. One day Marty Brennaman invited me into the radio booth, and I kept getting invited back. Our friendship goes back to his first year with the Reds. This is hallowed ground; you just don't walk into the booth. Eventually they got me a very comfortable chair directly behind Joe Nuxhall and next to Billy "Seg" Dennison. Seg and I have been friends from day one when he started at WLW helping me on my show. Dave "Yid" Armbruster sat next to Seg and produced the broadcasts. I went to games even in September when they were what seemed like fifty games out. I laughed so hard every night I was crying. If Marty got wound up—look out. The funniest stuff happened when the microphone was off. I was treated like a member of the booth, and he often mentioned my name. In between innings, Marty always asked me, "What's going on?" One night I said, "Did you see Tom Hanks, Ron Howard, and Dennis Miller? They have their own bus." He laughed and said it on the air. The television guys heard him and started scanning the private boxes, and they found them. They were on a guy tour just visiting a bunch of stadiums incognito. There was a rain delay, and they graciously met with the media. I started to include a couple of stories about some of the people who visited Marty and Joe and the crazy things that happened, but over the years I always respected—*What happens and is said in the booth, stays in the booth*. Trades, injuries, great gossip—I never used that material on my radio show. The old left-hander Joe Nuxhall was a real treat to be around. When I was a kid in the fifties, Pete Castiglione, the Pirates' third baseman, sold sports equipment for Kaufmann's department store in the off season, and my mother bought a catcher's mitt from him. Can you imagine a ballplayer today working in the off season? I told my friend Joe Nuxhall about Pete, and Nux said he'd work two, sometimes three jobs in the off season to make ends meet. Joe was the youngest player ever, fifteen years old, to play in the majors. He told me at times he'd take two street cars to get to the park. Once he borrowed a car, and on his way to Crosley Field, he was stopped by the police. Of course he didn't have a license, but the officer wished him good luck, and he was on his way. He knew the game and would turn around and give me a hand signal, pitcher not following through, or he was running on the pitch—that's why he scored. I will always be grateful to John Allen and my friend Marty Brennaman for taking care of me all those years.

This is a story I *will* share with you because it didn't happen in the booth but at the station. Marty Brennaman is a consummate professional. This was never more evident than one evening on Reds Line, a one-hour, one-night-a-week show that followed me afternoons on WLW during the off season. I said hello to Marty and his guest Reds' manager John McNamara. I was introduced to a female writer who was doing a story on the show. She was attractive but looked all business with her note pad. Her hair was tied back, she wore glasses and a very business looking outfit. During the first break she started to fan herself because it was hot in the studio. She proceeded to take off her jacket and let her hair down. After another five minutes she removed her shirt revealing a voluptuous figure and suddenly she was topless. Mac started sweating profusely and was red as a beet but Marty just acted like nothing happened. It was hilarious to watch. Mac was so flustered he couldn't talk, Brennaman is repeating questions over and over and this lady is taking notes and looking all business. Trumpy, although he never admitted he pulled off one of the best jokes ever on Marty, was all smiles. Seg Dennison was nearby, completely speechless. It was incredible until, out of nowhere several ladies were walking in the hall toward the studio. This masterfully executed prank was about to become a disaster but Trumpy headed off the ladies and told them they were not allowed near the studios because of a live broadcast. The League of Woman Voters had just concluded a meeting in our conference room located around the corner from our studios. Trumpy won that close call. I've included this story to exemplify what an incredible talent Marty is even under the most trying conditions.

Jimmy and Dad

On October 20, 1997, I was the guest speaker at DePauw University's Watson Forum. My son, Jimmy, was a junior at DePauw so it was extra special for me. Jerry Springer's television show was big at the time, and he packed the place a few weeks earlier. I was surprised when I got the same turnout. The college paper explained why I was there. "LaBarbara will bring an early understanding of the history of rock 'n' roll and how it evolved," said David Bohmer, director of the Center for Contemporary Media. "This guy was a major player in shaping music and creating a media form that had more influence on generations than any other media form."

I had a great time telling my story of rock music to a very attentive and responsive audience. It was an hour show with questions, but I think the loudest cheers came when I disagreed with a professor who believed the music caused disruption and violence to our youth. The show was taped and played back over Indiana cable for a month.

My son, Jimmy, spent part of his junior year studying at the University of Westminster in London. I took the opportunity to chaperon him and spend time as his roommate for eleven days. I wanted to explore and experience the culture of this land that gave us the great music of the British Invasion. While he was in class, I'd have lunch at a little pub on Baker Street where I noticed a number of ladies would come in and quickly drink a pint of ale and leave. Almost all of the London bars quit serving at 11:00 p.m. I was told if they didn't close, no one would be able to work the next day. One evening I asked the bartender to switch channels and put on the NCAA Basketball Tournament. Suddenly, a Brit starting yelling and told him not to change the channel; he was watching the Manchester soccer game. The guy later bought me a beer and explained he was from Manchester and once played in their farm system. They draft boys at a very young age to play, and if a team from another city takes you, then you would live with a family in that city. They know before you play high school soccer if you are going to play at the next level.

I called the program director of Capitol Gold in London and was invited to see the station. Jimmy and I were really impressed. He showed me the studios, and I met the air talent, or as they call them "presenters." We discussed their oldies play list, and I was surprised they weren't playing some British acts. Chad and Jeremy had a couple of hits in the states, but although they were from England, they never had a hit in their own country. Looking over their play lists, I knew most of the records, but he really surprised me when he complimented me by saying, "You're on the list of the 'Top Forty Disc Jockeys of All Time." He knew a great deal about me. I visited WCBS FM in New York a few weeks earlier, but the British studio equipment was far superior to ours. The Capitol stations were in a building that featured the Capitol Radio Restaurant on the first floor where they would sometimes broadcast shows.

Jimmy and I took the train to Liverpool for a weekend. Although we had tickets, we had to stand because all of the seats were reserved. Eventually we got a seat as passengers exited. I sat next to a teenage girl who was excited because she got close to Leonardo Di Caprio who was promoting *Titanic*. I later sat next to a man who explained their free medical care. He laughed and said if you have any money you have your own private doctor because it takes too long to get government care. When we got to Liverpool, I couldn't believe that the jukebox in the train station didn't have a single Beatles' song on it. In Liverpool, I hired a guide to take us to the Beatles' homes and show us the famous Beatles' landmarks. We visited Strawberry Fields and, as I looked around, I wondered what John Lennon saw that inspired him to write the song. The rebuilt Cavern Club was really tiny. We took in some of the nightlife and visited the "Yellow Submarine" in the harbor. It was a good weekend. I was glad I was sharing it with my son. When we got back to London, we stopped in a sports bar for a drink, but the place was packed, so we went to the second floor and sat in a room with a group of guys who were eating and watching the NCAA tournament. It was London's professional basketball team made up of several former college stars and, although the bar was closing, they stayed and let us drink and watch the games with them.

One of Jimmy's friends lived in Chelsea, and her next door neighbor had a picture with Mick Jagger. The lady was Mick's one-time girlfriend from the sixties, the recording star Marianne Faithful.

A couple of weeks after my British trip, I was with the English singer Eric Burden of the Animals. I mentioned how impressed I was with the British

Eric Burden, the Animals lead singer.

radio studio equipment. He wasn't surprised and said, "The Soho district was always way ahead of the States in audio equipment."

Sell, sell, sell

When I started on WGRR, I made just about what WSAI was paying me, not very much, but I knew I had the vehicle to really succeed. Financially, I was just about broke; my store had drained me. I worked every outside appearance I could, and I worked every endorsement deal I believed in. At one point, our production director Jim Blommel and I added up my endorsements, and they totaled around a half million dollars a year. I had taken the advice my radio friend Jim Scott gave me years before when I was fired from WLW. Jim had mapped out a plan for me to sell myself and get back on the air, and it worked. WCKY hired me. One of his ideas was to bring as much revenue in with endorsements as possible and did I ever.

Most guys read the commercial copy, and they're done. It's just a read. Blommel would throw a line to me like, "It has frosty, cold air conditioning," for a Joseph Chevrolet car commercial during a heat wave, or "You are riding your Vespa looking for people grilling and telling them not to use fork tongs on the Johnsonville brats—you might pierce the casing," and I would ad-lib a commercial. He was the best and most creative production director I ever worked with, and together we turned out spot after spot.

Recognition

Jim Richards was our station's general manager, and this was the third station where we worked together. J.R. respected my talent more than anyone I've ever worked with. He planned a big deal for my thirtieth anniversary on Cincinnati radio. Our promotion director Tracy Sunderhaus put it together. Mayor Roxanne Qualls gave me the key to the city along with a proclamation declaring, "Tuesday, May 18, 1999 as Jim LaBarbara Day" in Cincinnati. It was a busy day with a lot of old friends stopping by. Johnny Bench gave me an autographed bat, glove, and ball. We played catch a few times over the years, and I used his catcher's glove when I played in the Kid Glove celebrity games at Riverfront. I always wanted one. It was a great gift.

John Kiesewetter wrote in the *Enquirer,* "Professor marks 30th anniversary. LaBarbara said, 'I'm having more fun than ever.' He left Top-Forty radio in Cleveland to come to WLW in 1969. 'I was tired of playing Top-Forty records, screaming over records by the Rolling Stones and the Beatles, so I came to WLW, a more mature station. It's kind of ironic because now I'm playing the same things I did thirty or forty years ago.'"

I've been fortunate over the years to receive some nice honors. In 2010 the Cleveland Association of Broadcasters, at their Twentieth Annual Awards for Excellence in Broadcasting honored me with a Broadcast Legacy Award Induction. I was named one of the twenty legends in Cleveland broadcasting. My friend and mentor the late Bill Randle was on the list along with Jack Parr, the first host of the *Tonight Show*. I was humbled thinking of all the radio and television people there have been in Cleveland radio. My presenter was our WIXY midday guy Larry Morrow. That made it extra special. I was glad to be remembered.

The nicest honor I received was being inducted into the Radio/Television Broadcasters Hall of Fame, Class of 2000, in Akron, Ohio. WGRR didn't say much to me about it, and my program director, Chuck Finney, even scheduled me to do a remote the day before at Joseph Chevrolet with my friend Ben Bishop. Chuck had something up his sleeve. That remote was an overwhelming experience. Our promotions director, Tracy Sunderhaus, along with our assistant program director, Peter Zolenowski, had a giant party for me. The mayor of Cincinnati, Charlie Luken, proclaimed it Jim LaBarbara Day, and I was given another key to the City of Cincinnati. That started it—a long line of mayors from more than a dozen cities and townships honored me with my day and a key to their city. It was incredible. The gang from the station joined me, and all I could say was, "Thank you."

My family was with me at the Hall of Fame dinner, and we sat next to Mike Douglas's table. Mike's television show was in national syndication from the early '60s to the early '80s. He told me when he recorded the song "The Men in My Little Girl's Life" there wasn't a dry eye in the studio, and yes, he lived that song with his identical twin daughters. It was great to see Jack Armstrong again and to reminisce with another Italian, Dick Biondi. I thanked Biondi during my speech because if I had not listened to his show on WLS when I was in college, I would not have flunked out of premed and today I'd be a doctor instead of a disc jockey. I was especially happy to see Bill Randle; he told me he never goes to these events and only accepted because he knew I was going to be there.

Steve Popovich, the record company owner and former VP of Columbia/Epic Records, was the person I selected to introduce me. Steve was the record promoter from Cleveland working Erie who encouraged me to call WKYC in Cleveland and that was the beginning of everything. I never forgot that. He was very emotional when I asked him. Steve had a great career at Epic; he was credited with Boston's success and for reinventing Tom Jones. When I visited his New York office, there was a framed letter on his wall from Charlie Rich begging him to release him from his contract because they weren't recording him. After Steve read it, he got Charlie back in the studio to do "Behind Closed Doors" and "The Most Beautiful Girl." Both sold over a million, and Charlie was bigger than ever. The television show *WKRP in Cincinnati* premiered in 1978, and I had an idea. I called Steve because I wanted to record the theme song, but there wasn't a complete song at the time, and he couldn't get the rights to it. I think I could have made it a hit. "WKRP" was eventually recorded by Steve Carlisle, and it did make the national charts. Popovich's biggest success was Meatloaf's "Bat Out of Hell" release on his Cleveland International Records. He passed away in June 2010 and the industry lost a great friend.

They want me—no they don't

Halloween 2006 was one of the craziest days I ever experienced in radio. Early that day at WGRR the rumors were flying. (I was employed by CBS, but Entercom was in the building getting ready to take over our Cincinnati group of stations.) I met with the Entercom human resources person at 1:45 p.m. before I went on the air at 2:00 p.m. I wanted to make sure I was going to have insurance if I was let go. She asked my name, and said, "Jim, don't worry, we are keeping you." At 5:00 p.m., Jim Bryant, our general manager, came into the studio and asked me to play the record "American Pie." That's a seven-minute record, not a good sign, but I had already started my "Top Five at Five Countdown." I thought I was being fired, but instead Bryant said, "Cumulus just bought your contract." They were only taking the morning show, midday, and me. He told me this was a good move for me and that I could do my show tomorrow from my studio. Before the hour was up, he came in to say he was sorry, but I had to get all of my things out of the station that night. Several of us spent hours packing and moving to our new home. After moving boxes into Cumulus, we were told the deal hadn't been signed. A couple of hours later, the contract was signed. We were welcomed with open arms. Their national program director had been a fan of mine since my Cleveland days.

Six months later, my contract was up and not renewed. The program director was put on the air in a budget move. I was top four in the twenty-five to sixty-four demos, and number one in the thirty-five to sixty-four demos in my 2:00 to 7:00 p.m. shift. I brought in a lot of revenue to the station with personal endorsements, but the new owners in Atlanta couldn't care less. Did I mention I turned sixty-five three months earlier?

CHAPTER 23

"Motorcycle Rider of the Year"

I couldn't believe my wife, Sally, said yes, I could buy that little red 2003 Vespa motor scooter in the store window. I wanted a Vespa since I was a teen watching a group of Pittsburgh disc jockeys riding them. In the past, I was offered deals on motorcycles if I'd endorse them, but she said no. I respected her wishes because we had two young children, but now they were off to college. The guys in the Ten Year Lates Scooter Club advised me to buy the bigger 150cc ET4 because I'd be able to ride it anywhere. A couple of guys on motorcycles laughed at me when I took my driver's test, but I passed with no trouble—they both flunked, knocking over the cones. I rode that little scooter on I-71 to the radio station every day unless there was rain or snow. The Vespa makes me smile. It's classic Italian heritage, and it has to be cool—Marlon Brando and Dean Martin owned one. It became a part of my image, and I rode it in parades and to station events. A year later, I bought the bigger Vespa GT 200 Gran Turismo, the first one in Cincinnati. I love the freedom and speed of riding on two wheels. After reading that James Dean and Steve McQueen rode Triumph motorcycles, I bought a new, all black Triumph Bonneville.

I wasn't on the Triumph five minutes when I went flying. The Vespa is automatic; the Triumph isn't, and I let my hand off the clutch while it was in gear. I didn't go very far, but luckily I was wearing an armored jacket. I called Cycle Dynamics and got private riding lessons the next weekend. I was sitting in front of the Rabbit Hash General Store in Kentucky, and the more I saw it, the more I wanted a Harley Heritage Softail. Here we go again. I found a 1991 in excellent condition, and I surprised Sally, but she persuaded me to sell one of the three. I kept the Vespa and the Harley. It's funny, some bikers will turn their noses up at me if I'm on my scooter but not if I'm on my Harley. The older riders have respect for anyone on two wheels. I love the sound of a Harley: "Potato, potato, potato . . ." There is nothing like it. I don't practice meditation anymore; when I want to relax, I'll mount my Harley like some latter day cowboy and ride away from everything. In a car—a cage—you're looking out the window like a spectator. On my Harley, I'm a part of it, the wind against my body, the smells and the sounds—as I ride, I take it all in.

D. P. Freed, the owner of *Road Wheeler Motorcycle Magazine*, put me on the cover and named me the first ever "Rider of the Year" in 2007 and featured me in a two-page story: "The Music Professor, Radio Legend, Rider, and Friend." He praised my attendance at charity events and how much I promoted motorcycling on the air. "He proves again that bikers are everyday people, workers from all walks of life from just about every level of society." I was totally knocked out. I got started riding late in life because of other obligations. D.P. and I have explored the back roads of Kentucky on many occasions. I've ridden the big island in Hawaii from one end to the other by myself. I always look forward to riding with my old radio buddy Ernie "Fatman" Brown and the "NDN" Don Brockman and company. The Fatman is one of the most charitable people I know. Years ago when he was "down" people reached out and helped him— and his mission is to help others. All the bikers recognize the NDN. When you see a biker in a movie, he's trying to look like the NDN. He's no poser, he is the real thing. The troubled drug and alcohol

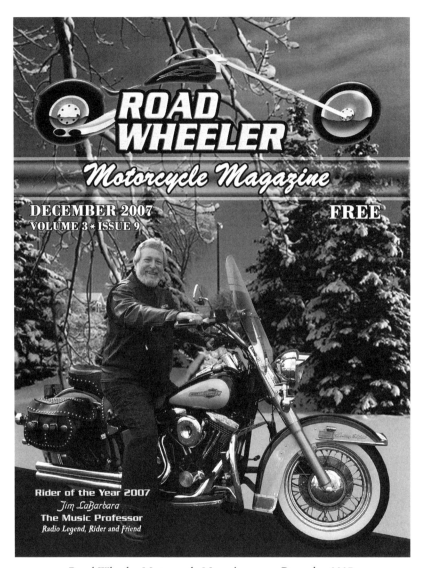

Road Wheeler Motorcycle Magazine *cover December 2007.*
I was honored to be named the Rider of the Year.
PHOTO COURTESY OF D. P. FREED

stage is in his rear-view mirror. He has the scars to prove he's been in more than a few bar fights. His weathered face speaks volumes and there is a story behind all of those tattoos. His long hair is pulled back in a ponytail and those are real rattlesnake rattles hanging from his ears. Grown men step aside for him, but at charity events little children gravitate toward him—they love him. The NDN has helped raise thousands of dollars for various causes over the years. He is the toughest guy I know, but if you talk to him on the phone, the last thing he says is "toodles." Life is never dull around the Fatman and NDN. Typically, we meet Sunday morning at the Fatman's house, and his wife, Lisa, cooks up an enormous breakfast before we take off. Some of our favorite rides are to the Ohio Renaissance Festival in Harveysburg; the Pork Festival in Eaton, Ohio; or just a leisurely ride for jelly beans and fudge in the canal town of Metamora, Indiana. I enjoy being a part of the biker community.

CHAPTER 24

What are you Going to do After Radio?

Sometimes I think doing a good radio show is like watching fireworks. There is that enjoyment and excitement at the moment, and then it's gone into the air. Hopefully a person connects with you and maybe feels your emotions, but then suddenly, you're gone, and most likely, they've forgotten you.

I mentioned earlier that in 1966, my high school friend Sonny Dudzinski visited me in Cleveland and, as he was leaving, he asked me, "What are you going to do after radio?" I explained this was my career, but he looked at me like I was crazy. That was a long time ago, and I still can't answer that question. My dream in radio was to work at a powerhouse station like WKYC in Cleveland, and I achieved that goal at a young age. Everything since then has been a gift. When I was in high school in the fifties, I never pictured myself getting old. One of the teenage idols, James Dean, died at a young age, and of course, there was the Buddy Holly plane crash.

A radio friend once told me that I was naïve to think I had friends in the radio business: "Jim, they were never 'real' friends to begin with, but merely business acquaintances who only had their own best interests at heart in dealing with you." He thought I needed a wake-up call because I wear my heart on my sleeve and tend to look at everyone as a friend. After all these years of doing what I enjoy most, I just can't think this is true.

I've had a wonderful fifty-year-plus love affair with radio. I will always have a great passion for her. It was just weeks after I turned sixty-five when she tossed me aside. I put on a few extra pounds, and my hair was turning gray, but I was still top four in the ratings. I was plugged into the water cooler talk and Cincinnati, and still making her a lot of money. We hit a few bumps along the road during those years, but we always got back together, and each time our love became stronger. I've tried to call her, but sometimes she won't even return my calls. I understand she's fickle, that's her prerogative, but I keep hoping that one day, she'll let me come back to that place I've loved for so many years.

Today I find myself often singing a part of a little known Jimmy Clanton record, "Old Rock 'n' Roller" written by K. Sullivan and R. Rice.

"There's an old rock 'n' roller who'd love to rock and roll again / He keeps thinking about the time when everything was going for him / He just dreams away about those good old days, and will it happen again? / Once it's in the blood, it's so hard letting go / He wants a second chance to ask the world to dance, and will it happen again? Will it happen again?"

How lucky can one guy get? I married a beautiful, intelligent woman who's put up with me all these years, and together we raised two wonderful children, Shelby and Jimmy. As a kid, I wanted to be the best baseball catcher who ever lived, and for years my best friend was Johnny Bench. I partied with some of the biggest names in the entertainment world. I interviewed the early rock stars I listened to as a kid: Bill Haley, Chuck Berry, Little Richard, Jackie Wilson, Phil Everly, and so many others. I was with the Beatles, the Rolling Stones, Neil Diamond, and John Denver. I better stop name-dropping, but it has been an exciting ride, and I had a good seat. I was sitting in the front seat during a time when rock 'n' roll music exploded. It was a time when radio played such an important role in the lives of baby boomers, and I was a small part of it.

Bibliography

Bench, Johnny. "A Practical Guide to Successful Living." *Guideposts* (May 1978).

Brown, Peter and Steven Gaines. *The Love You Make: An Insiders Story of the Beatles*. New York: McGraw-Hill Book Company, 1983.

Clark, Dick and Richard Robinson. *Rock, Roll & Remember*. New York: Thomas Y. Crowell Company, 1976.

Diorio, Al. *Borrowed Time: The 37 Years of Bobby Darin*. Philadelphia: Running Press, 1981.

Elliott, Ron. *Inside the Beverly Hills Supper Club Fire*. Paducah, Ky.: Turner Publishing Company, 1996.

Goldrosen, John. *The Buddy Holly Story*. New York: Quickfox, 1979.

Jackson, John A. *Big Beat Heat: Alan Freed and the Early Years of Rock & Roll*. New York: Schirmer Books, c1991.

Wilson, Mary. *My Life as a Supreme*. With Patricia Romanowski and Ahrgus Juilliard. New York: St. Martins Press, 1986.

Whitburn, Joel. *Joel Whitburn's Top Pop Artists & Singles, 1955–1978 / Compiled from Billboard's Pop Singles Charts, 1955–1978*. Menomonee Falls, Wis.: Record Research, c.1979.

Index

Anka, Paul 54, 180, 259
Apollo 11 134
Apollo program 24
Apollo Theater 280, 289
Apollo, Pa. 130
Arbitron 308
Arch Music 92
Arena Football League 324
Armbruster, Dave "Yid" 341
Armstrong, Jack 26, 62, 76, 81, 81–82,
        86, 347
Armstrong, Neil 134
Army National Guard 124
Army Reserve Band 100
Arnold, Eddie 246
"As Your Stomach Turns" 306
Aspen, Colo. 159
Association 62, 194
"At the Hop" 10, 92
Atkins, Chet 284
Atkins, Ted 256, 257
Atlanta Braves 126
Atlanta, Ga. 77, 292, 307
Atlantic Records 103, 254
Aunt Dora 64, 179, 227
Avalon, Frankie 10, 54, 254, 337, 338
Avco Broadcasting Corp. 111, 118–119,
        150, 151
Avenues 335
Axton, Mae Boren 265–266

B

B. Brown's Orchestra 273
B.J. Records 277
"Baby Love" 30
Bacharach, Burt 292
Back to the Future 311
Bailey and LaBarbara Show 313
Bailey, Bob 177
Baker, Chet 213
Baker, Ginger 106
Baker, LaVern 5, 6, 100, 252
Ballard, Florence 30, 312, 313
Ballards 337
Baltimore Colts 231
Baltimore, Md. 87, 231, 275
Band 305
Bare, Bobby 132, 133, 134
Barger, Sonny 83
Barnes, Betty 336
Barnett, Arnold 179
Barrett, Bill 112

Barrows, Sydney Biddle 314
Barto's Café 84
Barzie, Tino 248
Baseball Hall of Fame 186
Basgell, Monte 229
Bass, Billy 112
"Bat Out of Hell" 348
Beach Boys 202, 236, 237, 334–335
Beasley, Bob 306
Beatlemania 16, 27
Beatles 16, 26, 27, 31, 52, 185, 204, 236,
        258, 261, 271, 277–280, 283,
        286, 288, 325, 334, 344, 346,
        356
Beatty, Warren 180
Beauchamp, Al 160
Beaumont, Jimmy 291
Beckert, Glen 73
Bed Boat Race 195
"Behind Closed Doors" 348
Beiderbecke, Bix 10
Bel Air, Calif. 138
Belgian government 16
Bell, Gus 229
Bellevue, Pa. 230
Belushi, John 311
Ben Vereen Special 180
Bench, Johnnie 146
Bench, Johnny 116, 128, 136, 137, 141,
        142, 147–149, 153, 159, 168,
        171, 172–179, 181, 182, 184,
        187, 198, 208, 307, 346, 356
Bench, Ted 147
Benedetto, Anthony 312
Ben-Gals 300
Bennett, Buzz 257
Bennett, Tony (Anthony Benedetto) 206,
        207, 312
Bergy, Bill 147, 160
Berra, Yogi 183
Berry, Charles Edward Anderson. *See,*
        Berry, Chuck
Berry, Chuck 4, 95, 97, 286–288, 290,
        331, 356
Best, Pete 277–280
Bethany Methodist Church
        (Meadville) 114
"Better Man Than I" 57
Beverly Hills Hotel 180
Beverly Hills Supper Club 221
Beverly Hills, Calif. 138
Bienstock, Freddy 245

McPhatter, Clyde 5, 121
McQueen, Steve 351
Meadville, Pa. 12, 24, 36, 322
Meatloaf 348
The Medicine Show 294
Medley, Bill 31, 188, 271
Meister, Billy 316
Memphian Theater 264
"Memphis" 133
Memphis, Tenn. 103, 263, 265, 329
"The Men in My Little Girl's Life" 347
Mercury Records 242, 252, 254
Meredith, Don 159
Metamora, Ind. 354
Mexico 5
MGM 188
MGM Las Vegas 180
Miami, Fla. 215
Miamisburg, Ohio 155
Michael's Lounge 187
Michaels, Al 150
Michaels, George 269
Michaels, Johnny 108, 196
Michaels, Randy 308, 311
Michaels, Tom Cat 327
Mickey and Larry 120
Mickey Mouse Club 54, 154
Middletown, Ohio 168
Midsummer Rock 58, 119
Millan, Felix 126
Miller, Barbara 98
Miller, Dennis 341
Miller, Gary 4, 228
Miller, Harlan 98
Miller, Mitch 8, 246, 247, 251
Miller, Rodger 36
Miller, Roger 180
Miller, Ronnie 4, 228
Mills Brothers 117
Mills James 307
Mills Slot Machines 298
Milner, Dave 322
Milsap, Ronnie 158
Milton Berle Show 250
Milwaukee, Wis. 306, 315
Mineo, Sal 50
Minneapolis, Minn. 333
Miranda, Bobby 68
Mischell, Patricia 316
"Miss Ann" 337
Miss Cincinnati 300
Miss Kansas 175

Miss Ohio 61, 111
Miss Pennsylvania 18
Miss USA 300
Miss Vickie 109
"Misty" 152
Mitchell, Bobby 36
Modell, Art 151
Modern Dairy Milk 15
*Modern Radio Programming
    (Gaines)* 269
Moe's Main Street 251
Mojo Radio 339
Monday Night Football 158
Monkees 110, 329, 334
The Monkees 334
"Monkees Theme" 329
"Monkey" 83–84
Monroe, Marilyn 304
Montague, Magnificent 256
Monterey Pop Festival 330
Montgomery, Gary LeRoy 35, 83–85
Moods 282
"Moon River" 116
Moon, Keith 213
Moonglows 6
Moore, Bob 166
Moore, Hal "Hotdog" 86, 87
Moore, Joyce 103
Moore, Sam 103, 206
Moore, Scotty 244, 247, 264, 265, 267
"More" 115
"More Today, Than Yesterday" 223
Morgan, Joe 175, 182, 183, 187, 209
Morganna 128
Morning Zoo 339
Morris Minor convertible 14
Morrison, Jimmy 311
Morrow, Larry "the Duker" 90, 326, 347
Morrow, Vic 4
"The Most Beautiful Girl" 56, 348
Motown Records 30, 103, 257, 313
Motown Sound 214
Mount Adams 149, 153
Mountain 119
Mouseketeer 54
MTV 305
Mudfest 332
"Mulberry Bush" 7
Munoz, Anthony 186
Muppets 96
Murdock, Charlie 114–115, 118, 144,
    151, 162, 172, 305, 315